Media and Conflict in the Twenty-First Century

Media and Conflict in the Twenty-First Century

Edited by
Philip Seib

MEDIA AND CONFLICT IN THE TWENTY-FIRST CENTURY
© Philip Seib, 2005.

First published in 2005 by
PALGRAVE MACMILLAN™
175 Fifth Avenue, New York, N.Y. 10010 and
Houndmills, Basingstoke, Hampshire, England RG21 6XS
Companies and representatives throughout the world.

PALGRAVE MACMILLAN is the global academic imprint of the Palgrave Macmillan division of St. Martin's Press, LLC and of Palgrave Macmillan Ltd. Macmillan® is a registered trademark in the United States, United Kingdom and other countries. Palgrave is a registered trademark in the European Union and other countries.

ISBN 1–4039–6833–0

Library of Congress Cataloging-in-Publication Data

Media and conflict in the twenty-first century / edited by Philip Seib.
p. cm.
Includes bibliographical references and index.
ISBN 1–4039–6833–0
1. War—Press coverage. 2. War—Press coverage—United States.
3. Television and war. 4. Press and politics. I. Title: Media and conflict in the twenty-first century. II. Seib, Philip M., 1949–

PN4784.W37M43 2005
070.4'333—dc22   2004061673

A catalogue record for this book is available from the British Library.

Design by Newgen Imaging Systems (P) Ltd., Chennai, India.

First edition: June 2005

10 9 8 7 6 5 4 3 2 1

Printed in the United States of America.

Contents

Illustrations

Figures

Tables

Preface

Against a backdrop of conflict, the media facilitate mobilization of opinion, affect policymaking, and influence the different stages of waging war and making peace. Communications products range from the public diplomacy designed to help avoid or win support for conflict, to the real-time journalism that brings the battlefield vividly to the public. The intersections of communications and conflict are particularly important in a time when technology continues to transform communications fields and non-state actors add new and sometimes frightening dimensions to conflict.

The authors of this book have grounding in communications and political science disciplines, and so this volume looks at media and conflict from diverse viewpoints, ranging from theory to practical application. This diversity of outlook is the essence of the book. This volume illustrates that there is common ground shared by different approaches, and it will help anyone who is interested in communications and conflict, as joint or separate fields, to see the breadth of the range of relevant topics and draw from the findings of scholars with varied backgrounds. It covers conflict prevention, communications-enhanced interaction between public and policymakers, unconventional warfare, the use of communications technology to improve news coverage and mobilize publics, and changes in the content of news coverage.

The authors address ideas that are transforming the roles of the media. Eytan Gilboa's chapter analyzes the relationship between television news coverage and the making of U.S. foreign policy. The chapters by Steve Livingston et al., Cinny Kennard, Sean Aday, and Nel Ruigrok et al., look at the content of conflict coverage—what its components are and what effects it may have on the public and policymakers. The chapters by Robin Brown, Jayne Rodgers, and Kathy Fitzpatrick and Tamara Kosic examine the effects of communications tools on the mobilization of different levels of public opinion. Maura Conway reports about the ways that terrorist organizations have put the World Wide Web to work for their purposes. Philip Seib describes the news media's efforts to define new geopolitical alignments on which to base post–cold war coverage.

This material is wide-ranging but shares the common premise that understanding the pervasiveness and influence of media is essential to understanding the causes and conduct of conflict. In such understanding might be found ways to help resolve the conflicts that have already stained the twenty-first century.

Acknowledgments

This book began as a project of the Comparative Interdisciplinary Studies Section of the International Studies Association, and special appreciation is owed to section president Felicia Krishna-Hensel, who developed the basic plan for the book as part of the ambitious CISS publishing program. She also organized a workshop in Heidelberg at which many of the authors were able to try out early versions of their chapters. Some of the work was refined at other ISA meetings in Budapest, Montreal, and elsewhere.

At Palgrave Macmillan, editor Toby Wahl and everyone else involved with the book were supportive throughout and were a pleasure to work with.

The authors of these chapters are a diverse group—scholars from different fields and with varied backgrounds. I thank them all for their hard work in producing a volume that illustrates the complexity and breadth of the relationship between media and conflict.

CHAPTER 1

Effects of Global Television News on U.S. Policy in International Conflict

Eytan Gilboa

1. Introduction

The expansion of global all news television networks such as CNN International, BBC World, Sky News, and Fox News, and the emergence of new non-Western networks such as Al-Jazeera and Al-Arabiya have fascinated politicians, government officials, journalists, and scholars. This fascination resulted from a perception of the media in general, and television in particular, as being the most important power broker in politics. *Mediademocracy, medialism, mediapolitik, mediacracy,* and *teledemocracy* are but a few postmodern terms coined to describe this new media-dominated political system.[1] Application of the same perception to foreign policy and international relations yielded similar terms and concepts such as *telediplomacy* and *the CNN effect*.[2] A basic assumption lies behind all these concepts. It asserts that images of what is happening in the world are given greater significance than what really happens. Since television creates images, policymaking has primarily become what the veteran television journalist Robert MacNeil calls "a contest of images."[3] Based on his practical experience, former secretary of state Henry Kissinger confirmed this observation by commenting that officials asking for his advice used to ask him what to *do*, but now ask him what to *say*.[4] The "contest of images" perception has also dominated the discussion of the media's role in covering terror and war since the attacks of Islamic fundamentalist terrorists on New York and Washington in September 2001 and the U.S.-led wars in Afghanistan and Iraq.

Five characteristics best describe global television news coverage: (1) it is broadcast around the clock 24 hours a day; (2) it is transmitted in real time; (3) it is broadcast from every place in the world to every other place; (4) it is headline dominated; and (5) it is live event-oriented. One should note however, that networks repeat recorded news programs throughout the day. Two particular formats are more significant: the breaking news and the continuing crisis coverage characterized by a special logo, such as *War on Terrorism* or the *Middle East Crisis*. These formats create more pressure on editors, reporters, and leaders. Editors push reporters to constantly broadcast new pictures and supply new information; reporters push leaders to respond fast to unfolding events; and leaders push experts and diplomats to produce instant policy analysis and recommendations.

This chapter begins with a discussion of the most powerful possible effect of global television—taking over policymaking. Authors have defined this effect, also known as the CNN effect, in several different ways. In the early analysis of this concept, writers called it the "CNN curve," the "CNN complex," and the "CNN factor," each carrying multiple meanings with officials, journalists, and scholars. In recent years, however, researchers have predominantly associated the CNN effect with television forcing policy on politicians and policymakers primarily in connection with international conflicts. This study reveals an ongoing debate among politicians, government officials, journalists, and scholars, on the validity of the CNN effect hypothesis. The debates are conducted both internally within each group and among them, but these exchanges have not yet contributed significantly to resolving the issue.

This study distinguishes between effects of global coverage on outcome, as is the case with the CNN effect research, and effects on the policy process. It argues that the effects on policymaking are far more complex than is usually meant by the CNN effect. It suggests that no sufficient evidence has yet been presented to validate the CNN effect hypothesis, that this effect has been highly exaggerated, and that the focus on this hypothesis has deflected and diverted attention from the significant effects global television does have on policymaking in international conflict.[5] Theoretically, it is possible that under certain rare conditions television news does force policymakers to adopt a policy they oppose, and therefore the CNN effect concept should be preserved, investigated, and tested.[6] However, this study suggests that at this time "constraining" rather than "controlling" policymakers is perhaps a more useful analytical concept for analyzing the effects global television has on policymaking during international conflict. When considered in this way, global television is only one of several factors competing to influence decisions. "Constraining" refers to the pressure global coverage applies on leaders to respond quickly to events, to the limiting of policy options, and to changes in the work of experts, diplomats, and communications professionals.

A basic triangular relationship among the media, government, and public opinion anchors most studies of the effects global television is having on policymaking. In this context the media do not have power of their own, power resides with the public, and to the extent the media have power, it is derived from their perceived ability to stimulate or even shape public opinion.[7] The CNN effect hypothesis is based on this context of media effects. Yet this study departs from the triangular relationship and demonstrates effects that are more direct in their application and independent of public opinion.

The main purposes of this chapter are: (1) to systematically examine the direct and indirect effects global television coverage is having on the formulation and implementation of American foreign policy during international conflict; (2) to explore the consequences of these effects for politicians, appointed officials, and communication professionals; (3) to assess the quality of research conducted on the topic; and (4) to suggest preliminary paths for effectively coping with challenges and dilemmas. Research used to accomplish these purposes is qualitative and is based on interviews, testimonies, and writings of policymakers, journalists, and communication professionals, and on case studies of major international events of the last decade. The approach is interdisciplinary and is based on joint application of concepts and theories from the fields of both communication and international relations. The chapter begins with a critical analysis of the CNN effect hypothesis; it continues with the constraining effects of real-time coverage, and ends with dilemmas created by these effects for all the participants in the policy process.

Driving Policy

The term "CNN effect" first appeared in newspapers during the 1991 Gulf War, and was initially used to describe the adverse psychological, economic, and financial consequences of CNN's war coverage.[8] Later, journalists and commentators such as Daniel Schorr and Walter Goodman argued that CNN's coverage forced the West to reverse its nonintervention policy in the Kurdish rebellion against Saddam Hussein in the aftermath of the 1991 Gulf War and in the Somalian civil war.[9] Researchers of the CNN effect have employed a variety of confusing definitions. Several formulations address only the policy-forcing effect on humanitarian intervention decisions whereas others suggest a whole new approach to foreign policymaking and world politics.[10]

Feist wrote: "The CNN effect is a theory that compelling television images, such as images of a humanitarian crisis, cause U.S. policymakers to intervene in a situation when such an intervention might otherwise not be in the U.S. national interest."[11] Schorr defined the CNN effect as "the way breaking news affects foreign policy decisions," while Livingston and Eachus defined it "as elite decision makers' loss of policy control to news media."[12] According to Seib the CNN effect "is presumed to illustrate the dynamic tension that exists between real-time television news and policymaking, with the news having the upper hand in terms of influence."[13] Neuman expanded the range of effects by addressing the coverage's impact on the initial decision as well as on subsequent intervention phases including long-term deployment and exit strategies.[14] She described the effect in terms of a curve: television first forces policymakers to intervene militarily in a humanitarian crisis, and forces them again to terminate the intervention once the military force suffers casualties or humiliation.

Livingston, Wheeler, and Robinson suggested several different CNN effects. Livingston identified three effects: an accelerant to decisionmaking, an impediment to the achievement of desired policy goals, and a policy agenda-setting agent.[15] Wheeler distinguished between "determining" and "enabling" effects of television coverage.[16] The "determining" effect means policy forcing while the "enabling" effect means that coverage makes humanitarian intervention possible by mobilizing domestic support. Robinson adopted a somewhat similar distinction between "strong" and "weak" effects.[17]

Policymaker's Perceptions

The testimony of principal policymakers on the factors that had the greatest impact on their decisions provides evidence on the effects of global television. In May 1993, the then U.S. ambassador to the UN, Madeleine Albright offered the first official citation and explanation of the CNN effect: "Every day we witness the challenge of collective security on television—some call it the CNN effect," she told a subcommittee of the House Foreign Affairs Committee, "Aggression and atrocities are beamed into our living rooms and cars with astonishing immediacy. No civilized human being can learn of these horrid acts occurring on a daily basis and stand aloof from them."[18] Albright talked about the global news coverage of the humanitarian crises in Somalia and Bosnia. When asked to comment on factors that changed foreign policymaking, former secretary of state Lawrence Eagleburger emphasized the importance of the CNN effect: "The public hears of an event now in real time, before the State Department has had time to think about it. Consequently, we find ourselves reacting before we've had time to think. This is now the way we determine foreign policy—*it's driven more by the daily events reported on TV than it used to be*" (emphasis added).[19]

Former secretary of state James Baker III reinforced these perceptions when he wrote in his memoir: "The terrible tragedy of Tiananmen was a classic demonstration of a powerful new phenomenon: the ability of the global communications revolution to drive policy."[20] He added that since then "in Iraq, Bosnia, Somalia, Rwanda, and Chechnya, among others, the real-time coverage of conflict by the electronic media has served to create a powerful new imperative for prompt action that was not present in less frenetic time." Baker further elaborated on this conclusion in an interview with Marvin Kalb: "The 'CNN effect' has revolutionized the way policymakers have to approach their jobs, particularly in the foreign policy arena."[21] Several high-ranking American officials made more assertive statements. For example, Assistant Secretary of State John Shattuck wrote: "The media got us into Somalia and then got us out."[22]

Non-American officials have also expressed similar opinions. Former UN Secretary General Boutros Boutros-Ghali is quoted as complaining "CNN is the sixteenth member of the Security Council."[23] Former British foreign secretary David Owen observed that the media's calls for intervention in civil wars are not new, but "what is different today is the 'CNN effect.' The TV camera in Sarajevo recording minute by minute, hour by hour, day by day, in real-time . . . conveys an immediacy and has an impact that no newspaper . . . carries."[24] Another former British foreign secretary Douglas Hurd blamed foreign correspondents covering the Bosnian crisis for advocating military intervention by being the founding members of the "something must be done" school.[25]

Debating the CNN Effect

The preceding statements may imply that global television usurped policy control, as if leaders can no longer decide on the basis of interests, but are driven by emotional reactions of public opinion aroused by television coverage. Yet politicians and senior policymakers have offered diverse and often contradicting views on this claim. In a policy meeting, held on

July 17, 1995, President Bill Clinton is quoted as saying: "We have a war by CNN. Our position is unsustainable, it's killing the U.S. position of strength in the world."[26] Morris also heard him complaining: "TV reporters are doing their damnedest to get me to enter a war."[27] However, Clinton only talked about media "pressure" to intervene militarily in Bosnia. Although he was sensitive to both horrific violence and to the media coverage of his policies, he successfully resisted the pressure to change his policy of nonintervention for several years.

Other senior policymakers have also provided a more complex view of the effects of global news coverage. After serving as National Security adviser and chairman of the Joint Chiefs of Staff, Colin Powell observed "Live television coverage does not change the policy, but it does create the environment in which the policy is made."[28] Anthony Lake, a scholar and Clinton's first National Security adviser, acknowledged that public pressure, driven by televised images, increasingly played a role in decisionmaking on humanitarian crises, but added that other factors such as cost and feasibility were as important.[29] Finally, when commenting on Canada's policy toward the 1996 refugee crisis in eastern Zaire, the Canadian senior diplomat Brian Buckley wrote that the media was crucial in focusing international attention on the crisis, but "they did not determine the policy, the key decisions, or their implementation."[30]

Diplomats and journalists have also debated the CNN effect. One interesting exchange occurred in 1993 between the veteran diplomat George Kennan and CBS's reporter and anchor Dan Rather. On the day the U.S. Marines landed in Somalia, December 9, 1992, Kennan wrote in his personal diary that this was "a dreadful error of American policy" accepted by the public and the Congress because of television coverage.[31] "There can be no question that the reason for this acceptance lies primarily with the exposure of the Somalia situation by the American media, above all television. The reaction would have been unthinkable without this exposure. The reaction was an emotional one, occasioned by the sight of the suffering of the starving people in question." Almost a year later, he published this commentary in the *New York Times* (September 30, 1993, p. A25) eliciting a sharp denial from Rather titled "Don't Blame TV for Getting Us into Somalia" (October 14, 1993, p. A22). Rather asserted: "Reporters sometimes feel strongly about the stories they cover, and some may wish for the power to direct public opinion and to guide America policy—but they don't have it."[32] MacNeil followed up on this debate and summarized well the positions of the two sides. He added however, a single decisive variable: leadership. If a leader can define the national interest clearly, "television—however lurid, responsible or irresponsible—will not drive foreign policy. When he fails to do so, it may."[33]

The Scholarly Evidence

Scholarly and professional studies of the CNN effect present mixed, contradictory, and confusing results. Studies of the humanitarian interventions in Kurdistan and Somalia well demonstrate this record. Journalists and scholars such as Schorr, Shaw, and Ammon argued that television coverage of Saddam Hussein's massacre of Kurds forced the governments of the United States and Britain respectively to reverse their nonintervention policy.[34] Schorr wrote: "Score one for the power of the media, especially television, as a policy-making force. Coverage of the massacre and exodus of the Kurds generated public pressures that were instrumental in slowing the hasty American military withdrawal from Iraq and forcing a return to help guard and care for the victims of Saddam Hussein's vengeance." Yet the correlation Schorr found between media coverage and public opinion is not sufficient to establish a cause–effect relationship as well as a connection between public opinion and policy changes. Miller investigated the policy processes in the United States and Britain and found that CNN's coverage did not affect their policy in Kurdistan and his findings contradict the conclusions of Schorr, Shaw, and Ammon.[35]

The U.S. intervention in Somalia has been the second battleground for studies of the CNN effect and it also has yielded similar controversial results. Mandelbaum wrote: "television pictures of starving people" propelled the U.S. intervention.[36] Cohen observed that television "has demonstrated its power to move governments. By focusing daily on the starving children in Somalia, a pictorial story tailor-made for television, TV mobilized the conscience of the nation's public institutions, compelling the government into a policy of intervention for humanitarian reasons."[37] Mermin however, called this claim "a myth" and later added: "The case of U.S. intervention in Somalia, in sum, is not at heart evidence of the power of television to move governments; it is evidence of the power of governments to move television."[38]

Other studies also raised questions about the effects of CNN coverage on the U.S. decision to intervene in Somalia. Livingston and Eachus employed careful content analysis and interviews with decisionmakers in Washington and Africa, and they concluded that the U.S. decision "was the result of diplomatic and bureaucratic operations, *with news coverage coming in response to those decisions*" (emphasis added).[39] Riley also called the CNN effect "a myth" while Wheeler and Robinson agreed that the media had respectively a "weak" effect on the decisions to intervene in Kurdistan and Somalia.[40] Moreover, Gibbs argued that policymakers employed humanitarian justification but decided to militarily intervene in Somalia owing to strategic and economic considerations.[41]

A valid scientific approach to the study of the CNN effect requires two interrelated comparative analyses: (1) an assessment of global television's impact on a specific foreign policy decision in comparison to the relative impact of other factors; and (2) application of this procedure to several relevant case studies. Only a few researchers have systematically followed this procedure. Jakobsen examined the impact of the following factors on humanitarian intervention decisions: a clear humanitarian and /or legal case, national interest, chance of success, domestic support, and the CNN effect. He then examined the relative influence of these factors on decisions to intervene in several crises from the Gulf War to Haiti. He discovered that CNN's coverage was an important factor because it placed the crises on the agenda; but still the decision to intervene *"was ultimately determined by the perceived chances of success"* (emphasis added).[42] In a later study he furthered argued: "in situations when governments are reluctant to use force, interventions are unlikely to follow unless they can be conducted quickly with a low risk of casualties. Since this is rarely the case, media pressure on reluctant governments are most likely to result in minimalist policies aimed at defusing pressure for interventions on the ground."[43]

Robinson developed a sophisticated policy–media interaction model that predicts that media influence is likely to occur when policy is uncertain and media coverage is critically framed and empathizes with suffering people. When policy is certain, media influence is unlikely to occur.[44] Robinson applied this model to the crises in Bosnia and Kosovo and found that U.S. policy to defend the Gorazde "safe area" in Bosnia was influenced by the media because Clinton's policy was uncertain and the media strongly criticized him. In the Kosovo case, however, Clinton's air-war policy was clear and consequently the media failed to expand the operation to include ground troops.

Conclusion

This section reveals considerable debate and disagreement on the CNN effect hypothesis among leaders, officials, journalists, and scholars. The prevailing conclusion is that this effect has not dramatically changed media–government relations, does not exist, or has been highly exaggerated and may occur only in rare situations of extremely dramatic and persistent coverage, lack of leadership, and chaotic policymaking. Neuman and Buckley concluded that global communication has not changed the fundamentals of political leadership and international governance.[45] Strobel wrote: "The CNN effect implied by Kennan does not exist," and Seib also asserted: "There is a certain logic to the [CNN] theory, and it cheers journalists who like to think they are powerful, but there is a fundamental problem: It just ain't so, at least not as a straightforward cause-and-effect process."[46] Natsios, Gowing, and Jakobsen agreed that the CNN effect has been highly exaggerated.[47]

The CNN effect hypothesis has been defined very broadly, but to test it, this hypothesis has to be operationalized in a very narrow way. When this is done, as has been demonstrated in several studies, it becomes easier to disprove many of its claims and implications. Several studies confuse cause and effect relationship between coverage and policy. It is clearly necessary to distinguish between cases where a government wishes to intervene, and therefore not only does not object to media coverage of atrocities but also actually initiates or encourages it, and cases when a government is reluctant to intervene and consequently resists media pressure to do so. Global television cannot force policymakers to do what they intend to do anyway. Another problematic assumption confuses "control" and "pressure." There is a difference between "forcing" policymakers to adopt policy and "pressuring" them to do so. The "forcing" framework suggests that the media is taking over the policymaking process, while the "pressuring" framework considers the media as one of several factors competing to influence decisions. Finally, the CNN effect is now something of a misnomer. In the past one could identify CNN with global broadcasting and global broadcasting with CNN. That is no longer true. The emergence of several Western and non-Western global networks such as BBC World and Al-Jazeera ended CNN's global monopoly and with it the CNN of the "CNN effect."[48]

2. Chasing Real-Time Coverage

While there is not yet sufficient evidence to support the claim that global television is becoming a controlling actor in the formulation of policy in international conflicts, it certainly affects many important dimensions of foreign policy and diplomacy. As such, it may be "constraining" rather than "determining" policy. By constraining this study means that whereas global news coverage may alter or even disrupt the routine policymaking process, primarily the work of the professional bureaucracy, and leaders may have to reorder priorities, they do not feel forced to follow a particular policy called for by the media or implied by coverage.

Global television constrains the policy process primarily through the high speed of broadcasting and transmitting information. In the twentieth century, technology has reduced the time of information transfer from weeks to minutes. The time American presidents had to officially respond to the construction and destruction of the Berlin Wall clearly demonstrates this constraint.[49] In 1961, President Kennedy had the luxury of waiting eight days before making the first American official statement on the construction of the Wall. In 1989, President George Bush felt impelled to comment after less than eight hours on the destruction of the Wall. In less than 30 years the time for policy response has dramatically shrunk. One should note, however, that this condition is not always automatic. It depends on the circumstances of the challenge or the threat. Despite the dramatic coverage of the terrorist attacks on New York and Washington in September 2001, the media pressure was not powerful enough to require an immediate retaliation, and President George W. Bush took the time necessary to develop an adequate response. This section demonstrates how real-time coverage of international conflict competes with governmental sources of information and analysis, allows diplomatic manipulations, and produces instant judgments about policies and outcomes.

Competing Sources of Information

In traditional diplomacy, ambassadors and state representatives dominated several important areas of diplomacy: representing their countries, communicating their government's positions, negotiating and concluding agreements, gathering information about the countries to which they were posted, and recommending actions to policymakers back home. But the communication and information revolutions have substantially eroded the ambassadors' central position in all four areas. The 1992 U.S. presidential candidate Ross Perot made the following observation: "Embassies are relics of the days of sailing ships. At one time, when you had no world communication, your ambassador spoke for you in that country. But now, with instantaneous communication around the world, the ambassador is primarily in a social role."[50] Michael O'Neill former editor of the *New York Daily News* agrees: "thanks to the communications revolution and new technology, the old world of diplomacy is itself in ruins . . . And ambassadors become a threatened species, like snail darter fish."[51] Indeed, heads of state and ministers talk and negotiate directly, in secrecy or in public, with their counterparts. Their negotiations are conducted primarily through official and unofficial meetings and visits, but also via global television.

In addition, in many recent crises global television coverage has replaced ambassadors and experts as the source of critical information and evaluation on what is happening in the world. Several senior American officials acknowledged that diplomatic communications just cannot keep up with CNN.[52] Richard Haass, a former senior official of the National Security Council, also complained that "he could see an event or speech live on CNN at 2:00 p.m. but he had to wait three hours or more before the CIA could deliver its own updated news and commentary to the NSC office." In view of these gaps, it is no wonder that President Bush's press secretary, Marlin Fitzwater, said that in many international crises "we virtually cut out the State Department and the desk officers . . . Their reports are still important, but they often don't get here in time for the basic decisions to be made." Bush himself admitted during the 1990–91 Gulf crisis: "I learn more from CNN than I do from the CIA."[53]

Sometimes conventional diplomatic messages, regardless of their depth and sophistication, do not have the same effect on policymakers as do televised images from the field. Hurd acknowledged "when it comes to a distant but important conflict, even all the Foreign Office cables do not have the same impact as a couple of minutes of news video."[54] Fitzwater recalled that during the violence in Tiananmen Square they were getting reports and cables from the American embassy in Beijing, "but they did not have the sting, the demand for a government response that the television pictures had."[55] Similarly, during the 1991 Russian coup attempt, Boris Yeltsin's phone messages to Washington did not sufficiently impress Bush until the actual arrival of television broadcasts from Moscow showing Yeltsin's visible and viable resistance. Only then did the U.S. administration become convinced the resistance was serious, and proceeded to take actions to support Mikhail Gorbachev.[56]

Diplomatic Manipulations

Global television has also created new worldwide opportunities for propaganda, misinformation, and diplomatic manipulations. For example, leaders make what is described as a significant statement that is broadcast live on local or global television, hoping that what they say will in turn assume a dynamic of its own and undermine and confuse the plans of the rival side. Two examples from American–Iraqi confrontations illustrate this challenge. During the 1991 Gulf War, just before the beginning of the ground assault, Saddam Hussein made a statement designed to create the impression that he was ready to accept the allied conditions to end the war. Television anchors and reporters around the world quickly suggested that the war might be over, and leaders of U.S. allies jammed the White House switchboard to learn what the United States intended to do.[57]

Bush thought Hussein's peace plan was false but was worried that the Iraqi leader might snatch "a victory from the jaws of certain defeat."[58] He and Baker felt they had less than 30 minutes to dismiss the Iraqi deal or risk the disintegration of the coalition fighting Hussein. According to McNulty, Bush told the officials he assembled to deal with this challenge: "We've got to get on the air fast to answer all these people who either don't know what to do or want us to do something we don't want to do." Bush wanted to inform all 26 members of the international coalition confronting Iraq of the White House's position. Fitzwater said that the quickest and most effective way for transmitting this evaluation was CNN, because "all countries in the world had it and were watching it on a real-time basis."[59] In this particular case, both the challenge and the response were played on global television, but Bush won the game. He correctly identified the challenge and effectively neutralized it.

On Saturday, November 14, 1998, Saddam Hussein was much more successful in employing a similar tactic. In response to his defiance of UN resolutions on inspection and dismantling of weapons of mass destruction, Clinton authorized a military attack on Iraq. U.S. bombers were already in the air when CNN's reporter in Baghdad Brent Sadler broadcasted live a statement from an Iraqi official who said his government "positively" responded to an urgent letter UN Secretary General Kofi Annan sent to Hussein asking him to let the weapons inspectors come back. The Iraqi official added that the Iraqi government had faxed a commitment to that effect to the United Nations.[60] An official of the National Security Council watched this CNN live report and immediately called National Security adviser Samuel Berger who informed Clinton about the broadcast. While monitoring CNN for details, Clinton consulted with his senior advisers and immediately issued an order to abort the mission. Despite the renewed Iraqi commitment, Hussein continued to ignore the UN inspection resolutions and the U.S. demands that he comply with them. In this case, a broadcast on CNN prevented an action that was already underway.

Instant Judgments

Many editors think that because numerous networks and newspapers all chase the same facts the only way to distinguish one report from all the others, other than breaking the news story, is to produce a definitive thought about an event or a process. White House correspondent Kenneth Walsh called this new practice the battle for "insight scoops" and provided several examples to illustrate his observation.[61] Early in his presidency, Clinton ordered an attack on Baghdad, and CNN began to discuss the effects of this action on his presidency even before all the facts of the attack became known. Similarly, in September 1994, Jimmy Carter, Sam Nunn, and Colin Powell announced in a press conference that they had mediated an accord ending the military rule in Haiti and restoring the civilian government of President Jean-Bertrand Aristide. Minutes after the announcement a reporter called Clinton's communication director Mark Gearan and told him he was planning to write a story on whether the agreement represented effective diplomatic efforts or a flawed political settlement doomed to failure. Gearan said that this was a "ludicrously premature motion" motivated by "commercial pressure on reporters" to immediately analyze the news. "This is a dangerous trend," Gearan told Walsh, "If policymakers make decisions based on how they immediately [will] be judged, in many instances they are making bad decisions."

The tone of television coverage, not only its contents, may challenge policymakers. Fitzwater observed that presidents must be very careful in making policy statements when television "sets the tone or mood of response for America. A president has two options: lead that response and set the tone . . . or reflect that tone in some symbolic way."[62] If a president fails to recognize the television tone of events, he is likely to be judged "as out of touch or out of his head." Fitzwater ignored a third option: changing or overriding the tone. The Bush reserved approach to the dismantling of the Berlin Wall provides a good example of this constraint. The destruction of the wall was one of the most important events of the twentieth century, and television reporters expected Bush to immediately declare and celebrate a spectacular American and Western victory in the cold war. Bush thought however, that he should make only a low-key statement in order to avoid an embarrassment to Gorbachev and other Eastern European leaders, that could result in a policy reversal. Consequently, his approach looked uninspired and somewhat apathetic.[63] Fitzwater, however, thought that Bush failed to recognize the tone of the reports on the dismantling of the wall.

Representing television journalists in a pool organized to broadcast the president's message, CBS's Lesley Stahl wrote: "Bush with what looked like a frown, sat there so limply, he actually listed in his chair. And his voice, instead of expressing the excitement of the moment whined."[64]

Her reports and those of her colleagues reflected these observations. When told that he did not sound elated Bush replied "I am not an emotional kind of guy," but on several occasions he also said: "I'm not going to dance on the wall."[65] A decade later, Stahl explained in her book: "Bush's assuring the Soviets was the right approach," but she added "surely there was a way to satisfy the soul without threatening Gorbachev. Reagan would have found it." This case exemplifies careful diplomacy and poor communication strategy as Bush and Fitzwater did not even attempt to override the tone set by television for the event.

Conclusion

Leaders have always used the press, particularly the "elite newspapers," to obtain information and insights on other countries and world affairs. But the evidence presented in this section suggests that global television has become a much more immediate, dramatic, and powerful source. The faster pace of diplomatic exchanges conducted on global television has altered decisionmaking processes, particularly in acute crisis situations. Valuable information, observations, and suggestions from overseas diplomatic and intelligence sources may no longer arrive in time to have the desired influence on decisions, and when information does arrive in time, it has to compete with dramatic televised images and ongoing reportage of crises and foreign policy issues. Policymakers have also to take into consideration the tone of coverage, and deal with attempts of foreign leaders to undermine their policies and plans through messages delivered on global television, primarily via the "breaking news" format, which even increases the pressure for an immediate response.

Before the global communication revolution, a leader could have sent one message through local media to his people and another through foreign media to other peoples. Today this distinction has disappeared and a policy statement reaches, at the same time, both local and foreign audiences, including enemies and allies. Often, this audience multiplicity requires a balancing act that in turn may take considerable time to articulate. In addition, the result may have to be somewhat general and vague. The media however, apply pressure on senior officials to give them fast clearer responses, and if journalists do not receive what they want, they become critical of official policy. Moreover, in the past, when confronted with unfavorable coverage by local networks, leaders invoked patriotism and employed forceful persuasion to assure support for their policy. Today, however, they have also to cope with new networks such as Al-Jazeera whose reports tend to reflect an anti-American bias.

3. Facing Dilemmas

The development and expansion of global television networks and the faster speed of diplomatic exchanges on global television present major dilemmas to all the main participating actors in the foreign policy process: political leaders, experts, diplomats, editors, and journalists. Many of them have not yet recognized these dilemmas and those few who have are still searching for adequate answers. Former secretary of state Madeleine Albright recognized the advantages and disadvantages of global news coverage and said that global television coverage contributes to policymaking in international conflict: "because you know what's going on and there is a real-time sense about things," but she added: "it makes you have to respond to events much faster than it might be prudent, because facts may come in incorrect, but you don't have time to put them in context, so you respond just to a little nugget of fact, and when you learn the context later, things change."[66] Yet her response to this challenge and handling of the media, particularly in crisis situations, was problematic and controversial.[67]

While officials, scholars, and journalists have acknowledged the effects global television news is having on policymaking, they have hardly explored, particularly journalists, the effects global coverage is having on the work of journalists and editors that in turn also influences the policy process. Unlike Albright, most editors and journalists have yet to recognize the effects global news coverage is having on their own daily work and find ways to deal with them. This section presents dilemmas that politicians and officials face as a result of not having sufficient time for official response and of media's inherent impatience and tendency to create expectations that cannot be met in a short period of time. The section also demonstrates and discusses dilemmas that reporters and editors face and their possible consequences for decisionmaking in international conflict.

Time for Official Response

Scholars, officials, and journalists have expressed concern about the effect global television coverage is having on the pace of policymaking in international conflict. Historian Beschloss argued that the speed of this coverage may force hurried responses based on intuition rather than on careful extensive policy deliberation, and this may lead to dangerous policy mistakes. He asked whether under the pressure of global television Kennedy would have had the time to carefully consider options to resolve the highly inflammable Cuban missile crisis. Kennedy had 13 days to make decisions and to negotiate an acceptable agreement with the Soviets to end the crisis.[68] Clinton's press secretary, Dee Dee Myers also contrasted the time Kennedy had to make decisions in the Cuban crisis with today's practice. She explained: "If that happened now, Bill Clinton would have about 30 minutes, and Wolf Blitzer [CNN Reporter] and everybody else would be standing out on the North Lawn of the White House demanding action, or saying 'the president is indecisive.' So I worry that the time allowed leaders in crisis to make good decisions is compressed. That's a troubling development."[69] Daniel Schorr agreed with these concerns: "Think about the communication age we live in and the way nail-biting officials must make fateful decisions without time to think. And, if you are like me, you will worry a little bit when powerful people make snap decisions, trying to keep up with the information curve."[70]

It is difficult to correlate good decisions with the length of time available for policymaking. Great leaders may make the right decision fast and others may make wrong decisions even when they have weeks to deliberate all their options. It is logical to assume however, that in most cases, the more time leaders have for collecting information, consultation, and thinking, the greater is their chance to avoid major mistakes. The observations made by Beschloss, Myers, and Schorr point to a difficult dilemma political leaders often face. If they respond immediately without taking the time to carefully consider policy options, they may make a mistake. However, if they insist they need more time to think, or have no comment for the time being, they create the impression, both at home and abroad, of confusion or of losing control over events.

Following the traumatic experience of the 1979–81 Iran hostage crisis Carter's counsel Lloyd Cutler observed that if a president does not respond quickly to a crisis, the networks may report that his "advisers are divided, that the president cannot make up his mind, or that while the president hesitates, his political opponents know exactly what to do."[71] Representative Lee Hamilton also told *Time* magazine (April 25, 1994, p. 14) that real-time television coverage puts leaders on the spot before they are ready to respond: "policymakers are forced to react instantaneously. If you don't respond, it appears that you are ducking your responsibilities." Leaders often tend to resolve this dilemma by providing some response rather than requesting additional time to deliberate on a decision. Yet, an immediate response creates problems of its own, in that a statement on television becomes a commitment to a policy that leaders may find difficult to reverse or even change, if after careful consideration they decide that is the tack to take.

Live coverage of world events, the dramatic appeal of pictures, and the pressure on leaders to quickly adopt policy on the frenetic schedule of television programming, challenge the foreign affairs bureaucracy. Officials and experts face the following dilemma: how to compete effectively with real-time information provided on the screen without compromising professional standards of analysis and recommendations. If foreign policy experts, military and intelligence officers, and diplomats make a fast analysis based on incomplete information and severe time pressure, they might make bad policy recommendations. Conversely, if they take the necessary time to carefully verify and integrate information and ideas from a variety of sources, and produce in-depth reliable reports and recommendations, these may be irrelevant if policymakers have to make immediate decisions in response to challenges and pressure emanating from coverage on global television.

Impatience and Expectations

The "video clip pace" of global television coverage may create high expectations for instant results in both warfare and diplomacy. Former State Department spokesperson James Rubin said "The impatience of the media is one of the phenomena of the 24-hour news cycle. Three times a day, a new story line has to develop. And that creates an institutional impatience."[72] National Security adviser Condoleezza Rice also views the media as "a problem in policymaking" because "the media wants to know what the president has done for world peace today" while implementation often takes consistent long-term effort, "and if you are out there, having to report every day what you are doing is not very helpful."[73]

War, diplomacy, and other international processes are especially complex and take time to complete. The public expectations of instant results become dangerous in that failure to meet these expectations may result in huge disappointments and subsequent actions that further complicate international interactions. Wolf Blitzer's reports on CNN from the Pentagon immediately after the beginning of the 1991 Gulf War deeply concerned chairman of the Joint Chiefs of Staff Colin Powell because "it seems as if all that remained was to organize the victory parade."[74] Powell asked the Pentagon's spokesperson to tell Blitzer "This is the beginning of a war, not the end of ball game." Consequently, Blitzer modified the content and tone of his reports on the war. This exchange exemplifies these challenges and a successful response to them by a senior official.

During the initial phase of the 1999 NATO operations in Kosovo, Secretary of Defense William Cohen faced a similar challenge: "The pressure was on from the press to give us a day-by-day account of how successful you were today. And I think that builds a tempo into a campaign to say wait a minute, this is going to take some time."[75] Cohen's attempts to deal with this challenge were less successful than Powell's. A similar challenge appeared in the second week of the 2003 American-led war in Iraq. The U.S. and British forces slowed down the attack, soldiers were killed and taken prisoner, and the Iraqi government mounted an intensive propaganda campaign. The U.S. media became impatient and critical and thought the war was heading to a major disaster. Secretary of Defense Donald Rumsfeld was able to deal with the media impatience only because the coalition forces regrouped fast and went on to win a decisive and quick military victory over Saddam Hussein's forces.

Diplomatic media events and spectacular celebrations of breakthroughs in negotiations between enemies are significant because they prepare skeptical publics for a new era of cooperation and friendship.[76] On the other hand, because they are so dramatic and exciting, they create high expectations for rapid and efficient progress toward peace. But as American-sponsored Israeli–Arab peace processes demonstrate, even after initial breakthroughs and emotional speeches, difficult and long negotiations are needed to conclude agreements. The gap between the promise of media events and the actual results often create dangerous confusion and disappointments.[77]

The global war against terrorism represents a new major expectation challenge to policymakers. Following the terrorist attacks on the United States in September 2001, President George W. Bush realized that it would take a long period of time to combat the new fundamentalist Islamic terrorism and therefore, repeatedly cautioned the public not to expect rapid results and instead be prepared for a battle that may take years, maybe even a generation. The battle includes the use of economic and diplomatic measures that are less visible, slow to produce results, and difficult to evaluate. However, will the media and the public have the patience to wait years for victories in this campaign that may themselves be unclear and largely rhetorical? Global and local networks have already questioned the results of the war against terrorism and frequently pressed leaders to demonstrate success. No wonder that National Security Adviser Condoleezza Rice advised the media to recognize that "world affairs is not a scoreboard where you keep daily score of winning and losing."[78]

The media rich environment of policymaking in international conflict presents dilemmas to both policymakers and journalists. If policymakers provide premature assessments of events and processes that journalists demand, they may mislead the public and create false expectations. Conversely, if they refuse to cooperate with journalists, the latter are likely to produce their own evaluations that in turn also may create false expectations. If journalists press on policymakers to offer instant assessments, they may negatively affect sound policymaking, and if they refrain from such demands, they may stay behind in the race for scoops and sensational revelations.

Standards of Journalism

The global communication revolution presents professional and ethical dilemmas to editors and reporters that also affect policymaking in international conflict. Reporters are expected not only to report what they see and hear but also to understand and explain events to audiences around the world, albeit in a manner consistent with the time constraints of television. Due to technological advances it is possible today to carry in a few suitcases all the equipment needed to broadcast, and it takes only minutes to prepare for live reporting. Yet fast reporting may be incomplete at best and very inaccurate at worst.[79] Global news editors apply pressure on correspondents to file reports as soon they arrive in a relevant location. Often, though, while reporters are able to transmit pictures, they may not know the context and meaning of events, and do not have the time to absorb, reflect, and explain what they see. This is especially difficult for nonresident reporters, who are usually less familiar with the specific background of an event in a foreign place. However, owing to budget cuts in foreign bureaus and news production, increasingly such reporters are dispatched to cover foreign affairs. Consequently, their reports may be incomplete, distorted, and even misleading and leaders who use these reports as a significant source of information may adopt wrong policies.

Editors face an additional dilemma stemming from the emerging new highly accessible and affordable communication technologies, which allow almost anybody to videotape events. CNN receives footage from local stations as part of exchange deals, so the origins and bias of a tape can be unclear. In addition, the emergence of networks such as the Middle Eastern Al-Jazeera and Al-Arabiya has created a new pool of questionable sources and footage. Thus, editors receive an enormous outpouring of information coming from outside their normal and regular channels and sources. Gowing called this new phenomenon "the super-market of war videos" but the problem is not confined to war coverage.[80]

Editors are tempted to use these sources owing to the competition and constant pressure to adequately feed the 24-hour news cycle. The problem is how to select relevant materials under pressure, and the dilemma is whether to broadcast pictures that editors may not know when, where, and how they were videotaped. Marvin Kalb said this is one of the more serious problems facing television news.[81] NBC's Tom Wolzien said he was worried about overseas video because "by the time the tape gets on the air, nobody has the foggiest idea who made it or whether the pictures were staged."[82] But Rosenstiel argues that the consequences of this practice are actually far more severe: "The networks' loss of control over their pictures did more than make life tough: it lessened journalistic standards."[83] Thus, both policymakers and consumers must take these limitations into account.

The pressure of real-time all news channels may also confuse "a reporter's personal opinions and his relying of facts."[84] This confusion especially surfaced in coverage of the Israeli–Palestinian conflict and the civil war in Bosnia. Coverage of Palestinian–Israeli violence has been continuously infected by one-sided advocacy journalism. The pro-Palestinian bias began during the 1982 Israeli war in Lebanon and intensified during the first 1987–88 Palestinian Intifada (uprising) against Israel.[85] Lederman wrote: "many journalists maintain that their job is to be nothing more than a mirror on the society or event they are covering. No concept of journalism could be more fallacious . . . During the Intifada, television, in particular, sought both influence over foreign policy decision making and the prerogatives usually accorded neutral bodies in a political dispute."[86] This trend continued into the coverage of the second Palestinian Intifada that began in September 2000 and has been marred by numerous cases of anti-Israeli bias and media campaigns on behalf of the Palestinians.[87] A very serious example of this bias and distortion is the alleged massacre of Palestinians in the city of Jenin in April 2002, also known as the "Jenin massacre," that was widely reported but never happened.[88]

Several correspondents covering the Bosnia war crossed the professional lines, supported the Muslims, and vigorously advocated military intervention against the Serbs. The availability of all news global channels allowed them to mount a media campaign against one party to the conflict. Prominent journalists such as Christiane Amanpour, Martin Bell, and Ed Vulliamy strongly defended their one-sided coverage of the war.[89] Bell called his approach "journalism of attachment," and Vulliamy argued that

> in the examples of Bosnia, Rwanda, Cambodia, and elsewhere, the neutrality adopted by diplomats and the media is both dangerous and reprehensible. By remaining neutral, we reward the bullies of history . . . [and] create a mere intermission before the next round of atrocities. There are times when we as reporters have to cross the line . . .

News organizations, editors, and reporters often ignore the media campaigns on behalf of a particular side in an international conflict because it may question the standard media claim for fair, balanced, and objective coverage. The Bosnia coverage, however, inspired a debate among journalists. David Binder of the *New York Times* called the anti-neutrality argument "a garbage argument" and insisted that "our job is to report from all sides, not to play favorites."[90] Weaver explained: "Those who suffer more receive more media attention.[91] This has a distorting effect." In the case of Bosnia, he wrote, "the figures produced by the government in Sarajevo were accepted and broadcast with nowhere near the skepticism that greeted similar information coming from the Bosnian Serb leadership in Pale." Gowing also asserted that the attitude of Amanpour and her colleagues was neatly exploited by Bosnian ministers who "usually enjoyed a free ride, their increasingly exaggerated claims accepted as fact by callow interviewers and anchors in distant studios who did not have the knowledge or background briefings to know better."[92] The outcome, Gowing concluded, was a distorted and highly inaccurate coverage.

Conclusion

The fast pace of global television news presents difficult dilemmas to all the participants in deliberations on policymaking in international conflict including politicians, officials, journalists, and editors. These include the shortening of time for official response, the inherent media impatience and demands for immediate assessment of policies and events, and the pressure on reporters to constantly transmit pictures and reports even when their sources are questionable and the context is blurred. "Journalism of Attachment" and "advocacy journalism" have also challenged the professional community. Apparently, many participants in the media–policy dynamic interaction have not yet recognized the dilemmas and therefore are not making the necessary effort to deal with them. Surprisingly, perhaps, of all the participants, journalists and editors are the most reluctant to face the dilemmas global news coverage has presented for both policymakers and themselves.

4. Discussion and Conclusions

Policymaking in international conflict is highly complex and difficult. This study shows that the rise and the expansion of global television news coverage has made it even more complex. The September 2001 terror attacks and the U.S.-led wars in Afghanistan and Iraq have also challenged policymakers and journalists.[93] Whereas the most intriguing theory, the CNN effect hypothesis, has not been sufficiently validated, global television is increasingly becoming a source of rapid real-time information for policymakers, has accelerated the pace of diplomatic communication, and focused world attention on crises in places such as the Middle East, Bosnia, Somalia, and Kosovo. The fast pace of global television coverage has applied pressure on policymakers and foreign policy experts to respond even faster to international crises, while also allowing them to send significant messages that, in turn, have affected the outcomes of these events. The 24-hour all news channels and their fast broadcasting pace are also creating new challenging working conditions for journalists and reporters. Thus, the effects of global television on policymaking are much more complex and subtle than what is usually associated with the CNN effect.

The popularity of the CNN effect hypothesis and the attention it has received in all circles, including the policymaking and the media communities, and its consequences for both policymaking and research, deserve a separate comprehensive study.[94] Here, it is sufficient to suggest that this approach to the influence of global television represents an interesting case study in terminology and theory development. The concept was initially suggested by politicians and officials haunted by the Vietnam media myth, the confusion of the post–cold war era, and the communication revolution. Despite evidence to the contrary many leaders still believe that critical television coverage caused the American defeat in Vietnam.[95] Since then, many have viewed the media as an adversary to government policies in several areas, including humanitarian intervention and international negotiation. This background helps to understand why global television has been perceived as having a power to determine foreign policy, primarily in severe crisis situations, and why policymakers feel they need to neutralize the media before they implement significant foreign policy decisions.[96] This perception also explains why policymakers developed and employed new news management tactics such as "embedded journalism" to control coverage of war and terrorism.

This study demonstrates that global television affects the nuts and bolts of policymaking, and has created challenges and dilemmas for all the participants in the policy process. Political leaders face the following challenges and dilemmas: (1) how to avoid an immediate policy response to an unfolding event without being exposed as a weak leader who is confused and does not know how to handle a situation; (2) when responding, how to refrain from making a commitment to policy that might have to be reversed or changed; (3) how to include different appeals to domestic and foreign audiences in a single message; (4) how to flow with the fast pace of media events without creating too high expectations for too rapid results; and finally (5) how to maintain policy that is at odds with prevailing television tone, without alienating reporters and audiences. The professional foreign affairs bureaucracy face these dilemmas: (1) how to write and provide solid and well-founded information, evaluation, and recommendation for policy and still submit reports in time to be considered by leaders; and (2) how to effectively compete with video images that may be at odds with preferred policy.

Journalists face these challenges and dilemmas: (1) how to accurately report from any location and provide sufficient context and analysis under tremendous time pressure and limited knowledge on the events and processes covered; (2) how to report fairly on an international conflict when you believe one side is clearly the aggressor and the other is a victim; and (3) if reporters feel the need to take sides, how can they resist manipulations by the leaders of the party they support. Editors face these dilemmas: (1) how to avoid pressuring reporters sent overseas to file reports before they are ready, and still satisfy the everlasting hunger for real-time fresh and timely pictures; (2) how to select visuals from a large menu, including some from unknown sources, while still maintaining high professional standards; and (3) how to balance between one-sided reporting from journalists who believe they cannot be neutral in severe cases of violence, with the requirements of objectivity and fairness. There are no easy solutions to all these dilemmas, but the first task is to acknowledge that they exist and have significant effects.

This study suggests that all the participants in the foreign policy process have not yet sufficiently adapted to the new realities of global television coverage. Foreign policy experts, intelligence officers, and diplomats have lost several of their traditional functions to the journalists who are assuming some of these roles, and to spokespersons and communication experts, increasingly influential in inner governmental circles. News management techniques such as "embedded journalism" may be useful for a short period of actual combat but are highly problematic and controversial.[97] Similarly, the Pentagon's idea to create a special office for disinformation to help the global battle against terrorism was not likely to help the government in dealing with the global networks and fortunately was cancelled.

Successful coping with the challenges of global communication and efficient utilization of new and innovative media technologies require two sets of reforms in policymaking: first, in the training of leaders, high-level policymakers, and diplomats; second in the planning and implementation of policies.[98] Leaders must be prepared to handle the rapid pace of global communication and to avoid serious policy mistakes deriving from global television's demands for fast and effective responses, particularly in crisis situations. Thus, in addition to traditional and conventional strategic and diplomatic considerations, sophisticated policymaking in defense and foreign affairs today requires both sensitive understanding of the global media challenges and an efficient communication strategy for dealing with them. One of the most important principles of successful leadership and governance is the talent and ability to adjust to changing circumstances. Leaders and organizations are now more aware of the challenges of global television but need to address them more effectively.

This study also shows that in contemporary international conflicts reporters function as important participants and not only as observers. This places a heavier responsibility on journalists to report more accurately on what they see and hear. There is no in-depth discussion of the global coverage effects within the media professional community. Writings by television journalists such as Nik Gowing and Dan Rather are still scarce. Reforms in the training and conduct of both reporters and editors are required as well as constant close monitoring of media performance. Owing to the rapidly changing nature of both global communication and international relations, it is probable that the roles and effects of global television will increase as will their complexity and challenge. Researchers will have to devote more attention to these effects and understand them better, while policymakers and journalists will have to make a greater effort to cope with them.

Notes

The author wrote this work while serving as a fellow at the Shorenstein Center on the Press, Politics, and Public Policy, at the Kennedy School of Government, Harvard University. He thanks the center's director Alex Jones and associate director Dr. Pippa Norris for the invitation to conduct research at the center. He also thanks Thomas E. Patterson, Bradlee professor of Government and the Press at the Shorenstein Center, Richard N. Kaplan, former president of CNN-U.S., and Ambassador Jonathan Moore, former deputy assistant secretary of state, for making valuable comments on an earlier draft of this essay. He also thanks Caroline Cooper and Parker Everett for their research assistance.

1. See David Gergen, "Diplomacy in a Television Age: The Dangers of a Teledemocracy," in S. Serfaty, ed., *The Media and Foreign Policy* (New York: St. Martin's Press, 1991), pp. 47–63; and Lee Edwards, *Mediapolitik: How the Mass Media have Transformed World Politics* (Washington, D.C.: The Catholic University of America Press, 2001).

2. See Royce J. Ammon, *Global Television and the Shaping of World Politics: CNN, Telediplomacy, and Foreign Policy* (Jefferson, NC: McFarland, 2001).

3. Robert MacNeil, "The Flickering Images that May Drive Presidents," *Media Studies Journal*, Vol. 8 (Spring 1994), p. 125.

4. Cited in Johanna Neuman, *Lights, Camera, War: Is Media Technology Driving International Politics?* (New York: St. Martin's Press, 1996), p. 270.

5. Eytan Gilboa, "The CNN Effect: The Search for a Communication Theory of International Relations," *Political Communication*, Vol. 22, 2005.

6. Eytan Gilboa, "Global Communication and Foreign Policy," *Journal of Communication*, Vol. 52 (December 2002), pp. 731–748.

7. See Michael Gurevitch, "The Globalization of Electronic Journalism," in J. Curran and M. Gurevitch, eds., *Mass Media and Society* (London: Edward Arnold, 1991), pp. 178–193; W. Lance Bennett, "The Media and the Foreign Policy Process," in D. Deese, ed., *The New Politics of American Foreign Policy* (New York: St. Martin's Press, 1994), pp. 168–188; Brenda M. Seaver, "The Public Dimension of Foreign Policy," *Harvard International Journal of Press/Politics*, Vol. 3 (Winter 1998), pp. 65–91; Brigitte L. Nacos, Robert Shapiro, and Pierangelo Isernia, eds., *Decisionmaking in a Glass House* (Lanham, MA: Rowman and Littlefield, 2000).

8. I used Lexis-Nexis to identify the first reference to the term CNN effect in the print media. John Rohs, a lodging industry analyst, made the first reference to the term when he told the *New York Times* on January 28, 1991: "Restaurants, hotels, and gaming establishments seem to suffer from the *CNN effect*. People are intensely interested in the first real-time war in history and they are just planting themselves in front of the TV."

9. Daniel Schorr, "Ten Days that Shook the White House," *Columbia Journalism Review* (July–August, 1991), pp. 21–23; Walter Goodman, "Critic's Notebook, Re Somalia: How Much Did TV Shape Policy?" *New York Times*, (December 8, 1992), p. C20.

10. Michael J. O'Neill, *The Roar of the Crowd: How Television and People Power are Changing the World* (New York: Times Books, 1993); Ammon, *Global Television and the Shaping of World Politics*; Edwards, *Mediapolitik*.

11. Samuel Feist, "Facing Down the Global Village: The Media Impact," in R. Kugler and E. Frost, eds., *The Global Century* (Washington, D.C.: National Defense University Press, 2001), p. 713.

12. Daniel Schorr, "CNN effect: Edge-of-Seat Diplomacy," *Christian Science Monitor* (November 27, 1998), p. 11; Steven Livingston and Todd Eachus,

"Humanitarian Crises and U.S. Foreign Policy: Somalia and the CNN effect Reconsidered," *Political Communication*, Vol. 12 (December 1995), p. 413.

13. Philip Seib, *The Global Journalist: News and Conscience in a World of Conflict* (Lanham, MD: Rowman and Littlefield, 2002), p. 27.

14. Neuman, *Lights, Camera, War*, pp. 15–16.

15. Steven Livingston successfully applied these variations to a typology of military interventions created by Haass and to several case studies: "Beyond the 'CNN effect': The Media–Foreign Policy Dynamic," in P. Norris, ed., *Politics and the Press: The News Media and their Influences* (Boulder, CO: Lynne Riener, 1997), pp. 291–318; "Media Coverage of the War: An Empirical Assessment," in A. Schnabel and R. Thakur, eds., *Kosovo and the Challenge of Humanitarian Intervention: Selective Indignation, Collective Action, and International Citizenship* (Tokyo, New York, Paris: United Nations University Press, 2000), pp. 360–384; Richard Haass, *Intervention: The Use of American Military Power in the Post–Cold War World* (Washington, D.C.: Carnegie Endowment for International Peace, 1994).

16. Nicholas J. Wheeler, *Saving Strangers: Humanitarian Intervention in International Society* (New York: Oxford University Press, 2000), p. 300.

17. Piers Robinson, "The Policy–Media Interaction Model: Measuring Media Power During Humanitarian Crisis," *Journal of Peace Research*, Vol. 37, No. 5 (2000), pp. 613–633; "Operation Restore Hope and the Illusion of a News Media Driven Intervention," *Political Studies*, Vol. 49, No. 5 (2001), pp. 941–956; *The CNN Effect: The Myth of News, Foreign Policy and Intervention* (London and New York: Routledge, 2002).

18. Madeline Albright, *"Building a Collective Security System,"* statement before the subcommittee on Europe and the Middle East and on International Security, International Organizations, and Human Rights of the House Foreign Affairs Committee (Washington, D.C.: Department of State, May 10, 1993).

19. Cited in David Pearce, *Wary Partners: Diplomats and the Media* (Washington, D.C.: Congressional Quarterly, 1995), p. 18.

20. James A. Baker III, *The Politics of Diplomacy* (New York: G.P. Putnam's Sons, 1995), p. 103.

21. Marvin Kalb, "Report First, Check Later, Interview with James A. Baker III," *Harvard International Journal of Press/Politics*, Vol. 1 (Spring 1996), pp. 3–9.

22. John Shattuck, "Human Rights and Humanitarian Crises: Policymaking and the Media," in R. Rotberg and T. Weiss, eds., *From Massacres to Genocide: The Media, Public Policy and Humanitarian Crises* (Cambridge, MA: The World Peace Foundation, 1996), p. 174.

23. Cited in Larry Minear, Colin Scott, and Thomas G. Weiss, *The News Media, Civil War, and Humanitarian Action* (Boulder, CO: Lynne Rienner, 1996), p. 4.

24. David Owen, "A Clinician Caution: Rhetoric and Reality," in K. Cahill, ed., *Preventive Diplomacy: Stopping Wars Before They Start* (New York: Basic Books, 1996), p. 308.

25. Douglas Hurd, *The Search for Peace* (London: Little, Brown, and Company, 1997), p. 11.
26. Bob Woodward, *The Choice* (New York: Simon and Schuster, 1996), p. 261.
27. Dick Morris, *The New Prince: Machiavelli Updated for the Twenty First Century* (Los Angeles, CA: Renaissance Books, 1999), p. 165.
28. Timothy J. McNulty, "Television's Impact on Executive Decisionmaking and Diplomacy," *Fletcher Forum of World Affairs*, Vol. 17 (Winter 1993), p. 80.
29. James Hoge, Jr., "Media Pervasiveness," *Foreign Affairs*, Vol. 73 (July–August 1994), p. 139.
30. Brian Buckley, *The News Media and Foreign Policy: An Exploration* (Halifax, Nova Scotia: Centre for Foreign Policy Studies, Dalhousie University, 1998), p. 39.
31. George Kennan, *At a Century's Ending: Reflections, 1982–1995* (New York: Norton, 1996), pp. 294–297.
32. Dan Rather continued the debate in speeches and writings. See, e.g., in "The United States and Somalia: Assessing Responsibility for the Intervention," in E. Girardet, ed., *Somalia, Rwanda, and Beyond: The Role of the International Media in Wars and Humanitarian Crises* (Geneva: Crosslines Global Report, 1995), pp. 27–43.
33. MacNeil, "The Flickering Images," p. 130.
34. Schorr, "Ten Days that Shook the White House," 1991, p. 21; Martin Shaw, *Civil Society and Media in Global Crises* (New York: Pinter, 1996); and Ammon, *Global Television and the Shaping of World Politics*, pp. 96–105.
35. Derek Miller, Measuring Media Pessure on Security Policy Decisionmaking in Liberal States: The Positioning Hypothesis. Paper Presented at the Annual Convention of the International Studies Association, New Orleans, March 2002.
36. Michael Mandelbaum, "The Reluctance to Intervene," *Foreign Policy*, Vol. 95 (1994), p.16.
37. Bernard Cohen, "A View from the Academy," in W.L. Bennett and D. Paletz, eds., *Taken by Storm: The Media, Public Opinion, and U.S. Foreign Policy in the Gulf War* (Chicago, IL: The University of Chicago Press, 1994), pp. 9–10.
38. Jonathan Mermin, "Television News and American Intervention in Somalia: The Myth of a Media-Driven Foreign Policy," *Political Science Quarterly*, Vol. 112 (Fall 1997), pp. 385–403, and *Debating War and Peace: Media Coverage of U.S. Intervention in the Post-Vietnam Era* (Princeton, NJ: Princeton University Press, 1999).
39. Livingston and Eachus, "Humanitarian Crises and U.S. Foreign Policy," p. 413.
40. John Riley, Rethinking the Myth of the CNN effect. Paper Presented at the Annual Convention of the American Political Science Association, Atlanta, September 1999; Wheeler, *Saving Strangers*, p. 300; Robinson, "Operation Restore Hope," p. 941.
41. David Gibbs, "*Realpolitik* and Humanitarian Intervention: The Case of Somalia," *International Politics*, Vol. 37 (March 2000), pp. 41–55.

42. Peter V. Jakobsen, "National Interest, Humanitarianism or CNN: What Triggers UN Peace Enforcement after the Cold War?" *Journal of Peace Research*, Vol. 33, No. 2 (1996), p. 212; and "Focus on the CNN effect Misses the Point: The Real Media Impact on Conflict Management is Invisible and Indirect," *Journal of Peace Research*, Vol. 37, No. 2 (2000), pp. 131–143.

43. Jakobsen, "Focus on the CNN effect," p. 138.

44. Robinson, "The Policy–Media Interaction Model"; and *The CNN Effect*, pp. 25–35.

45. Neuman, *Lights, Camera, War*, p. 16; Buckley, *The News Media and Foreign Policy*, p. 44.

46. Warren P. Strobel, *Late-Breaking Foreign Policy, the News Media's Influence on Peace Operations* (Washington, D.C.: United States Institute of Peace Press, 1997), p. 5; and Philip Seib, *The Global Journalist*, p. 27.

47. Andrew S. Natsios, *U.S. Foreign Policy and the Four Horsemen on the Apocalypse: Humanitarian Relief in Complex Emergencies* (Westport, CT: Praeger, 1997), p. 124; Nik Gowing, "Media Coverage: Help or Hindrance in Conflict Prevention?" in S. Badsey, ed., *The Media and International Security* (London: Cass, 2000), p. 204; Jakobsen, "Focus on the CNN effect," p. 133.

48. Eytan Gilboa suggested that owing to the expansion of global news networks the term CNN effect should be replaced by a broader and more neutral term: "controlling actor." See his "Global Communication and Foreign Policy," pp. 733–735.

49. Philip Seib, *Headline Diplomacy: How News Coverage Affects Foreign Policy* (Westport, CT: Praeger, 1997), pp. 103–106.

50. Neuman, *Lights, Camera, War*, pp. 270–271.

51. O'Neill, *The Roar of the Crowd*, pp.177–179.

52. David Hoffman, "Global Communications Network was Pivotal in Defeat of Junta," *Washington Post* (August 23, 1991), p. A27. See also McNulty, "Television's Impact on Executive Decisionmaking," pp. 71–73.

53. Lewis A. Friedland, *Covering the World: International Television News Services* (New York: Twentieth Century Fund Press, 1992), pp. 7–8.

54. Cited in Nicholas Hopkinson, *The Media and International Affairs after the Cold War* (London: HMSO, Wilton Park Paper 74, 1993), p. 11.

55. Hoge, "Media Pervasiveness," p. 140.

56. Friedland, *Covering the World*, pp. 42–45; Robert J. Donovan and Ray Scherer, *Unsilent Revolution, Television News and American Public Life, 1948–1991* (Cambridge: Cambridge University Press, 1992), p. 317.

57. McNulty, "Television's Impact on Executive Decisionmaking," pp. 70–71.

58. George H.W. Bush and Brent Scowcroft, *A World Transformed* (New York: Knopf, 1998), pp. 474–475; See also McNulty, "Television's Impact on Executive Decisionmaking," pp. 70–71; and Tom Rosenstiel, "The Myth of CNN," *The New Republic* (August 22 and 29, 1994), pp. 27–33.

59. Cited in Walter B. Wriston, "Bits, Bytes, and Diplomacy," *Foreign Affairs*, Vol. 76 (September–October 1997), p. 174.
60. Schorr, "CNN Effect: Edge-of-Seat Diplomacy," p. 11; Feist, "Facing Down the Global Village," pp. 715–716.
61. Kenneth T. Walsh, *Feeding the Beast: The White House Versus the Press* (New York: Random House, 1996), pp. 288–289.
62. Marlin Fitzwater, *Call the Briefing* (New York: Times Books, 1995), p. 264.
63. Seib, *The Global Journalist*, pp. 23–25.
64. Lesley Stahl, *Reporting Live* (New York: Simon and Schuster 1999), pp. 355–356.
65. Michael R. Beschloss and Strobe Talbott, *At the Highest Levels: The Inside Story of the End of the Cold War* (Boston: Little, Brown, 1993), p. 135.
66. Nicholas Kralev, "Around-the-Clock News Cycle: A Double-Edged Sword, An Interview with Secretary of State Madeline K. Albright," *Harvard International Journal of Press/Politics*, Vol. 6 (Winter 2001), pp. 105–108.
67. Thomas W. Lippman, *Madeleine Albright and the New American Diplomacy* (Boulder, CO: Westview Press, 2000).
68. Michael Beschloss, *Presidents, Television, and Foreign Crises* (Washington, D.C.: The Annenberg Washington Program, 1993).
69. Cited in Bradley Patterson, Jr., *The White House Staff: Inside the West Wing and Beyond* (Washington, D.C.: Brookings Institution Press, 2000), pp. 130–131.
70. Schorr, "CNN effect: Edge-of-Seat Diplomacy," p. 11.
71. Lloyd Cutler, "Foreign Policy on Deadline" *The Atlantic Community Quarterly*, Vol. 22 (Fall 1984), pp. 223–232.
72. Cited in Dean Fischer, "State of Tension," *American Journalism Review*, (April 2000), p. 39.
73. Nicholas Kralev, "The Media—a Problem in Policymaking, Interview with Condoleezza Rice," *Harvard International Journal of Press/Politics*, Vol. 5 (Summer 2000), p. 88.
74. Colin L. Powell, *My American Journey* (New York: Random House, 1995), p. 508.
75. Marvin Kalb, "Be Skeptical, but in a Crisis Give us the Benefit of the Doubt, Interview with William S. Cohen," *Harvard International Journal of Press/Politics*, Vol. 5 (Spring 2000), p. 8.
76. Daniel Dayan and Elihu Katz, *Media Events: The Live Broadcasting of History* (Cambridge, MA: Harvard University Press, 1992).
77. Eytan Gilboa, "Media Diplomacy in the Arab–Israeli Conflict," in E. Gilboa, ed., *Media and Conflict: Framing Issues, Making Policy, Shaping Opinions* (Ardsley, NY: Transnational Publishers, 2002), pp. 193–211.
78. Kralev, "The Media—a Problem in Policymaking," 2000, p. 88.
79. Seib, *The Global Journalist*, p. 13.
80. Gowing, "Media Coverage," p. 217.
81. Jacqueline Sharkey, "When Pictures Drive Foreign Policy," *American Journalism Review* (December 1993), p. 16.

82. Tal Sanit, "The New Unreality: When TV Reporters don't Report," *Columbia Journalism Review* (May–June, 1992), p. 17.

83. Rosenstiel, "The Myth of CNN," p. 30. See also Brenda Maddox, "How Trustworthy is Television," *British Journalism Review*, Vol. 10 (1992), pp. 34–38.

84. Gowing, "Media Coverage," pp. 219–220.

85. Joshua Muravchik, "Misreporting Lebanon," *Policy Review*, Vol. 23 (Winter 1983), pp. 11–66; Zeev Chafets, *Double Vision: How the Press Distorts America's View of the Middle East* (New York: Morrow, 1985).

86. Jim Lederman, *Battle Lines: The American Media and the Intifada* (New York: Holt, 1992), pp. 237–238.

87. See, e.g., Trevor Asserson and Elisheva Mironi, The BBC and the Middle East: A Critical Study (London: unpublished manuscript, 2002); Barbara Amiel, "Disinfect the BBC Before it Poisons a New Generation," *Daily Telegraph*, Internet edition (July 9, 2003); Daniel Seaman, "Can the BBC Operate Responsibly?" *Jerusalem Post*, Internet edition (July 15, 2003). CAMERA, Committee for Accuracy in Middle East Reporting in America, has documented numerous cases of distorted and biased reporting on Israel and the Arab–Israeli conflict in the Western media. See www.Camera.org.

88. Charles Krauthammer, "Jenin: The Truth," *Washington Post* (May 3, 2002), p. A27; Sharon Sadeh, "How Jenin Battle became a 'Massacre,' " *The Guardian*, London (May 6, 2000), p. 7; Hirsh Goodman, and Jonathan Cummings, eds., *The Battle of Jenin: A Case Study in Israel's Communications Strategy* (Tel Aviv: Jaffee Center for Strategic Studies, Tel Aviv University, Memorandum No. 63, 2003).

89. Christiane Amanpour, "Television's Role in Foreign Policy," *Quill* (April 1996), pp. 16–17; Martin Bell, "TV News: How Far should We Go?" *British Journalism Review*, Vol. 8 (1997), pp. 7–16; Ed Vulliamy, " 'Neutrality' and the Absence of Reckoning: A Journalist's Account," *Journal of International Affairs*, Vol. 52 (Spring 1999), pp. 603–620.

90. Sherry Ricchiardi, "Over the Line," *American Journalism Review* (September 1996), p. 27. For a critique of "journalism of attachment" see Gregory McLaughlin, *The War Correspondent* (London: Pluto Press, 2002), pp. 153–198.

91. Tim Weaver, "The End of War: Can Television Help Stop It?" *Track Two*, 7 (December 1998), Internet edition, 1–4.

92. Gowing, Media Coverage, pp. 221–222. See also James J. Sadkovich, *The U.S. Media and Yugoslavia, 1991–1995* (Westport, CT: Praeger, 1998).

93. See, e.g., Brigitte L. Nacos, *Mass-Mediated Terrorism: The Central Role of the Media in Terrorism and Counterterrorism* (Lanham, MD: Rowman and Littlefield, 2002); Bradly S. Greenberg, ed., *Communication and Terrorism, Public and Media Responses to 9/11* (Cresskill, NJ: Hampton Press, 2002); Barbie Zelizer and Stuart Allen, eds., *Journalism after September 11* (London and New York: Routledge, 2003).

94. See Gilboa, "The CNN Effect."

95. Daniel Hallin, *The Uncensored War* (Berkeley, CA: University of California Press, 1986).

96. Eytan Gilboa, "Secret Diplomacy in the Television Age," *Gazette*, Vol. 60 (June 1998), pp. 211–225.

97. See, e.g., Bill Katvosky and Timothy Carlson, *Embedded: The Media at War in Iraq* (Guilford, CT: The Lyons Press, 2003); Danny Schechter, *Embedded: Weapons of Mass Deception, How the Media Railed to Cover the War on Iraq* (Amherst, NY: Prometheus Books, 2003); Howard Tumber and Jerry Palmer, *Media at War: The Iraq Crisis* (London: Sage, 2004); Philip Seib, *Beyond the Front Lines* (New York: Palgrave, 2004).

98. For detailed analysis and recommendations see Eytan Gilboa, "Television News and U.S. Foreign Policy: Constraints of Real-Time Coverage," *Harvard International Journal of Press/Politics*, Vol. 8 (Fall 2003), pp. 97–113. See also Evan Potter, ed., *Cyber-Diplomacy: Managing Foreign Policy in the Twenty-First Century* (Montreal and Kingston: McGill-Queen's University Press, 2002).

CHAPTER 2

International News and Advanced Information Technology

Changing the Institutional Domination Paradigm?

Steven Livingston, W. Lance Bennett, and W. Lucas Robinson

In a recent critique of American politics and journalism, sociologist Herbert J. Gans emphasizes the importance of analyzing news according to the defining structural elements of the media. "Journalistic work," says Gans, "is almost always performed under difficult conditions of one kind or another, and most of the important imperfections . . . reside in the structures of the news media."[1] We share this perspective and use it as our point of departure for the development of a news gatekeeping model.[2] There are several useful but incomplete gatekeeping models found throughout the political communication research literature. Each model tends to emphasize important aspects of news selection and production processes while underutilizing alternative factors. Developing a more complete news gatekeeping model would contribute to the development of more sophisticated political communication theory. With that objective in mind, we present the basic outline of a multigated news gatekeeping model and apply it to a preliminary analysis of media coverage of the war in Iraq.

There are at least four distinct gatekeeping models scattered about the political communication research literature. We refer to them as the (1) reporter-driven; (2) organizationally driven; (3) economically driven; and (4) technologically driven news gatekeeping models. Each of these four models in turn has at least six defining characteristics. They are: (1) the decision basis of news selection; (2) a distinct information gathering and organizing style; (3) differing understandings of the role of the reporter; (4) a particular concept of the public; (5) a particular understanding of press–government relations; and (6) an overarching gatekeeping norm. We will begin by outlining the four gatekeeping models and then selectively consider the six defining characteristics. Our principal objectives are: (1) to provide the reader with an introductory outline of the multigated gatekeeping model; and (2) its application in an effort to explain emerging trends in media–state relations, particularly concerning military–media relations during the U.S. war against Iraq. Although we believe the model outlined here can be adapted to a variety of press systems around the world, our primary focus in this chapter is on the press system in the United States.

1. A Multigated Gatekeeping Model

At least four news gatekeeping models can be found in the political communication literature. The reporter-driven news gatekeeping model centers on the role of newsgathering professionals. According to this model, to understand news selection processes one must focus on the social and professional norms of journalists, and on the socialization processes of the profession.[3] The economically driven news gatekeeping model focuses on the economic constraints and incentives in newsgathering. According to this understanding of news selection processes, news construction is constrained by the economic imperatives of commercial media.[4] An organizationally driven gatekeeping model emphasizes the bureaucratic or organizational context of news. In this view, news is the product of a system of exchange between institutionally based reporters and officials.[5] Reporters are given access to a steady and predictable supply of information that is typically provided by official government sources. Finally, a fourth news gatekeeping model emphasizes the role of technology. News is, according to the technology-driven model, the product of a given state of technological development.[6] A simplistic technological determinism is avoided when one considers the interactive nature of news and technology. The predilection to pursue dramatic and visually compelling stories in real time places a premium on the development of technology that facilitates such coverage. News values lead to technologies, just as technologies encourage a particular sort of news.[7]

Rather than isolating economics, technology, or the role of professional journalist norms and values, a multigated gatekeeping model allows us to examine the interactions among the various pressures and incentives captured by each of the constituent models. They blend and merge together, creating a mélange of influences. The defining elements of the technologically driven gatekeeping model can, for instance, be used to accentuate journalistic independence by providing alternative sources of information. For example, high-resolution remote-sensing satellite imagery now provided by private firms enables news organizations to independently verify bomb damage assessments or analyze nuclear weapons facilities in a manner not unlike an intelligence organization.[8] Videophones can also empower journalists as enterprise journalists, documenting the effects of battle while capturing a dramatic but information-rich account of war. Alternatively, new technologies can fuel pursuit of banal entertainment, such as the use of microwave relays and helicopters to transmit the latest car crash on the local freeway. If it bleeds it leads.

Different news organizations place greater emphasis on different elements of the four gatekeeping models. Prestigious press such as the *New York Times, The Wall Street Journal,* and *The Washington Post* tend to carve out hybrids of the organizationally driven and reporter-driven models, though there is concern that economically driven gatekeeping elements are encroaching on even these bastions of elite American journalism. Until at least its merger with Time-Warner, CNN tended to combine elements of the technologically driven model with the organizationally driven and reporter-driven models. In the view of many contemporary critics, news consists of content driven by the entertainment values of the economically driven gatekeeping model.

From a more distant perspective, the four gatekeeping models capture the shifting dynamics of particular eras in journalism. As Bennett noted in the original formulation of the multigated gatekeeping model, "During any period, one or more of the factors may be dominant in the quartet, but the relations among dominant and submissive factors settle into an equilibrium that journalists come to recognize in terms of commonly accepted working conditions [e.g., established levels of personal autonomy, known organizational routines, recognized economic limits, and stable applications of technology]."[9] When one or more of the dominant elements fades or is eclipsed by another element (or combination of elements), a new equilibrium emerges. The penny press, for example, was the product of a particular level of technological development (mechanical presses and sophisticated distribution systems), economic conditions (emerging mass audiences, urbanization, and consumerism and the shift to advertising-based revenue streams), and the growth of complex organizational structures (assigning reporters to police beats, city hall, and state assemblies). Bennett uses the example of the rise of a national, mass audience news system in the mid-twentieth century to make this same point.[10] From roughly 1950 to 1980, the mass audience news system was distinguished by the rise of network television, the introduction of nightly network newscasts, the creation of a mass audience, and comparatively modest economic constraints on news organizations. This mass audience media system began to atrophy toward the end of the twentieth century. The development of segmented media such as cable television and the Internet undermined the logic of mass audience marketing and, therefore, mass audience programming of all sorts, including news.[11]

Following landmark studies beginning in the 1970s by Leon Sigal (1973), Herbert Gans (1979), Lance Bennett (1990), and Daniel Hallin (1985, 1986), among others, scholarship centered on the democratic limitations of a media system dominated by the views and interests of government and other political elites.[12] More recent critiques tend to focus more on the effects associated with the growth of corporate media and the rise of entertainment values in the news.[13]

Thomas Patterson, for instance, found that as a result of corporate profit pressures, so-called hard news—news concerning politics and policy—has been eroded by soft news and infotainment features.[14] Countless seminars, conferences, symposia, and an enormous volume of literature have documented the effects of economic pressures on traditional gatekeeping based on reporter judgment and professional editorial standards.

This shift in media scholarship signals the occurrence of a reorientation of the principal influences of the four gatekeeping models. Periods of media equilibrium such as the mass audience media system of the mid-twentieth century are punctuated by periods of disruption, such as we've seen as a result of corporate consolidation of the media, changing information, and communication technology. Following the Communication Act of 1996 and the more recent Federal Communication Commission ruling expanding the ability of media corporations to own multiple media outlets in a given market it seems reasonable to conclude that we are still in the midst of a transitional period. There are, however, indications of what the new patterns look like. The point of our analysis is to get a better handle on the state of the contemporary media environment, particular concerning state–media relations. A comprehensive understanding of what may emerge in the next era of news gatekeeping requires consideration of the rich interactions among new technological and economic changes with the still-dominant organizational and individual level news practices.

We can gain a clearer sense of the interactive links among the four gatekeeping models with a closer examination of their key distinguishing elements. We turn to that task in the next section.

2. Six Key Elements

There are at least six defining elements of each of the four gatekeeping models found in the research literature.[15] We cannot provide a full accounting of each of these six elements in the space available here.[16] Instead, we will focus on those we believe will assist us the most in thinking about news coverage of the war in Iraq in 2003. (See table 2.1.)

Table 2.1   A multigated model of news gatekeeping

Defining elements	Core gatekeeping principles			
	Reporter-driven	Organizationally driven	Economically driven	Technologically driven
Decision basis	Personal (implicit news values)	Bureaucratic (professional journalism values and editorial standards)	Business (profits and demographics)	Immediacy and utilization of technical capacity
Information gathering and organizing	Investigation enterprise journalism	Beats and assignments (official pronouncements, pack journalism)	Marketing formulas (infotainment)	Systemic transparency
Journalistic role	Watchdog	Record keeper, intermediator/ translator	Content provider	Transmitter
Conception of public	Intellectually engaged citizens (public interest)	Social Monitors (is my world safe?)	Entertainment audience (consumer content)	Voyeur
Media–government relations	Personalized (cultivated source relationships)	Symbiotic (routinized informationand status exchange)	Commodified (manipulative transactions)	Real-time, event-driven, requiring official reaction
Gatekeeping norm	Independence (what the journalist decides is news)	Objectivity-fairness (officials and establishedinterests define news)	Plausibility (If plausible, would it make a good story?)	Eye-witness

Decision Basis

The first defining element is the decision basis: what criteria rest at the center of a purely reporter-driven, economically driven, organizationally driven, or technologically driven news decision? The ideal reporter-driven decision basis, for instance, seems nearly instinctual in nature, involving an engrained sense of what constitutes a "good story." Discussions of this sort of journalism among seasoned veterans are often steeped in the folklore of cub reporters, crusty green-eyeshade editors and hard-bitten veteran journalists. News decisionmaking is anchored by the reporter's own sense of what constitutes a good story.

The economic-driven decision basis, on the other hand, is driven by market research and the profit motive. Accordingly, profit is at the heart of the news decision basis. The line between entertainment and news is blurred, both within a story and within the media corporate product structure. For example, this is evident in the way CBS News pursued a contemporary version of checkbook journalism when its parent corporation, Viacom, offered former U.S. Army POW Jessica D. Lynch a bundle of big-budget deals as an inducement to reaching an agreement for an exclusive interview with CBS News. The combination of programs included a book contract with Simon & Schuster, an MTV concert special, and a made-for-television movie.[17]

The decision basis for the technologically driven gatekeeping model centers on utility maximization of technical capacity. In other words, the possession of helicopters, mobile satellite uplinks, or any other costly newsgathering tool creates incentives for their regular use. Along the way, "news" tends to be defined according to criteria that emphasize the use of this sort of technology. A premium is placed on covering—live if possible—dramatic events with striking visual elements, action, and suspense. Live pictures of police chases, for example, have become staples of local news organizations armed with helicopters and live transmission equipment.

Given the central role of technology in our analysis of the media and the war in Iraq presented below, it is worth taking a moment for a more detailed discussion of the news decision basis according to the technologically driven gatekeeping model.

For television news (and to a lesser extent radio and Internet news services) going live is an end in itself.[18] Evidence of this is seen in the habit of television news to utilize high-tech transmission equipment to report live from a location that otherwise offers little intrinsic news value. Examples of this include reporting live from the location of an event long over, or defining as "news" any dramatic event that happens to be available at the time of the broadcast, even if it is devoid of larger social or political significance.[19]

Crime stories complete with yellow tape around the crime scene and tearful victims offer another example of news content driven by technology and economics, whether the segment is live or an edited package. According to the results of a study of local news conducted by the Center for Media and Public Affairs, crime stories dominated most programs.[20] The telling irony behind this phenomenon is the fact that at the time crime news shot up in the 1990s crime was actually on the decline.[21] Murder rates across the nation, for example, declined by 20 percent over the 1990s, while the number of murder stories on network news programs soared some 700 percent between 1993 and 1996.[22] The orientation of television news toward crime in the 1990s was not an aberration. Network news more than doubled the time devoted to entertainment, disasters, accidents, and crime, while reducing the coverage of environment, policymaking, and international affairs.[23]

Reporting live is now as much a part of the commercial packaging or branding of a news organization, as it is a serious tool of journalism. Viewers are encouraged to equate professional competence with an ability to report live from venues associated with otherwise mundane or banal events. Indeed, news as synthetic drama—facilitated by live reports—may be the perfect counterpart to what Daniel Boorstin called pseudo-events. A pseudo-event, said Boorstin, comes about "because someone has planned, planted, or incited it."[24] It is an artificial event concocted for the purpose of being covered by the news media.

Institutionally based pseudo-events offer news organizations a ready and predictable supply of information that can be presented as news. These are news values deeply rooted in the organizationally driven gatekeeping model. Adding a patina of drama through live reports introduces news decisionmaking values more closely associated with the economically driven news gatekeeping model. Official institutions and the officials in them still dominate the news agenda and frames of reference, but in the context of news programming with an added dose of drama. Something quite similar to this dynamic explains at least some of the media content and practices during the war in Iraq. In essence, war news presented by the embedded reporters was institutionally based, despite the battlefield environment. The embed program extended the reach of institutionally based reporting. Indeed, with the dangers of the battlefield, the war correspondent in Iraq was utterly dependent on his military sources/protectors/ fellow countrymen. At the White House, State Department, or

Pentagon beat, a reporter's next story depends on getting along and going along with the routines and expectations of the institution. For the war correspondent in Iraq, his next story and his life depended on those he was assigned to cover. We will pick up on this line of reasoning more in the discussion section below.

If banal or controlled news were the only stories concerning news decisionmaking and technology, news gatekeeping analysis would be a rather straightforward and comparatively simple task. We could simply say that technology is used in the service of dramatic but banal news that is intended to deliver audiences to advertisers. The elements of the technologically driven gatekeeping model blend only with the economically driven gatekeeping model. This of course is not the case; not all dramatic events captured by advanced information and communication technology are synthetic, banal, nor can they be dismissed as mere dramatic window dressing for an otherwise routine interaction between government institutions and the news media. Wars, famine, terrorist incidents, civil unrest, environmental and natural disasters all have intrinsic political, economic, and social significance. Political communication and public policy research literature is replete with references to the potentially destabilizing effect associated with media coverage of unplanned and unpredicted events. Roger Cobb and Charles Elder (1984) speak of triggering events that reorient public and policy agendas into new and unexpected directions.[25] Public policy scholars such as John Kingdon (1984), Bryan Jones and Frank Baumgartner (1993), and Thomas Birkland (1997) have spoken of "focusing events," a term of reference for a concept nearly identical to Cobb and Elder's earlier reference to triggering events.[26] Political communication scholars refer to the related concept of event-driven news to refer to the effects on the media agenda of dramatic, unexpected events that have a significant impact on politics and policy debates. Regina Lawrence's examination of the videotaped beating of Rodney King offers the most thoughtful and compelling example of this sort of research.[27] In international affairs and foreign policy decisionmaking, references to the CNN effect rest on a similar premise: dramatic, usually unpredicted events covered by the media alter the foreign policy priorities of officials charged with managing the affairs of state.[28]

Whether referred to as triggering events, focusing events, event-driven news, or the CNN effect, a wide array of scholarship from across several disciplines has recognized the potential effects associated with news reports of dramatic, unplanned events. For scholars who are interested in formulating general rules concerning news gatekeeping decisionmaking and technology, the challenge is coming up with a way of distinguishing politically significant event-driven news from banal pseudo-events. The boundary between pseudo-events and event-driven news is unstable and permeable. Even the most carefully crafted pseudo-event has the inherent potential to degenerate into farce, folly, and mayhem. Political leaders misspeak, have awkward or clumsy habits, or miscalculate the effects of a synthetic event. At other times disruptive outside elements such as protesters pull a scripted event off into unanticipated directions. Nearly all staged events involve a gamble for institutional actors who are intent on controlling the pace and framing of news. Election campaign debates, presidential press conferences, and even staged events on aircraft carriers at times drift off course. Despite these dangers, from the perspective of officials in government, the deeper danger is found in ceding control of the agenda to journalists. That is why even in war, officials will find ways to control as best as possible journalists empowered by new technologies. How this was accomplished in the Iraq war is discussed below.

Information Gathering and Organizing Style

A particular information gathering and organizing style is the second of our six defining elements of each gatekeeping model. The information gathering style of the organizational gatekeeping model centers on routine exchanges of information and prestige among institutional actors. When assigned to specific institutions or organizations, reporters gather news from the daily interactions with officials and their spokespersons. They go to press conferences and briefings, conduct interviews, solicit and sometimes receive leaks, and generally define news in terms of official pronouncements and activities. As Leon Sigal noted 30 years ago in his classic study of the organizational basis of newsgathering, because reporters cannot witness most news events directly they must, "locate themselves in places where information is most likely to flow to them." Efficiency dictates "newsgathering through routine channels." The result is that the reporter "looks to official channels to provide him with newsworthy material day after day. To the extent he leans heavily on routine channels for news, he vests the timing of disclosure, and hence the surfacing of news stories, in those who control the channels."[29] In this way, official frames of reference and interpretation have tended to dominate public deliberations.

Conversely, according to the reporter-driven gatekeeping model, news is the product of scoops, inside information, investigative prowess, and—fundamentally—journalistic independence. According to its ideal, reporters are there to comfort the afflicted and afflict the comfortable. Again, the folklore of American journalism is populated by archetypes: I.F. Stone, Edward R. Murrow, Bob Woodward and Carl Bernstein, and Seymour Hersh, to name a few of the more noteworthy examples. Reporter independence offers the clearest line of demarcation between the traditional reporter-driven gatekeeping model and the other three models.

The information gathering style of the organizational model emphasizes a reporter's close adherence to the norms and expectations of the organizations involved in routine transactions or exchanges of information and status. The mark of a good reporter is found in his or her familiarity with the "workings of the building," as Pentagon reporters sometimes put it.[30] They are often experts in their own right on the arcane substance of policy, players, regulation, and procedures. Former NPR and ABC correspondent Cokie Roberts offers an example of such a reporter. Roberts grew up roaming the halls of the institution she would cover in her career as a journalist.[31] Organizational reporters are also familiar with the patois of the institutions they cover and therefore serve as translators and propagators of institutionally sanctioned language. This is particularly true of the Pentagon with its dizzying array of acronyms and jargon.[32] Stanford linguist Geoffrey Nunberg remarked "Embedded reporters produce embedded language, the metallic clatter of modern military lingo: acronyms like TLAM's, RPG's and MRE's; catchphrases like 'asymmetric warfare,' 'emerging targets' and 'catastrophic success'—the last not an oxymoron, but an irresistibly perverse phrase for a sudden acceleration of good fortune." Rather than working outside the system—the ideal of the reporter-driven model—news media are integral components of the governing system.[33]

The newsgathering and organizing style of reporters in the economically driven gatekeeping model centers on the collection of believable accounts of reality. Reports are filed according to a lower threshold of plausibility, rather than verified and conditional statements of fact. The decision basis of the economically driven model is rooted firmly in business terms: profit maximization through tailoring content to appeal to desired audiences. The information gathering and organizing style of this model centers on the development of information formats that deliver the most profitable audiences to advertisers.

The relationship between press and government officials is in a sense similar to the newsgathering and organizing style of the organizationally based model. There, news organizations and government institutions are involved in the cooperative production of news that benefits each respective institution. Politicians set agendas and frame issues in their regular exchanges with journalists. Similarly, economically driven news is based on the co-production of news that fits the commercial formulas of news organizations. Just as is true of the organizationally driven gatekeeping model, officials in the economically driven gatekeeping model are expected to manipulate journalists through well-staged events and dramatic announcements. The principal difference between the two models hinges on the nature of the staged events and desired content. The content of the economically driven gatekeeping model tends to be sensationalistic, highly personalized, and devoid of political significance, at least as traditionally construed. Rather than news concerning policies and politics, one is fed a steady diet of scandal, personal profiles, and other light news fare. News is entertainment; entertainment is news.

Finally, the technologically driven news gatekeeping model organizes newsgathering according to immediacy. News is what is happening now. Of course there are other expressions of technology in addition to its ability to collapse time and space in reporting live from distant locations.[34] The Internet and electronic archives such as Lexis-Nexis allow fast and easy access to a virtual library of obscure facts, past articles, and entire encyclopedias in moments.

Role of the Journalist

A third defining element of each of the four ideal gatekeeping models is the perceived role of the journalist. The role of the journalist according to the organizational model is defined by accuracy, access, and accommodation. Standards of professionalism so understood require the reporter to represent the views and positions of key institutional actors, thereby encouraging further access. To succeed, the reporter must play by the formal and informal rules established by the institution he or she covers. The idealized role of the reporter-driven model, on the other hand, is of the intrepid investigative journalist who attacks the powerful without fear or favor. This view is perhaps rooted in the Progressive era's faith in the restorative powers of publicity. During the Progressive era, notes cultural historian Stuart Ewen, the term publicity "had not yet assumed today's connotation of mendacious cunning. If anything, it was understood as a crystalline light by which an unraveling society and its toxic contradictions might be illuminated and brought to order."[35] The role of the journalist is to gather the facts that expose wrongdoing, the first step in reform.

The technology-driven gatekeeping model emphasizes a less intellectual, more visceral understanding of news and the role of the reporter. The technology-enabled reporter is an immediate extension of the eyes and ears of distant audiences. Rather than a collector and conveyer of facts, as in the Progressive-era ideals of the reporter-driven gatekeeping model, the technologically driven model is rooted in the immediate effects of sensory perception and emotion. Reporters are active agents, positioning themselves—often at great personal risk—in relation to a story that allows audiences to watch and react to events unfolding live before them. In the process, reporters often find themselves becoming a part of the story itself. For example, during the war against Iraq, embedded journalists utilized the latest technology to report the advance of U.S. forces toward Baghdad. In the process, they served as "force multipliers," underscoring to the Iraqi political and military establishment that resistance was hopeless. In conjunction with the practice of Secretary of Defense Donald Rumsfeld to speak directly to the Iraqi leadership during Pentagon press conferences, images of the rolling behemoth heading toward Baghdad sent a clear message to Iraqi officials: surrender. In this way, media technology was an integral part of the story.

Conception of the Public

Each gatekeeping model has a distinct concept of the public. Rooted in the Progressive era's faith in publicity, the reporter-driven gatekeeping model understands citizens in relation to earlier Jeffersonian ideals of democratic participation. Citizens are active information seekers, engaged in civic affairs.[36] If the outward orientation of the organizational reporter is to the institutional beat, the outward orientation of the reporter-driven ideal is toward the active citizen. In contrast, the economically driven newsroom understand the public as audience members defined by demographics. News programming is determined by demographic determinants. The clearest evidence of this is found not just in the nature of the news but also in the character of the advertising. The health and medical advertising of broadcast nightly news is oriented toward the demographic profile of its aging audience. On the other hand, one is unlikely to see Depends and Viagra advertisements while watching MTV news.

In comparison to the reporter-driven model, the technologically driven gatekeeping model places less faith in the intellectual capacity of the public. The public is understood more in terms of an audience, people who respond viscerally to stimuli. Viewing the news is as much an emotional experience as it is an intellectual one. Yet unlike the economic model's bottomless capacity to titillate an audience with the gross and sensational (think here of reality programming such as "Fear Factor" and quasi-news programs such as "Cops") the sometime sensational visual images of technologically enabled news can actually facilitate a deeper understanding of events. For instance, the enormity of the suffering of refugees in Somalia in 1992 or of genocide victims in Rwanda in 1994 were understandable only as a consequence of television pictures made possible by satellite uplinks.[37]

Media–Government Relationship

There is also variation among the gatekeeping models concerning the proper relationship between the media and the government. According to special protections given the press by the Constitution, journalism in the United States presumably has a special relationship to government. As noted by Bennett, there are the "symbiotic, mutually dependent relations nurtured by the economically protected organizational model of journalism, versus the commodified, negative, and manipulative relationships that develop under an economically dominant model of news construction."[38]

The technologically driven gatekeeping model offers a more complex and unpredictable view of reporter–government relations. Indeed, it is this very relationship that most concerns us here. "Event driven news," says Lawrence, "is cued by the appearance of dramatic news events and the 'story cues' for reporters that arise out of those events."[39] In her view, the organizational gatekeeping model—what she calls the institutional domination paradigm of news—explains much but not all news content and public problem definitions. "In institutionally driven news, political institutions set the agendas of news organizations; in contrast, as event-driven news gathers momentum, officials and institutions often respond to the news agenda rather than set it."[40] Lawrence notes that problems and problem definitions arising out of event-driven news are "more volatile and difficult for officials to control or to benefit from and are more open to challengers."[41] In this view, officials are sometimes challenged by the breaking news environment of the technologically enabled news organization and they are rarely in complete control of an issue agenda.

Livingston and Bennett (forthcoming) have found clear empirical evidence for at least a part of this claim: there has indeed been an increase in the frequency of event-driven news stories over the past decade. Officials are also more often found responding to these sorts of stories. But it remains to be seen whether or to what degree this development has resulted in an erosion of official control over the policy agenda. Our initial research of news coverage of the war in Iraq suggests that officials are still very much in control of news.

In summary, each constituent gatekeeping model of the multigated model differs according to several defining elements. Of these defining elements, we consider the tension found between, on the one hand, the

e for institutional access found in the organizationally driven
kekeeping model and the desire for the breathless immediacy and
drama found in the breaking event-driven news of the technologically
driven gatekeeping model on the other. Preliminary evidence and casual
observation suggests that elements of the organizational gatekeeping
model are most clearly evident in the reporting of the war in Iraq by U.S.
reporters and that whatever nascent independence technology might
afford the reporter in the field was, for the most part, unrealized.

Reporting the War

We collected television news coverage of the war in Iraq for a 32-day
period overlapping the start of the bombing and ground campaign
through to the declared end of the war following the fall of Baghdad.
The American news networks (Fox, CNN, ABC, CBS, NBC) were
recorded 24 hours a day for 32 days.[42] In May 2003, a team of graduate
students at George Washington University began coding the newscasts,
focusing first on the prime news programs aired each evening.

Though it is too early to draw definitive conclusions, initial results
suggest that the Pentagon's "embed" program served to extend the reach
of the institutional domination paradigm—a reflection of the defining elements of the organizationally driven gatekeeping model—into
the field of battle. Rather than atrophying in the face of advancing technologies and event-driven news, the organizationally driven gatekeeping
model seems alive and well, at least in the case of war reporting from Iraq.

While videophones were used by the embedded reporters to report
combat as it was happening, few of the reports extended beyond the immediate perspective of the U.S. military. Reports of the initial tank incursion
through the heart of Baghdad, for instance, said that thousands of Iraqis
were killed in several hours of fighting. Yet despite the presence of technologies that would allow the broadcasting of the human toll of war, there was
practically no coverage of casualties. Only in three cases were videophones
used to show casualties; and beyond videophones, only 7.3 percent of
stories coded show civilian casualties. Other results support the conclusion
that technology was used conservatively by news organizations:

(1) 2.7 percent of stories coded show Iraqi troop casualties versus
    3.5 percent showing U.S. troop casualties (only one story that
    shows British troop casualties).
(2) 28.6 percent of all stories coded focus on the battle for control of
    Baghdad.

Protests against the war were practically nonexistent on American television news. A total of 17 images of protests are shown: 8 in the United States, 1 in Europe, and 8 in an Arab/Muslim country.

Who serve as sources in the news? U.S. officials, including military personnel, constitute the majority of news sources, just as one would expect according to the organizationally driven gatekeeping model. Approximately one-third of all sources in the news were U.S. officials so defined.

(1) U.S. political officials speak in 13.2 percent of stories coded.
(2) British political officials speak in 0.8 percent of stories coded.
(3) Iraqi political officials speak in 3.4 percent of stories coded.
(4) Soldiers (US/Coalition) speak in 20.3 percent of stories coded.
(5) Among analysts, retired military/CIA speak in 6.9 percent of stories coded thus far; the Muslim community is represented in 0.5 percent of stories coded thus far (3 in the United States, 1 in the Middle East); academics in the United States speak in 3 percent of stories coded thus far; and "think tank" analysts speak in 2 percent of stories coded.
(6) Iraqi civilians speak in 9.7 percent of stories coded.

According to these preliminary results, elements of the organizationally driven gatekeeping model are most evident in American television news coverage of the war in Iraq.

3. Discussion

 new media

(Since 1999, media technology has become more mobile and significantly less controllable.[43] For instance, in April 2001 a CNN reporter/producer used a videophone to cover the departure of the crew of an American EP-3 surveillance plane that had been forced to land after colliding with a Chinese fighter aircraft. This was the first ever unauthorized television transmission from China.) Unlike the large and easily identified KU-band satellite uplinks often used by the networks to transmit from places such as Afghanistan, videophones are small, discrete, and unregulated at border crossings. They can literally be carried over one's shoulder. But their most important attribute is the ability to transmit acceptable quality video images live from any spot on earth(The line from event to global audience runs directly from the camera operator or reporter.)

During the 1990–91 Persian Gulf War, the only live transmissions occurred in the vicinity of the large and mostly immobile satellite uplink equipment found in Saudi Arabia. Combat reporters were dependent on military couriers to physically transport copy back to the Joint Information Bureau where it could be relayed to Washington, New York, Atlanta, and elsewhere. This placed the military in a position of organizational gatekeeper.[44] This stands in sharp contrast to the experience of reporting from Afghanistan a decade later. Journalists were free to roam in Afghanistan, limited only by brutal force and dangerous conditions.[45] Reporting from outside the confines of government institutional structures had its drawbacks, of course. One was that the technologically enabled reporter was dependent on his or her own wits and resourcefulness in finding news. Peter Baker of *The Washington Post* lamented that he spent six months "without ever speaking to an American soldier. We were shut out, leaving readers with only part of the story and, in my view, leaving journalists at greater risk as they roamed around the war zone without any military cooperation."[46]

With the embed program, reporting the war in Iraq was different, though perhaps no less dangerous. Organizationally driven news content places a premium on access to officials. Reporters exchange a degree of independence for the benefits of a steady flow of "news." To reiterate Leon Sigal's conclusion of 30 years ago, at the heart of the organizational newsgathering model is a consideration of logistics and efficiency. Because reporters cannot witness most news events directly they must, "locate themselves in places where information is most likely to flow to them." Because efficiency dictates, "newsgathering through routine channels," the reporter "vests the timing of disclosure, and hence the surfacing of news stories, in those who control the channels."[47] That is, essentially, what happened in Afghanistan. American news organizations ceded control of news to the Pentagon in exchange for access and a greater degree of safety. When asked why he abandoned his initial intention of covering the Iraq war as a unilateral—an independent reporter unassigned to a military unit—one reporter said, "It's just too dangerous. I'm not a cowboy. I want to come home to the kids in Washington."

Howard Kurtz, *The Washington Post* media correspondent, noted the importance of danger in explaining why correspondents were reluctant to cover the war from outside the confines of the embed program:

The dangers of wandering around Iraq were underscored yesterday when a BBC cameraman was killed by a land mine. An Australian cameraman and British television reporter were also killed in Iraq last month, and two *Newsday* correspondents and two freelance photographers were imprisoned by the Iraqis for a week before being released Tuesday.[48]

But danger alone doesn't explain the organizationally driven news content found in the reporting of the war in Iraq. Another part of the answer is found in the Pentagon's deft exploitation of the economic imperatives of television news. As we have noted above, technology can accentuate the gatekeeping norms of the reporter-driven model, placing a premium on independence and the desire for a good story. Alternatively, it can service the "breaking news at 11" mentality of the economically driven model. The embed program reinforced the latter.

4. Origins of the Embed Journalist Program

With movies such as "Top Gun," "Pearl Harbor," and "Black Hawk Down," Hollywood producer Jerry Bruckheimer was well known to the Pentagon. In 2001, Bruckheimer visited the Pentagon to pitch an idea he had for a new reality-based television show. Also in attendance was Bertram van Munster, the creator of the *Cops*. *Cops* "embeds" journalists with local police departments while they perform their duties, including car chases, arrests, and an occasional shoot-out. Bruckheimer and van Munster suggested a program about the U.S. forces in Afghanistan, a program they would call *Profiles from the Front Line*. It would be a prime time television series that followed the U.S. forces in Afghanistan. As with *Cops*, they were after human stories told through the eyes of the participants. The program was aired on ABC not long before the war in Iraq. In short, the origins of the embed program are found in a Fox reality television program.

Profiles from the Front Lines was filmed by eight teams of two or three "reporters" over several months. According to the Pentagon's project officer for the series, the interactions of the film crew and military personnel provided "a prelude to the process of embedding" media representatives in military units for war coverage. "Though they weren't reporting on a daily basis, they were with the unit—living with the unit and reporting on what different individuals or units were involved in. With each passing day, week, month came a better understanding."[49]

In the view of one entertainment critic reviewing *Profiles*, the program made no attempt to "discuss policy issues and whether troops should be there. Rather, it focuses on a variety of individuals, explaining who they are, what they do, and what they think and feel about their efforts."[50] George Wilson, a veteran war correspondent who covered Vietnam for *The Washington Post*, was embedded with a marine artillery unit in Iraq. His assessment of embed reporting echoes the entertainment reporter's criticism of *Profiles From the Front*. He described the Iraq war coverage as looking around and telling the reader: " 'These are magnificent kids, and I'm here in the dirt with them and I'm eating MREs [meals, ready to eat], and I'm sleeping in the sand.' There's nothing inherently wrong with that kind of reporting, but because it was so dominant, the larger story—namely, the near absence of organized resistance—was lost amid all the 'purple prose'."[51]

The embed program gave news organizations what they wanted: access to the war from a relatively manageable environment (surrounded by the might of the most powerful military in history). As with *Cops* and other reality television programming, access meant hearing and seeing the drama and action almost entirely from the perspective of the institutional actors. The gatekeeping hybrid was formed by elements of the economically driven and organizationally driven gatekeeping models.

It is important to keep in mind, however, that other conflicts, or even different moments of the same conflict, will assemble elements of the multigated gatekeeping model in different ways. After the Iraq war became the Iraq occupation, another synthesis emerged, one that combined the investigative reporting of Seymour M. Hersh with the technological power of ubiquitous digital photography. The prison abuse scandal at Abu Ghraib illustrates the technological gatekeeping model at work. Photographs of soldiers abusing Iraqi prisoners led to an international crisis for the United States. Technology was an enabler of tough investigative journalism.

As with any model, ours must be measured according to its ability to explain phenomena in a relatively complete and economical fashion. We believe the multigated gatekeeping model meets that objective.

Notes

1. Herbert J. Gans, *Deciding What's News: A Study of CBC Evening News, NBC Nightly News, Newsweek, and Time*, 1st ed. (New York: Pantheon Books, 1979), p. 45.
2. W. Lance Bennett, "Branded Political Communication: Lifestyle Politics, Logo Campaigns, and the Rise of Global Citizenship," in M Micheletti, A. Follesdal, and D. Stolle, eds., *The Politics Behind Products: Using the Market as a Site for Ethics and Action* (New Brunswick, NJ: Transaction Books, forthcoming).
3. W. Breed, "Social Control in the Newsroom," *Social Forces*, Vol. 33, (May 1955), Mark Fishman, *Manufacturing the News* (Austin: University of Texas Press, 1980).
4. Ben Bagdikian, *The Media Monopoly*, 5th ed. (Boston, MA: Beacon Press, 1997); Doug Underwood, *When MBAs Rule the Newsroom: How the Marketers*

and Managers Are Reshaping Today's Media (New York: Columbia University Press, 1993); Robert Waterman McChesney, *Rich Media, Poor Democracy: Communication Politics in Dubious Times* (Urbana: University of Illinois Press, 1999).

5. Leon V. Sigal, *Reporters and Officials: The Organization and Politics of Newsmaking* (Lexington, MA: D.C. Heath, 1973); Timothy E. Cook, *Governing with the News: The News Media as a Political Institution, Studies in Communication, Media, and Public Opinion* (Chicago: University of Chicago Press, 1998); Gans, *Deciding What's News: A Study of CBS Evening News, NBC Nightly News, Newsweek, and Time*; W. Lance Bennett, "Toward a Theory of Press-State Relations in the United States.," *Journal of Communication*, Vol. 40, No. 2 (1990).

6. Bruce A. Bimber, *Information and American Democracy: Technology in the Evolution of Political Power, Communication, Society, and Politics* (Cambridge, U.K., New York: Cambridge University Press, 2003); Steven Livingston, "Transparency and the News Media," in Finel Bernard and Kristin Lord, eds., *Power and Conflict in the Age of Transparency* (New York: St. Martin's Press, 2002); Philip M. Seib, *Going Live: Getting the News Right in Real-Time, Online World* (Lanham, MD: Rowman and Littlefields, 2001); Bill Kovach and Tom Rosenstiel, *Warp Speed: America in the Age of Mixed Media* (New York: Century Foundation Press, 1999); Johanna Neuman, *Lights, Camera, War: Is Media Technology Driving International Politics?* 1st ed. (New York: St. Martin's Press, 1996).

7. Michael Schudson makes a similar point concerning the relationship between technology and the creation of mass circulation newspapers in the nineteenth century. Newspapers invested in the creation of technology that would expand production and lower costs. As Schudson notes, "Indeed, it may be more accurate to say that the penny press introduced steam power to American journalism than to say that steam brought forth the penny press," Michael Schudson, *Discovering the News: A Social History of American Newspapers* (New York: Basic Books, 1978), p. 33.

8. Steven Livingston and W. Lucas Robinson, "Mapping Fears: The Use of Commerical High-Resolution Satellite Imagery in International Affairs," *Astropolitics*, Vol. 1, No. 2 (2003).

9. Bennett, "Branded Political Communication: Lifestyle Politics, Logo Campaigns, and the Rise of Global Citizenship."

10. Ibid.

11. Joseph Turow, *Breaking up America: Advertisers and the New Media World* (Chicago: University of Chicago Press, 1997).

12. Sigal, *Reporters and Officials: The Organization and Politics of Newsmaking*; Gans, *Deciding What's News: A Study of CBS Evening News, NBC Nightly News, Newsweek, and Time*; Bennett, "Toward a Theory of Press-State Relations in the United States"; Daniel C. Hallin, "The American News Media: A Critical Theory Perspective," in J. Forester, ed., *Critical Theory and Public Life*, (Cambridge, MA: MIT Press, 1985); Daniel C. Hallin,

The "Uncensored War": The Media and Vietnam (New York: Oxford University Press, 1986).

13. Gerald J. Baldasty, *The Commercialization of News in the Nineteenth Century* (Madison, WI: University of Wisconsin Press, 1992); M.X. Delli Carpini and B.A. Williams, "Let Us Infotain You: Politics in the New Media Environment," in W. Lance Bennett and Robert M. Entman, eds., *Mediated Politics: Communication and the Future of Democracy* (New York: Cambridge University Press, 2001); Neil Hickey, "Money Lust: How Pressure for Profit Is Perverting Journalism," in *Columbia Journalism Review* (Columbia Journalism Review, July/August 1998); Underwood, *When MBAs Rule the Newsroom: How the Marketers and Managers Are Reshaping Today's Media*. Other systems of organizing eras of media and communication can be found in Bimber, *Information and American Democracy: Technology in the Evolution of Political Power* Chap. 1. There is no clear point of demarcation between these two foci, and indeed they clearly overlap. One model does not necessarily replace another. Instead, it is a matter of shifting emphasis.

14. T.E. Patterson, *Doing Well and Doing Good: How Soft News and Critical Journalism Are Shrinking the News Audience and Weakening Democracy—and What News Outlets Can Do About It* [online pdf] (2000 [cited]); available from www.ksg.harvard.edu/presspol/Research_Publications/Reports/softnews.pdf.

15. Like all ideal types, the six defining elements outlined here are abstractions and as such do not exist in pure form in the real world. We will find that different combinations of our ideal types best explain media practices of a given era, news organization, or even individual cases.

16. Bennett, "Branded Political Communication: Lifestyle Politics, Logo Campaigns, and the Rise of Global Citizenship"; Steven Livingston and W. Lance Bennett, "Gatekeeping, Indexing, and Live-Event News: Is Technology Altering the Construction of News?," *Political Communication,* Vol. 20, No. 4 (Fall 2003).

17. L. Moraes, "CBS News Defends Its Multi-Pronged Pitch to Lynch," *The Washington Post,* June 17, 2003. By mid-June 2003 the value of Lynch's story began to decline as further investigation revealed that the Pentagon, initially benefiting from its dominant position as primary framer of war news, had embellished her exploits on the battlefield. Rather than emptying her magazine of bullets into her assailants just before being shot and stabbed (as the original story had it), Lynch suffered her life-threatening injuries as the vehicle she was riding in crashed at the onset of the battle. Nor did her rescuers shoot their way into the hospital where she was under treatment by Iraqi doctors. Instead, the U.S. soldiers were met at the door of the hospital and directed to Lynch, kept at the time in the best room in the hospital (N. Kristof, "Saving Private Jennifer," *New York Times,* June 20, 2003.) The Pentagon's ability to spin Lynch's story into a heroic epic suggests elements of the organizationally driven gatekeeping model, while the

subsequent investigations that debunked the story suggest elements of the reporter-driven gatekeeping model (Dana Priest, William Booth, and Susan Schmidt, "A Broken Body, a Broken Story, Pieced Together Investigation Reveals Lynch—Still in Hospital after 67 Days—Suffered Bone-Crushing Injuries in Crash During Ambush," *The Washington Post*, June 17, 2003.)

18. Seib, *Going Live: Getting the News Right in a Real-Time, Online World.*

19. The famous Los Angeles freeway chase of O.J. Simpson in his white Ford Bronco comes to mind as one example of this, though examples are evident during almost any newscast.

20. Lawrence K. Grossman, "Does Local TV News Need a National Nanny?" in *Columbia Journalism Review* (Columbia Journalism Review, July/August 1998).

21. Something similar to this occurred in the late 1980s and early 1990s regarding terrorism news. At a time when, according to several statistical sources, the actual number of terrorist events was on the decline around the world, the number of U.S. media stories about terrorism rose. See Steven Livingston, *The Terrorism Spectacle* (Boulder, CO: Westview Press, 1994).

22. For a more complete review of the burgeoning of crime stories at a time of dropping crime rates, see Bennett, "Branded Political Communication: Lifestyle Politics, Logo Campaigns, and the Rise of Global Citizenship."

23. Center for Media and Public Affairs, Bennett, "Branded Political Communication: Lifestyle Politics, Logo Campaigns, and the Rise of Global Citizenship."

24. Daniel J. Boorstin, *The Image: A Guide to Pseudo-Events in America* (New York: Harper and Row, 1961), p.11.

25. Roger W. Cobb and Charles D. *Elder, Participation in American Politics: The Dynamics of Agenda-Building,* 2nd ed. (Baltimore: Johns Hopkins University Press, 1983).

26. John W. Kingdon, *Agendas, Alternatives, and Public Policies,* 2nd ed. (New York: HarperCollins College Publishers, 1995); Frank R. Baumgartner and Bryan D. Jones, *Agendas and Instability in American Politics* (Chicago: University of Chicago Press, 1993); Thomas A. Birkland, *After Disaster: Agenda Setting, Public Policy, and Focusing Events, American Governance and Public Policy* (Washington, D.C.: Georgetown University Press, 1997).

27. Regina G. Lawrence, *The Politics of Force: Media and the Construction of Police Brutality* (Berkeley: University of California Press, 2000).

28. Steven Livingston and Todd Eachus, "American Network Coverage of Genocide in Rwanda in the Context of General Trends in International News," in Susanne Schmeidl and Howard Adelman, eds., *Early Warning and Early Response* (New York: Columbia International Affairs online, 1998); Steven Livingston, "Beyond the CNN Effect: The Media-Foreign Policy Dynamic," in Pippa Norris, ed., *Politics and the Press: The News Media and Their Influences* (Boulder, CO: Lynne Rienner Publishers, 1997).

29. Sigal, *Reporters and Officials: The Organization and Politics of Newsmaking,* p. 119 (emphasis added).

30. One of the authors served as associate director of the Defense Writers Group between 1997 and 2001. The Defense Writers Group held regular breakfast and dinner meetings between high-ranking Pentagon and intelligence officials and the national press corps. At least once a month, officials such as the chairman of the joint chiefs of staff, the secretary of defense, or the director of central intelligence would meet with reporters from the major national news outlets at a local Washington, D.C. hotel. Over the course of this author's affiliation with the Defense Writers Group, he witnessed a remarkable continuity in attendance. Reporters such as Jamie McIntyre of CNN and David Martin of CBS, Dana Priest of *The Washington Post*, and a host of less familiar names who write for the professional trade publications such as *Defense Daily, Defense Weekly, Air Force Magazine*, and Jane's Defense publications, remained largely unchanged. There is very little actual turnover in the institutional beats, or at least on the sometimes arcane Pentagon beat. This impression was enforced by biannual participation in the Robert R. McCormick Tribune's Cantigny Conferences on the military and the media. These conferences also bring together top officials with seasoned and tested defense correspondents. Over the course of a decade, there has been practically no change in the roster of correspondents attending the conference; defense officials have been less consistent as officers and civilian officials have a higher rate of career advancement and turnover.

31. Robert's father and mother were both members of Congress.

32. At times, it would seem this role as translator of Pentagon terms has also served as a signifier of the reporter's ability to "fit in" with the troops. During the 2003 war against Iraq, correspondents and other media commentators began using the lexicon of the military as if it were the patios of the population at large. The Third Infantry Division, for example, became the "third ID." The specialized language of subgroups and specialized organizations serve as bases of tribal identities. This is no less true of the Pentagon and the press corps desires to fit in with the institution it covers.

33. Cook, *Governing with the News: The News Media as a Political Institution.*

34. Steven Livingston and Douglas Van Belle, "The Effects of New Satellite Newsgathering Technology on Newsgathering from Remote Locations," *Political Communication* (forthcoming).

35. Stuart Ewen, *Pr! A Social History of Spin* (New York: Basic Books, 1996), p. 48.

36. See Gans, *Deciding What's News: A Study of CBS Evening News, NBS Nightly News, Newsweek, and Time*, pp. 55–61.

37. Livingston, "Beyond the CNN Effect: The Media-Foreign Policy Dynamic"; Livingston and Eachus, "American Network Coverage of Genocide in Rwanda in the Context of General Trends in International News"; Livingston, "Transparency and the News Media."

38. W. Lance Bennett, *News: The Politics of Illusion*, 5th ed., *Longman Classics in Political Science* (New York: Longman, 2003).

39. Lawrence, *The Politics of Force: Media and the Construction of Police Brutality*, p. 9.

40. Ibid.
41. Ibid.
42. This data collection was made possible by a generous grant from Arthur Kent.
43. Livingston, "Transparency and the News Media"; Livingston and Belle, "The Effects of New Satellite Newsgathering Technology on Newsgathering from Remote Locations"; Livingston and Bennett, "Gatekeeping, Indexing, and Live-Event News: Is Technology Altering the Construction of News?"
44. John J. Fialka, *Hotel Warriors: Covering the Gulf War, Woodrow Wilson Center Special Studies* (Washington, D.C.: Woodrow Wilson Center Press; distributed by the Johns Hopkins University Press, 1992).
45. Eight journalists were killed in just one month of fighting in Afghanistan in 2001. B. Bearak, "The Media: 3 Photographers in Tora Bora Are Detained by Afghan Fighters," the *New York Times*, 2001.
46. Peter Baker, "Inside View," *American Journalism Review*, May, 2003.
47. Sigal, *Reporters and Officials: The Organization and Politics of Newsmaking*, p. 119 (emphasis added).
48. H. Kurtz, "Start Shredding the News: Are the Revenue-Hungry Networks Ready to Dump Dinner Hour Broadcasts?" *The Washington Post*, March 18–24, 2002.
49. J. Gillies, "Putting a Face on Those Who Serve," *The Washington Post*, March 9, 2003.
50. Ibid.
51. Liz Marlantes, "The Other Boots on the Ground: Embedded Press," *The Christian Science Monitor*, April 23, 2003.

CHAPTER 3

Getting to War

Communications and Mobilization in the 2002–03 Iraq Crisis

Robin Brown

1. Introduction

Just as politicians and diplomats are struggling to come to terms with the impact of the communications revolution in international politics, so too are the academic fields of International Relations and International Communications. Although it is a decade since the twin impacts of satellite television and the Internet began to attract serious attention, scholars are still struggling to understand how to locate innovations in communications within the practice of world politics. Very often discussions are anecdotal or simplistically generalized, reaching conclusions that either the communications revolution is sweeping away the states system or is largely unimportant or that it is having some impact but it is not quite clear what.[1] There is a growing body of work that allows us to move beyond these generalizations but much of this is dispersed across relatively specialized debates on topics such as transnational advocacy networks, transparency, deliberation or information warfare and is only just beginning to find its way back into the mainstream theoretical debate.[2] This chapter sets out to offer one way of making sense of the impact of the communications revolution in contemporary international politics.

The core of the argument is that the diffusion of communications technologies, ranging from the telephone to the Internet, is producing a more open, more public political environment and that this environment modifies the type of political strategies that work. The argument that publicness and transparency change the nature of human behavior is hardly new: Kant argued that the principles that guided human action could only be ethical if they were public.[3] The argument developed here is about political effectiveness rather than ethical requirements. In a nutshell, this new communications environment affects the ability of states or other political actors to get things done. An environment where information is more easily available and where communication is cheap, changes the extent to which different groups can become involved in political issues and their ability to influence outcomes. The ability of groups to mobilize resources in pursuit of their political agendas is modified. While authors have frequently pointed to the importance of new communications technologies for non-state actors, there are consequences for states just as much as other groups.[4] The argument developed here is that this new, more open environment does not *determine* political outcomes but modifies the dynamics of the processes that occur. In this new environment the strategies by which agents mobilize power, change as does the effectiveness of those strategies.

This broad theoretical argument is illustrated with reference to the 2002–03 Iraq crisis. The interpretation developed here is that the Iraq crisis as such can be seen as an effort by groups within the U.S. government to mobilize political support for the removal of the Iraqi regime. This effort was partially successful in that it gained sufficient support within the U.S. administration and political system and among a number of other governments to bring about the overthrow of the Saddam regime. However, in the face of countermobilizations led by France, among others, the U.S. efforts were unsuccessful in gaining the support of many important governments and the United Nations and even less successful in gaining public support. The mismatch between the new environment of mediated international politics and the political strategy pursued by the Bush administration accounts for much of the political damage that the United States has sustained in the period since the fall of Saddam.

This chapter comprises four parts. The first part makes a case for the importance of mobilization as a neglected phenomenon in politics. The second outlines some of the issues involved in developing a model of mobilization processes. The third part examines the changes in the international environment that have been produced by the growing penetration of information and communications technologies while the final part provides a preliminary examination of the crisis. It should be noted that the duration and complexity of the crisis as well as the growing volume of material becoming available particularly as a result of investigations into the production and use of intelligence in the United States and United Kingdom means that the interpretation of the crisis offered here is necessarily tentative.

2. Locating Communication: The Problem of Power and the Dynamics of Mobilization

In order to understand how innovations in communications technologies affect the nature of international politics, it is necessary to understand how they fit in. As with most of the social sciences, international relations has tended to ignore issues of media and communications.[5] Neither of the dominant theoretical perspectives in international relations, realism and constructivism, has paid significant attention to these issues. Realism treats international relations in terms of a set of agents (states) that are located within a structure defined by the distribution of capabilities; constructivism tends to treat international relations as a set of states located within a structure defined by a set of norms. In realism, states are assumed to act in accordance with their interests defined by material gains; in constructivism, states act in accordance with norms of appropriate behavior. In both these cases it is simply not clear how communications fits into the picture. Explicit discussion of how to resolve this issue is rare, the exception being the work of Buzan and Little who argue that in the context of an international system, the increases in "interaction capacity" offered by improvements in transportation and communication have theoretically significant consequences and James Rosenau's argument that technologically enabled individuals are a significant part of "postinternational politics."[6]

Although explicit attention to the theoretical implications of media and communications are relatively rare, recent work in international relations (IR) theory has indicated a number of routes by which the issue could be integrated. For instance, there has been considerable attention to the formation of social identities and to the process by which norms change.[7] This has led to an extremely interesting debate about the role of communications in social interaction between those who adopt a "rationalist" or rational choice perspective where agents have fixed objectives so that in interaction, communication is used to manipulate the opponent's expectations or to issue threats. On the other side of this debate are those influenced by discussions of deliberative democracy.[8] Here the assumption is that agents who engage in communication may well change their preferred outcomes, redefine their interests, and possibly reach consensus. There are a number of intermediate positions where communication may not lead to consensus but still has an impact on preferences.[9]

A more radical strategy is to argue that the tendency to focus on the analysis of structures and agents in mainstream IR theory has tended to divert attention away from social processes. Social theorists such as Norbert Elias, Pierre Bourdieu, and Anthony Giddens have argued that pursuing the explanation of social phenomena through a focus on the characteristics of agents or structures tends to lead to reification. Instead social theory should focus on processes and relationships.[10] This emphasis echoes concerns in the study of communications and in social theory more generally. Social theorists concerned with capturing the dynamics of society have argued that discussion of social action should give due attention to the location of social action in time and space. These are precisely the dimensions of social action that are often emphasized in discussions of the impact of communications technologies. By making it easier to reach out across space or by reducing the time for information to be transmitted, these technologies modify the context for social action.[11]

In consequence this chapter argues that one profitable route into the intersection between communications technology and political life is through attention to the ways in which political actors seek to mobilize support for their projects. Mobilization is a term that is frequently used in political life—a leader mobilizes his or her supporters—but in the literature of social science it is really only given serious attention in two areas: first in a military context of mobilization of forces and second, and more importantly, in the study of social movements. However, it can be argued that mobilization is a much more general social process. In the context of structurationist social theory, mobilization becomes the basic building block of social action. For instance, in the work of Anthony Giddens, the structural properties of a social situation are conceptualized as rules and resources.[12] Social action is the process by which an agent mobilizes these resources. Rather than mobilization being something specific to social movements this type of social mobilization can be seen as a special case of a much more common form of activity. Power can be understood as an ability to mobilize resources. This means that power is not an unproblematic property of an agent but something dependent on the relationships that exist in a specific circumstance. Power is about the ability to persuade people to go along with you. This ability is highly dependent on the context and the issue within which the attempt is played out. The ability to mobilize support involves access to material resources and to ideational ones. It requires attention to agents and to the impact of their environment on their behavior. Importantly it points toward a concern with time (when is this happening and what else is going on?) and with space (where is this happening?).

This analysis requires a process-oriented approach that does not sit easily with traditional international relations theories. If we postulate a world where information flows relatively easily it becomes increasingly difficult to separate domestic processes from international ones and creates a situation where transnational, international, and multiple domestic political fields are increasingly interdependent. By suggesting mobilization as a universal process we have to recognize that it occurs in multiple locations simultaneously on different scales. This necessitates an awareness of the way in which actions in multiple political games in multiple places interact with each other.[13]

It then follows that changes in the communications environment are changes in the political environment in terms of what agents know and in terms of who and what they can act on—that is the attempt to mobilize support for and against. An environment where information flows more freely will be different if only through the increased knowledge of the actions of third parties.

If we are to look at international politics from the perspective of mobilization then the significance of institutions—such as states—is as mobilizations of bias; by structuring the world in particular ways they facilitate mobilization around particular issues and discourage it around others.[14]

In looking at processes of mobilization we need to consider five sets of questions. First, who is attempting to mobilize support? What are they seeking to achieve? What resources do they have to gain support with? Relevant resources can range from money to prestige to contacts. Second, whom are they trying to enlist in their support? How attractive is the appeal of the mobilizer to them? Third, what is the nature of the relationship between the mobilizer and mobilizee? Are there elements in the relationship that will predispose them to work together? Is it possible for the mobilizer to reach the target of the mobilization attempt? Fourth, we need to consider the context within which the mobilization attempt is taking place. These contextual factors play a major role in determining whether particular initiatives succeed or fail. To what extent are events focusing attention on an issue or competing with it? To what extent do existing institutions support or hamper the initiative? To what extent are broader events facilitating a focus on the issue and are other groups also reacting to the issue? Finally, assuming that our mobilizer is trying to enlist support to influence the behavior of a third party, how does that third party respond? Does it seek to organize support for itself among the groups that are being targeted for mobilization (competitive mobilization) or among different groups (countermobilization)? Does it seek to block the mobilization of support by our initiative (anti-mobilization)?[15]

The central contribution of a mobilizational approach is that it forces us to focus on *process* rather than on structure or agent. It suggests that power understood as the ability to influence outcomes is highly contingent, evanescent, and also found in the most surprising places. This promises a stronger connection between the theoretical concerns of the discipline and the actual practice of world politics. At its most fundamental level a mobilizational approach treats politics as a temporal activity. How successful are mobilizational attempts? Do they fade away or do they become an institutionalized part of the landscape? This temporal focus helps to create the link between the structures of politics and the apparently chaotic day-to-day reality.

The analysis of mobilization forces us to cut across some of the dualities that hamper contemporary theorizing. It forces us to link agency with the structural and contextual situation. We need to examine the strategies of political actors but we cannot ignore the context in which they are employed. A central criticism of extant constructivist approaches has been their failure to develop a theory of agency or to account for variations in outcomes between cases; a mobilizational approach overcomes this problem.[16] Mobilization cuts across the distinction between material and ideational factors. The current interest in constructivism emphasizes the role of norms and ideas in shaping outcomes yet outcomes are in part dependent on the resources of those that share particular norms and ideas. The diffusion of ideas and norms is in turn dependent on the existence of the material bases of communication.[17]

Although mobilization is a perspective that can be applied to any form of political action, it allows us to make a connection between technological innovation and political change rather than seeing technology as a determining factor that is firmly located in the institutions and strategies of political life.

3. The Changing Environment for Mobilization

From a mobilizational perspective the state can be seen as an organization that imposes a particular bias on processes of mobilization. States are structures that exist to mobilize resources from particular territories. The ability to do this varies between states and across time. From a shorter term perspective there is the issue of what states choose to use their resources to do. Many of the claims about the impact of new communications technologies are about the ability of states to mobilize resources in comparison with the past or with other agents.[18] Taken together, these claims suggest considerable changes in the possibilities for mobilization.

Before looking at the impacts that are particularly associated with communications a number of other changes in the contemporary political environment need to be identified:

(1) Long run changes in principles of political legitimacy. If we look at domestic politics it is now extremely difficult to find countries where power is not exercised in the name of the people. Two centuries ago it would have been very difficult to find countries where this was the case. A century ago it was possible to justify war in the name of the nation. Today international actions are (mostly) justified by reference to universal values and international norms. The increasing visibility of political actions increases the need to justify them and changes the nature of those justifications. The expanding scope of conflict and new norms of legitimacy are essentially equivalent to democratization and greater public involvement.

(2) The increasing scope of international governance regimes: compared with a century ago there are now a hugely increased number of international governance regimes that impose common standards on international actors. Failure to act in accordance with them may become a source for international criticism and hence generates pressure to comply.

(3) Plurilateral politics: Philip Cerny coined the term plurilateral to indicate a situation with multiple actors of different types. Applied to the international realm, new norms, expanded governance regimes, and more information open the way for greater involvement by more actors and by more types of actors.[19]

(4) Blurring of the international/domestic divide: the consequence of this is a growing connection between international and domestic political areas. International events have an impact in the domestic sphere and vice versa.

These changes provide the context for a number of other developments that are more directly related to the way that innovations in communications affect political practice.

(1) Multiple groups/shared media: these structural developments have some more specific consequences in the realm of information and politics. The expansion of the political universe gives a greater role to the public and quasi-public media as a means of communication between involved groups. Not only does the increasing number of information gathering sources and means of dissemination make it harder to keep things secret but political action also increasingly involves public action.

(2) Multiple sources of information reduce the ability of any political agent to act as a sole definer. Historically governments have been able to act as the sole source of information on foreign events and by doing so define the problem. In the contemporary environment this becomes more difficult. Not only are there other sources of information but the expertise is also available to contest official interpretations.

(3) Importance of credibility: in this environment where information is contested it becomes increasingly important to be credible in the interpretation of information. Further, moral capital becomes more useful as a source of influence.[20]

(4) Schattschneider effect: a fundamental impact of increasing transparency lies in the realm of what can be called the Schattschneider effect. Essentially, the more public a conflict becomes the greater the potential for initially uninvolved groups to intervene and by doing so to change the potential outcome. Communications technology is a powerful instrument for "socializing" conflict that is involving more people. Secrecy is a tool for restricting who can become involved.[21]

(5) In practical terms the growing transparency of the political realm means that agents who want to attract attention (or find themselves attracting attention) need to focus on the practice of news management and strategic communication. This means that they need to communicate their message consistently and repetitively in order to put it across and ensure that their declaratory line is consistent with their practice. In an increasingly transparent environment ensuring consistent communications becomes more difficult as it becomes more essential.

Taken together these factors suggest a pattern of politics where it becomes more important to communicate in a credible way, where justifications and appeals need to fit with the characteristics of the new environment and where more people can be reached by mobilizational appeals and where people are better able to draw their own conclusions about the fit between justifications and actions. Broadly speaking this is the world that fits with the arguments about political transformation advanced by Keohane and Nye and Arquilla and Ronfeldt.[22]

4. Making Sense of the Iraq Crisis

The remainder of this chapter examines the crisis preceding the Anglo-American attack on Iraq in March 2003. This is not intended to be a formal test of the position outlined above but rather an exploratory exercise to investigate its plausibility. In a global perspective the crisis was an immensely complex event that even with a full range of memoirs and archives will inevitably remain highly controversial. The crisis was marked by mobilization on multiple scales and arenas; within the U.S. government, toward U.S. allies and neutrals in order to gain their support, by an emergent antiwar bloc that involved traditional antiwar groups, domestic political agents, and governments. Additionally the Iraqi regime mounted a distinct countermobilization in order to undermine the U.S. mobilization. All these arenas of conflict were linked by instantaneous flows of information that caused the whole game to shift as actors realigned their positions on the basis of developments in other arenas of conflict. The crisis not only shows us how diplomacy works in a highly mediated international environment but also gives us clues to the strategies that work.[23]

Although it is not proposed to mount a formal test of a mobilization perspective against realist or constructivist positions, and it is doubtless possible to develop treatments from either of these positions, the crisis can be seen as a protracted struggle over which interests or which norms should guide action. Even if it is argued that the crisis was ultimately shaped by interests or norms, the interests or norms that guided action only did so at the end of a protracted process of contestation. Therefore it is this process that deserves attention. Particularly with hindsight it can be argued that the impact of the war and its aftermath can only be understood by reference to the processes of mobilization that actually produced the conflict.

U.S. Policy Toward Iraq 1991–2001

In many respects the 2002–03 Iraq crisis was simply the continuation of a crisis that originated with the Iraqi invasion of Kuwait in August 1990. The end of hostilities in 1991 left Saddam in power but subject to a regime of sanctions, weapons inspections, autonomous Kurdish safe havens and no fly zones patrolled by British and American aircraft. At the end of the 1991 conflict Western decisionmakers had assumed that the Baathist regime was so weakened that it would inevitably collapse. Saddam's continuing hold on power led to a situation of continuing political warfare where Iraq sought to undermine the U.S. policy of containment just as the United States sought to undermine the Iraqi regime. Over time the appetite of the other members of the Security Council for confrontation with Iraq eroded but not to the extent that there was a willingness to simply abandon the sanctions regime. In 1998 UN weapons inspectors were withdrawn creating a situation where monitoring of Iraqi arms programs became more difficult but also preventing the conclusion of the inspection programme and the dismantling of the whole sanctions regime.

In the United States policy toward Iraq became an issue in the conservative movement's critique of the Clinton administration. In January 1998 the conservative think tank The Project for a New American Century sent a letter to President Clinton warning of the threat that Iraq posed to regional and U.S. security and calling for the overthrow of the regime. The same year President Clinton signed the Iraq Liberation Act effectively enshrining the removal of Saddam's regime as U.S. policy. Despite this there was little energy behind the policy. Conservative groups took notice of the analyses of international terrorism put forward by Laurie Mylroie who argued that activities attributed to transnational groups such as Al-Qaeda should be seen as products of a war waged by Saddam Hussein against the United States.[24] Further, conservative thinkers began to argue that the Arab–Israeli conflict should be understood not as an obstacle to democratization in the region but a product of that lack of democratization. The implication being that instead of pushing a negotiation process the United States should seek to remove repressive regimes. While the conservatives had high hopes for the new Bush administration (among the signatories of the 1998 letter were Donald Rumsfeld, Paul Wolfowitz, and Richard Armitage) the early months of the Bush administration showed little urgency in moving against Iraq.

This situation was to change with the attacks of September 11. The attacks shifted the agenda of the administration toward dealing with these threats. At one level the attacks crystallized the warnings of the bipartisan Hart–Rudman commission about the vulnerability of the continental United States to mass casualty terrorism. At another level the new situation created a permissive environment for the advocates of action against Iraq. In his study of decisionmaking in the U.S. government, John Kingdon makes the point that often solutions exist independently of problems but that a changing political context tends to link solutions to problems.[25] After September 2001 changing circumstances made action against Iraq thinkable. The possible intersection between rogue states, weapons of mass destruction, and transnational terrorism had reached the top of the agenda. It is now clear that immediately after the attacks consideration was being given to action against Iraq. This view was rejected on the grounds that there was no direct evidence linking Iraq to Al-Qaeda and in the absence of this evidence it would not be possible to sustain an international coalition in favor of the war on terrorism.[26]

Nevertheless it does appear that very rapidly after September 11, a consensus emerged in the U.S. government that it was necessary to deal with the Iraq problem. Iraq was a country that was hostile to the United States and was pursuing the development of weapons of mass destruction. This posed a direct threat to its regional neighbors and if placed in the hands of organizations such as Al-Qaeda, to the United States itself. Where there was no consensus was about the timing of action against Iraq and how it was to be achieved. The drivers of the crisis appear to be the group centered on Vice President Dick Cheney and the Secretary and Deputy Secretary of Defense Donald Rumsfeld and Paul Wolfowitz. This group rapidly reached the conclusion that Saddam Hussein must be removed by force. From the end of 2001 this was a position that was consistently pursued by this faction. In reconstructing the crisis, however, the central issue is that this position does not appear to have become the position of the administration until the end of 2002 and was not consistently enunciated as the policy of the administration until immediately before the outbreak of war. This led to multiple levels of ambiguity. The administration was not clear as to what its position was and given this could not be clear to anyone outside the administration what the policy was. From September 2001 to March 2003 the president clearly enunciated the demand that Saddam Hussein should be removed from power. However, examination of presidential statements during the period show that at points he opened ways for Saddam to remain in power and at others the timescale and mode of removal were ambiguous.

In his State of the Union address on January 29, 2002, President Bush identified Iraq as part of the "Axis of Evil" and it appears that a decision had been taken to confront Iraq with the aim of overthrowing the government. During the spring of 2002 military planning was underway for an attack against Iraq. However, the actual execution of this would be delayed by the need to carry out the diplomatic preparations and to replenish stocks of smart weapons depleted in Afghanistan. During this extended phoney war period the conflict within the administration would be waged between the unilateralists and the multilateralists.

This struggle was to hamper the ability of the United States to mobilize support for the conflict and to confuse other countries as to what America was doing. The immediate effect of the Axis of Evil speech was to trigger a wave of unease among European allies. In autumn Colin Powell had warned against including Iraq in the initial phase of the conflict in order to avoid such a split. In February and March it was clear that the United Kingdom was already onside. In a public comment Tony Blair made it clear that he fundamentally agreed with the sentiment behind the "Axis of Evil" of speech. Reports in the British media suggested that the United States had asked for 25,000 British troops for an attack on Iraq and that the diplomatic strategy would be to launch a drive for new inspections and if this failed to prepare public opinion for war. In March Vice President Cheney was dispatched to London and then the Middle East. In April Blair traveled to the Bush ranch in Crawford, Texas to discuss the forthcoming confrontation. During that spring attention was diverted from Iraq by the escalation of the Palestinian crisis. It was being estimated that an attack could not occur before autumn at the earliest and was more likely to occur in the spring of 2003.[27]

During the summer uncertainty continued. There were leaks to the press about the developing war plan. In public statements Bush, Blair, Wolfowitz, and others made it clear that Saddam must be removed. In parallel, opposition to a conflict developed. The secretary general of the United Nations Kofi Annan warned against war, within the American political elite even associates of George Bush senior went public with concerns about the war. The key date in the development of American policy appears to have been Monday August 5. Colin Powell had dinner with the president and persuaded him that a broad international coalition was vital to the prosecution of the war.[28] During August discussions within the administration continued until September 12, when President Bush went before the United Nations against the advice of his vice president. In his speech he warned of the danger that Iraq posed to international security and argued that Iraq's history of noncompliance was a challenge to the organization itself. Although the decision to work through the United Nations was welcomed with some relief the initial U.S. position was that Iraq had 30 days to comply under penalty of "all necessary means," that is, force, and that the United State itself would judge whether there had been full compliance.

During September and October President Bush was able to gain a high level of domestic support. Both houses of Congress passed resolutions authorizing the use of force during the second week of October. While Democrats expressed disquiet with the situation the approaching election encouraged a view that this was not the time to risk challenging the president. White House officials emphasized a relatively moderate line that only by persuading Iraq that there was credible threat of war would it be possible to avoid it. In the mid-term elections the Republicans gained control of both houses of Congress.

The Security Council proved a tougher nut. Three of the five permanent members were opposed to the Anglo-American position. Less than a week after the president's speech, Iraq accepted the return of weapons inspectors and France, Russia, and China were expressing the view that there was no need for a new resolution. On October 1, the United Nations and Iraq reached an agreement that would permit full inspections everywhere in Iraq with the exception of the presidential palaces. This agreement was not acceptable and the United States was able to delay the return of inspectors until a new tougher resolution had been passed. This was to take another month. France and Russia in particular were able to considerably soften the draft resolution. There was no explicit authorization for the use of force and the weapons inspectors reported back to the Security Council, which would consider the situation. These negotiations were accompanied by growing pressure from the United States and the United Kingdom. In the daily White House press briefings, the president's press secretary Ari Fleischer frequently commented on the fact that the United Nations was running out of time. The United Kingdom released a dossier claiming that Iraq could use chemical weapons at 45 minutes' notice. U.S. officials pointed to links between Iraq and Al-Qaeda. Three days after the mid-term elections the Security Council passed resolution 1441. Five days later Iraq indicated that it would accept the terms of the resolution.

Almost immediately it was clear that the U.S. military and political preparations for war were continuing. The United States facilitated and supported meetings of Iraqi exile groups and preparations for the movement of forces to the Gulf continued.

The four months that followed revolved around the issue of whether the United States and the United Kingdom could persuade the other 13 members of the Security Council to pass a resolution authorizing a military attack on Iraq. Here the United States seems to have made a major miscalculation. The U.S. policy seems to have been based on the assumption that either clear-cut evidence of Iraqi weapons of mass destruction would emerge or that Iraqi noncooperation with the new inspection regime would be so blatant that other countries would support this resolution and at least not obstruct military action. Military preparations themselves were evidence of resolve and would contribute to Iraqi cooperation but of course once they were completed would allow an attack to proceed without delay. The problem was that there was not to be any "smoking gun" of discovered weapons or blatant noncooperation. When banned weapons were discovered—missiles capable of ranges that exceeded those permitted—the Iraqis moved to destroy them as ordered. While a smoking gun would not have automatically led to an authorization for war it would have redefined the situation in a way that permitted greater support in the Security Council and provided the diplomatic cover for governments to support the war. Thus the activities of the weapons inspectors came to attract a considerable body of contestation in the media as the United States sought to emphasize the inspectors' criticisms of Iraqi behavior and to question the competence of the inspectors.

The final month before the outbreak of war saw increasing tension as both the United Kingdom and the United States made it clear that rejecting a second resolution would not prevent war because they would attack anyway and the antiwar countries sought to minimize the extent to which they had to directly confront the United States and issue a veto.

U.S. Strategy in the Region

The area of the world where the U.S. strategy was most successful and by extension the Iraqi strategy failed was in the Gulf region. The minimum necessary support for the U.S. military option to be viable was for countries in the region to provide access to ports, bases, and airspace for U.S. and British forces. Here there seems to have been a degree of inconsistency between the public and private stance taken by some of these states and. One of the most illuminating examples of this happened a month before the conflict when OPEC announced that in case of war it would act to stabilize oil prices by increasing supply. This was in effect a Saudi announcement that it was with the United States and that Iraq could not expect support from that direction. The splits among the Arab countries were so severe that a plan to send an Arab League delegation to Baghdad had to be scrapped.

The diplomatic complexity of the crisis was increased by the parallel efforts to prepare the military dimension of the crisis. In particular, the United States sought access to Turkey to permit an opening of a second front in the North. This opened three additional diplomatic fronts, with

Turkey itself, with NATO, and with the EU. Turkey was engaged in a dialogue with the EU to determine a firm date for admission to the EU. The United States appears to have attempted to exert some diplomatic pressure on the EU to aid the Turkish case. Whether or not this pressure backfired, the EU refused to set a date for Turkish admission. The United States attempted to gain access to NATO resources to support a conflict with Iraq both in general terms and to provide protection to Turkey. This request was resisted by France, Germany, and Belgium on the grounds that as diplomacy had not been given sufficient time to run its course at the United Nations, military preparations were premature. This triggered a serious diplomatic rift within the alliance. The U.S. motivation was to provide additional insurance (military and diplomatic) for Turkey to encourage U.S. access to the north of Iraq. In the end the Turkish parliament rejected the U.S. request despite support from the government and from the Turkish armed forces.

Iraq's Counterstrategy

In the wake of the September 11 attacks, Iraq seems to have recognized the increased threat to the regime that the United States posed. The response seems to have been a diplomatic offensive in the Gulf region and the broader Arab world in order to, at best, produce a block of states that would work against an American attack, or at worst vaccinate against U.S. attempts to mobilize the support that it needed. As a result Iraq sought to repair its relations with its neighbors making concessions to Iran and Kuwait, seeking to reintegrate itself into the Arab family and making ostentatious demonstrations of support for the intifada. Despite this diplomatic strategy Hans Blix was surprised by the reluctance of Iraq to fully cooperate with the United Nations in readmitting weapons inspectors. This can be seen as a major strategic error. Among governments and intelligence services the view was almost universally held that Iraq was pursuing illegal weapons policies—the argument was over what to do about this—and only a fully cooperative position could have begun to break down these suspicions.[29]

During the extended autumn crisis, regional and global television channels provided ample opportunity for Iraq to put its views across and to challenge U.S. framings of the situation. As the United States made accusations and released information about particular sites Iraq took journalists to see them, undercutting American accusations. This growing tactical expertise in challenging the U.S. case was not sufficient to offset the basic strategic errors.

The Antiwar Bloc

Mobilization against the war was global in its scope and multifarious in its sources. In the Islamic world there was mobilization based on the American war against Islam. In the Middle East, U.S. support for Israel was significant. In Europe, there was suspicion of US power. In the United States, there was concern that this was really a war for oil. In the United Kingdom, concerns about the war triggered the largest political demonstration in British history.

Across the whole 14 months prior to the attack on Iraq it is possible to detect a steady hardening of attitudes among German and French political elites culminating in a clear willingness to prevent the United Nations from passing a resolution authorizing an attack on Iraq. As soon as the possibility of action against Iraq began to be floated in early 2002 Western European governments began to make it clear that they were reluctant to participate in such action. Over time these views were made more explicit, there was a movement through no participation without a UN resolution, to no participation without a second UN resolution, to no participation under any circumstances, to UN inspectors need more time to outright opposition and finally the threat of veto and explicit attempts to mobilize Security Council votes against a second authorizing resolution.

How can we explain this hardening of the governmental opposition to the war? At least three factors were at work. First, a concern to limit U.S. ability to dictate to the rest of the world and by doing so gain the diplomatic prestige taking this independent line. Second, the United States had simply failed to persuade the opposing countries of their case for war. Given that the predominant frame was in terms of a threat, France and Germany were simply not convinced that the threat was so pressingly urgent that military action was required or even if that was conceded that military action was prudent. The final possibility was concern over the political consequences. All European countries had sizeable antiwar public opinion and it appears that both the French and German governments derived some domestic political advantage from taking an antiwar stance. Of course there was the possibility that public opinion would respond to political leadership but even in the United Kingdom where the case for war was most strongly made, public opinion was against war.

The result was an escalating conflict between those governments that opposed the conflict led by France and Germany and those that were in favor led by the United Kingdom. These conflicts were fought out in the media, in NATO, and the EU. Although a sizeable number of

European governments took explicit pro-war positions public opinion remained hostile.

5. Analysis

The analysis developed here suggests that whereas the U.S. "war party" was successful in mobilizing support for action against Iraq in the U.S. government and assembling the minimum necessary coalition for the conflict (essentially diplomatic and political support from the United Kingdom, access rights from regional states plus overflight rights) it comprehensively failed to sell the war more broadly. This can be attributed to the success of the antiwar coalition in raising the costs of participation through mobilizing public opinion, not to mention persuading governments to oppose the war on normative, political, or strategic grounds.

The U.S. problem seems to have been attributable to the lack of consistency in its own strategy. While there appears to have been agreement on the need to do something about Saddam there was no consensus about what should be done and how this should be achieved. First, if there was a clear commitment to the overthrow of the regime it was not clearly communicated even in the president's statements. At times it appeared that a change in the behavior of the Iraqi government would constitute "regime change." Even if there was clear agreement on the objectives there was ambiguity over the strategy to achieve it. Second, this ambiguity over ends injected some uncertainty over the role of the military buildup—was it a way to provide a credible threat to back a coercive strategy or was it simply a preparation for invasion? Third, what was the role of international support in the strategy? Was the objective to secure a minimal level of support to allow military access or a high level of diplomatic consensus?

The difficulty for the United States seems to be have stemmed at worst from an inability to decide its position on these three questions or at best from an inability to communicate its position. This uncertainty both undermined the effectiveness of American diplomacy but also encouraged other actors to work against it. Much of the texture of the crisis seems to have had its source in the uncertainty over what the United States was doing. If the United States had simply issued an ultimatum to Iraq and made its military preparations, the clarity of the situation would probably have opened some doors and persuaded other countries not to get actively involved in opposing the U.S. action. In some senses the apparent embrace of the diplomatic process encouraged diplomatic maneuvering.

From the information now available it appears that the group that did have a clear picture of the desired outcome was the group around Donald Rumsfeld and Dick Cheney. This group had a clear-cut view of the desired outcome—the military occupation of Iraq by U.S. forces. The challenge that they faced was how to get there. In mobilizing support for this action, at a minimum they had to gain support from the president, the military, and the Congress plus get access to the military facilities that they needed in the Gulf. This can be seen as a relatively small mobilization compared with that achieved by George H.W. Bush in 1990–91—he enjoyed the public support of the United Nations, NATO, the EU, and most of the Arab world. In 2002–03 this commitment to a small mobilization was to have fateful consequences. Whereas Rumsfeld and company would have doubtless preferred a more extensive mobilization they were unwilling to risk their goal to achieve it. A larger coalition would have had the effect of changing the timescale for conflict or even of shifting the objective to something that could be supported by the other members of the coalition—for instance, the disarmament of Iraq. The war party was not confident that it could create a larger coalition and still maintain its objective.

Despite this consistent view, the public face of the administration (and still more the coalition) was that the priority was to remove the threat from Iraq and that this might be achievable by disarmament. This opened the way to a key ambiguity in the autumn of 2002: was support being sought for an attack on Iraq or for a credible threat of war that would create pressure for cooperation? Playing on this ambiguity allowed the administration to gain Congressional and diplomatic support—by supporting a hard line partners were creating a credible threat that would open the way to a diplomatic solution.

A third element of the strategy was through a communications strategy that sought to build support for war through maximizing the threat from Iraq, minimizing the costs and risks of action, and maximizing the benefits. Coupled to this was a strategy of denigrating opponents and critics of the war. The emphasis on the threat took the form of placing the most threatening interpretation on questionable intelligence. It has been argued that the Office of the Secretary of Defense was unwilling to face up to likely postwar problems because that would have increased the costs of the war and hence potential opposition.[30]

Much of the postwar diplomatic and political damage is attributable to the strategies and tactics used to reach the Cheney/Rumsfeld goal. Any attack on Iraq was likely to create negative attitudes toward the United States but the damage has been exacerbated by the perception that the United States was not serious about diplomacy. Frank Schimmelfenig has made the argument that in international negotiation states can find themselves "rhetorically entrapped"—the willingness to use certain language and to enter into dialogue can create a situation where states find themselves pursuing goals that they did not intend to. The costs of backing out are too great.[31] This case both supports and challenges his position. By involving the United Nations, the United States was rhetorically entrapped but still chose to walk away at the cost of being seen as unreliable and manipulative by diplomatic partners and their public. In the same way that some of the diplomatic moves were made simply for short-term advantage without considering their long-term implication the same is true of the use of intelligence. The failure to find weapons of mass destruction has been a major blow for the credibility of the United States and its intelligence services. Either they were wrong or that the United States (and U.K. leadership) wrongly exaggerated the intelligence available. As Keohane and Nye argue, one of the consequences of the information revolution in international politics is to place a growing importance on credibility as a source of power.[32]

Recent literature about influence in international politics has made use of at least four mechanisms of influence. First, the traditional rationalist models of instrumental calculation of interest. Second, constructivist views about the importance of identity and norms in shaping action; third, approaches that draw on the logic of argumentation; and fourth, concepts of social environment where agents are pressured into compliance without necessarily being persuaded in a cognitive sense.[33] The Iraq crisis demonstrates the interdependence of all these mechanisms. Agents may be persuaded that an action is normatively correct but still attempt to gain a payoff for doing the right thing. They may be persuaded that an action is the wrong thing to do but still be coerced or bribed into undertaking it. Their instrumental calculations will be influenced by the arguments deployed by the main interlocutors but also by their perceptions of the reactions of third parties whether the publics or allies or other reference groups. Their attitude and willingness to make commitments will depend on their beliefs about whether negotiating partners will be able to deliver on their commitments but this in turn may depend on their beliefs about how the others third parties will respond. For instance, public opinion in the negotiating partners' country may, in the end prevent them from delivering on their commitments.

This whole crisis can be seen as being about creating a set of beliefs about the future in a complex web of agents where the position of many of the agents depended on their own perceptions of the positions of ay of the others. In this complex environment it was a constant struggle to "get the ducks in a row." Relatively small changes in the perceived position of one agent would bring about shifts in others. In this radically decentralized system the media provided the link between the agents.[34]

This tends to support an argument made in some discussions of the impact of transparency—rather than clarifying diplomatic positions the growing volume of information tends to create greater ambiguity, making diplomacy harder to manage. This is a particular problem with democracies.[35] For instance, part of the difficulties between France and the United States reflected uncertainty about the other's position. Much of the European reportage suggested that the administration was split between a pro-war camp led by Cheney, Rumsfeld, and Wolfowitz and an antiwar camp led by Colin Powell. In retrospect it appears that there was a difference between these two camps about the timing of the attack and the degree of effort that should have been be made to develop a multilateral coalition. In the case of France, there were persistent media reports that France would participate in a conflict. For the French, the belief that there was an antiwar grouping within the administration encouraged collaboration with the diplomatic process whereas for the State Department the belief that France could be persuaded to participate had a similar effect. It is the dissipation of these misperceptions that led to some of the bitterness that developed in the final weeks of the crisis.

In attempting to mobilize support the United States was able to make use of both traditional tools of secret diplomacy and more public mediated strategies. It appears that conventional diplomacy was effective in generating support in the least democratic areas in Saudi Arabia and the Gulf. In more democratic states governments found themselves trapped between U.S. diplomatic pressure and public opinion that was largely hostile. In Europe, the United States was more successful in gaining support from governments rather than the public, and where support was offered it was amidst substantial public opposition. It is striking that the United States was unable to gain the support of the non-permanent members of the Security Council for a second resolution. Countries like Mexico and Chile felt that the consequences of supporting the United States were worse than not.[36] Part of the reason for this can be found in the public nature of the crisis. The United States failed to persuade the public outside the country that war was the best strategy. Here the growing diversity of global media organizations tended to undermine the ability to shape coverage.[37]

6. Conclusions

The Iraq crisis provides mixed lessons about the impact of communications technologies in international politics. The United States was able to mobilize the support that it needed for the overthrow of Saddam Hussein's regime but it did so at the cost of considerable damage to its reputation. The failure to find stockpiles of weapons of mass destruction and the political instability in Iraq in the wake of the war has reinforced these political costs.

In general terms the diffusion of communications technologies contribute to the creation of a political order marked by an increase in transparency. This is not to say that every development or action becomes visible. The volume of information may mean that many developments simply do not attract attention. In general as actions become more visible they have to be justified in terms of generalizable values. Greater transparency implies a situation where other governments or public have the opportunity to form an opinion, to express it, or take action on an issue. This type of order runs contrary to the realpolitik expectation that action takes place in conformity with narrowly defined self-interest and in all likelihood in secret. Realpolitik sees action as sui generis adapted to the narrow needs of the situation. In contrast a transparent order has an affinity with universal public norms. Yet contemporary international politics is a mix of realpolitik and noopolitik. If the logic of the current international situation is toward a liberal order much action occurs that is not consistent with these norms. This in turn may require a strategic response. The result is a constant tension between self-interest and accountability that is most problematic for the United States. As the most powerful actor it has the opportunity to operate with the greatest impunity but it is also the most visible actor and a proponent of liberal norms.

This change in the political environment has an impact on the nature of effective political action. In particular high profile actors must engage with broader public in rational argument and be concerned to demonstrate consistency with international norms. Of course, part of the U.S. case for war with Iraq was that international norms needed to change—that the combination of rogue states with weapons of mass destruction and terrorist groups created a new imperative for action. This is certainly an arguable case but the difficulty stemmed from the perception that the norm was being advocated to justify a particular case. One of the most problematic developments for the administration was the appearance of a parallel crisis with North Korea that claimed to have developed nuclear weapons. The reluctance of the administration to be diverted from Iraq by what many observers saw as a more immediately threatening situation tended to undermine the credibility of the norm. Similarly the administration's framing of the crisis with Iraq as being about the need to enforce UN resolutions was challenged by reference to American support for Israel that had not complied with resolutions. Such inconsistency encouraged framings of the crisis that suggested that there were other hidden reasons for the United States' willingness to confront Iraq, such as oil or support for Israel.

In a more public international realm the requirements of effective political communications become more important. In domestic politics it has long been recognized that representatives of a party need to stay "on message"—to select a message and then to ensure that all representatives consistently say the same thing. Actions need to be consistent with the message. In an environment with pervasive media coverage it becomes increasingly difficult to say different things to different audiences and for this to remain unnoticed. At the same time inconsistencies reflecting differences with a government can lead to a loss of leverage as other agents discount what is said to them. This lack of consistency was noticeable in the comments of U.S. spokespersons and in the comments and actions of the French government. Of course, if a government lacks an agreed policy the media is likely to reflect this but if the government does have an agreed policy that is not being reflected in media coverage there is a problem with its communications strategy. This is not to suggest that all that is required is good communications but it does suggest that a more transparent world is one where representations and arguments matter more than in the past. The ability to mobilize support in closed meetings through appeals to self-interest remains highly important but the visible face of diplomacy is both growing and becoming more important as a result of the diffusion of communications technologies. Failure to recognize may not prevent actors in the international realm from achieving their goals but it will inevitably increase the price they pay.

Notes

1. For examples of these three positions see Ronald Deibert, *Parchment, Printing and Hypermedia: Communication in World Order Transformation* (New York: Columbian University Press, 1997); and Eugene B. Skolnikoff, *The Elusive Transformation: Science Technology and the Evolution of International Politics* (Princeton: Princeton University Press, 1993); Warren P. Strobel, *Late Breaking Foreign Policy* (Washington, D.C.: U.S. Institute of Peace, 1997).

2. For examples of this work see Margaret Keck and Kathryn Sikkink, *Activists Beyond Borders: Advocacy Networks in International Politics* (Ithaca, NY: Cornell University Press, 1998); Bernard Finel and Kristin Lord, eds., *Power and Conflict in the Age of Transparency* (New York: Palgrave, 2000); Marc Lynch, *State Interests and Public Spheres* (New York: Columbia University Press, 1999); John Arquilla and David Ronfeldt, *The Emergence of Noopolitik: Towards an American Information Strategy* (Santa Monica, CA: Rand Corporation, 1999).

3. Immanuel Kant, "Perpetual Peace" in Lewis White Beck, ed., *Kant on History* (Indianapolis, IN: Bobbs-Merrill, 1963).

4. For studies that focus on the implications for NGOs see Keck and Sikkink, *Activists Beyond Borders*; Ronald Deibert, "International Plug 'n' Play? Citizen Activism, the Internet and Global Public Policy," *International Studies Perspectives*, Vol. 1, No. 3 (2000), pp. 255–272.

5. For critiques of political science, geography, and social theory to engage with issues of media and communications see respectively John Downing, *Internationalizing Media Theory* (London: Sage, 1996); Stephen Graham and Simon Marvin, *Telecommunications and the City: Electronic Spaces, Urban Places* (London: Routledge, 1996), pp. 2–11; John B. Thompson, *The Media and Modernity: A Social Theory of the Media* (Cambridge: Polity, 1995).

6. Barry Buzan, Charles Jones, and Richard Little, *The Logic of Anarchy* (New York: Columbia University Press, 1993); Barry Buzan and Richard Little, *International Systems in World History* (Oxford: Oxford University Press, 2000); James N. Rosenau, "Information Technologies and the Skills, Networks and Structures that Sustain World Affairs," in James N. Rosenau and J.P. Singh, eds., *Information Technologies and Global Politics: The Changing Scope of Power and Governance* (Albany, NY: State University of New York Press, 2002).

7. For instance Audie Klotz, *Norms in International Relations* (Ithaca, NY: Cornell University Press, 1995).

8. Jürgen Habermas, *Between Facts and Norms* (Cambridge: Polity, 1996); James Bohman, *Public Deliberation: Pluralism, Complexity and Democracy* (Cambridge, MA: MIT, 1996); James Bohman and William Rehg, eds., *Deliberative Democracy* (Cambridge, MA: MIT, 1997); Jon Elster, "Strategic Uses of Argument" in Kenneth J. Arrow, Robert H. Mnookin, Lee Ross, and Amos Tversky, eds., *Barriers to Conflict Resolution* (New York: Norton, 1995); Marc Lynch, "Why Engage? China and the Logic of Communicative Engagement," *European Journal of International Relations*, Vol. 8, No. 2 (2002), pp. 187–230 and *State Interests and Public Spheres*.

9. In addition to the works by Lynch see Thomas Risse " 'Let's Argue!': Communicative Action in World Politics," *International Organization*, Vol. 54, No. 1 (2000), pp. 1–40; and Frank Schimmelfenig, "The Community Trap: Liberal Norms, Rhetorical Action and the Eastern Enlargement of the European Union," *International Organization*, Vol. 55, No. 1 (2001), pp. 47–80.

10. Norbert Elias, *What is Sociology?* (London: Hutchinson, 1978), Anthony Giddens, *The Constitution of Society: Outline of the Theory of Structuration* (Cambridge: Polity, 1984); Pierre Bourdieu and Löic Wacquant, *Invitation to Reflexive Sociology* (Chicago: Chicago University Press, 1992); for an application to IR see Patrick T. Jackson and Daniel Nexon, "Relations Before States: Substance, Process and the Study of World Politics," *European Journal of International Relations*, Vol. 5, No. 3 (1999), pp. 291–333.

11. Harold Innis, *The Bias of Communication* (Toronto: University of Toronto Press, 1951); Joshua Meyrowitz, *No Sense of Place: The Impact of Electronic Media on Social Behaviour* (New York: Oxford University Press, 1985).

12. Giddens, *Constitution of Society*, chap. 1.

13. Of course recognition of the complexities of such overlapping games is not new, for instance, Norton Long, "The Local Community as an Ecology of Games," *American Journal of Sociology*, Vol. 44, No. 2 (1958), pp. 251–261; George Tsebelis, *Nested Games: Rational Choice in Comparative Politics* (Berkeley CA: University of California Press, 1990).

14. E.E. Schattschneider, *The Semisovereign People* (New York: Holt, Rinehart and Winston, 1960).

15. A more detailed treatment of these issues can be found in Robin Brown, *Mobilizing the Bias of Communication: Information Technology, Political Communications and Transnational Political Strategy*, paper presented at the American Political Science Association Convention, Washington, D.C., September 2000.

16. Jeffrey T. Checkel, "The Constructivist Turn in International Relations Theory," *World Politics*, Vol. 50, No. 3 (1998), pp. 324–348; Martha Finnemore and Kathryn Sikkink, "International Norm Dynamics and Political Change," *International Organization*, Vol. 52, No. 4 (1998), pp. 887–917.

17. Emmanuel Adler, "Seizing the Middle Ground: Constructivism in World Politics," *European Journal of International Relations*, Vol. 3, No. 3 (1997), pp. 319–363 at 323–324; Sidney *Power in Movement* (Cambridge: Cambridge University Press, 1998), pp. 19–25.

18. For instance, Deibert, *Parchment, Printing and Hypermedia*; Arquilla and Ronfeldt, *The Emergence of Noopolitik*.

19. Philip G. Cerny, "Plurilateralism: Structural Differentiation and Functional Conflict in the Post Cold War World Order," *Millennium*, Vol. 22, No. 1 (1993), pp. 27–51.

20. Robert O. Keohane and Joseph S. Nye, "Power and Interdependence in the Information Age," *Foreign Affairs*, Vol. 77, No. 5 (1998), pp. 81–94.

21. Schattschneider, *Semisovereign People*; Robin Brown, "The Contagiousness of Conflict: EE Schattschneider as a Theorist of the Information Age," *Information, Communication and Society*, Vol. 5, No. 2 (2002), pp. 258–275.

22. Arquilla and Ronfeldt, *Emergence of Noopolitik*; Keohane and Nye, "Power and Interdependence in the Information Age."

23. The discussion developed here is based on a chronology of the Iraq crisis initially developed from public actions and statements (including provision

of material by the media) by political actors and contemporaneous media coverage. The assumption underpinning this is that, in large part, these statements, actions, and media coverage constructed the crisis for those involved as participants. This examination of the public face of the crisis has been supplemented by memoirs, official reports, and retrospective statements as they have become available. Given the duration and complexity of the crisis, this analysis is necessarily preliminary and tentative.

24. Laurie Mylroie, *Study of Revenge: Saddam Hussein's Unfinished War Against America* (Washington, D.C.: American Enterprise Institute, 2000); Gary Schmitt, "State of Terror: War by Any Other Name. . . .," *The Weekly Standard*, November 20, 2000.

25. John W. Kingdon, *Agendas, Alternatives and Public Policies* (New York: Longman, 1995).

26. Bob Woodward, *Bush at War* (New York: Simon and Schuster, 2002), p. 49 and *Plan of Attack* (New York: Simon and Schuster, 2004), p. 25.

27. Michael Donovan, "Iraq: Washington Prepares for Another War," *CDI Eye on Iraq*, April 25, 2002 available on line at www.cdi.org

28. Woodward, *Plan of Attack*, pp. 148–153.

29. Hans Blix, *Disarming Iraq: The Search for Weapons of Mass Destruction* (London: Bloomsbury, 2004), pp. 63–67.

30. James Fallows, "Blind into Baghdad," *The Atlantic* (January–February 2004), pp. 52–77.

31. Schimmelfenig, "The Community Trap."

32. Keohane and Nye, "Power and Interdependence in the Information Age," p. 89.

33. Lynch, *State Interests and Public Spheres*, and "Why Engage?"; Risse, "Let's Argue"; Schimmelfenig, "The Community Trap"; and Alastair Iain Johnston, "Treating International Institutions as Social Environments," *International Studies Quarterly*, Vol. 45, No. 4 (2001), pp. 487–516.

34. There is a tendency to underestimate just how central the media are as a source of information in foreign policy. See Robin Brown, "Spinning the World: Spin Doctors, Mediation and Foreign Policy" in François Debrix and Cynthia Weber, eds., *Rituals of Mediation: International Politics and Social Meaning* (Minneapolis, MN: University of Minnesota Press, 2003), pp. 160–162.

35. Bernard Finel and Kristin Lord, "The Surprising Logic of Transparency," *International Studies Quarterly*, Vol. 43, No. 2 (1999), pp. 315–339.

36. Woodward, *Plan of Attack*, pp. 343–344.

37. Philip Seib, *Hegemonic No More: Western Media, the Rise of Al-Jazeera, and the Influence of Diverse Voices*, paper prepared for the International Studies Association Convention, Montreal, March 2004.

CHAPTER 4

The Internet, Politics, and Missile Defense

Jayne Rodgers

1. Introduction

One downloadable poster by missile defense[1] activists depicts a smiling George W. Bush with a laughing Paul Martin, the Canadian prime minister. Labeled "Dumb and Dumber," with reference to the 1994 movie of the same name, an arrow pointing to Bush says "Started missile defense again" and one to Martin stating "He wants Canada to participate . . ."[2] A postcard on the same website, with an image of an astronaut floating above earth, is addressed to Paul Martin, and is labeled "Earth to Paul! Keep Weapons Out of Space—Keep Canada Out of Missile Defence."[3] Posters and postcards with variations on these themes are common on activist sites worldwide, and are often preprinted with protest text and addressed directly to the minister responsible for security policy. Activism against missile defense, like many other civil campaigns of this kind, is simultaneously entertaining and deadly serious, and provides an opportunity for social engagement around issues of profound human consequence.

It is the ways that the connections and discontinuities in the interpretations of this human consequence are made manifest online that are the concerns of this chapter. The Internet, frequently characterized as the driving force of global activism, is examined as a technological conduit, a mechanism through which the politics of protest against missile defense are explored. It is suggested here that political engagement against the project demonstrates how the Internet facilitates new forms of activism but just as often serves to provide a mechanism for the continuation of older ways of networking and sharing information. Missile defense is a project that has endured, in one form or another, since World War II. Online activism against it is obviously a relatively new phenomenon. We have, therefore, a situation where a long-term policy objective is subject to challenge by new and evolving technological and social networks.

The main aim of this chapter is to advance our thinking about the Internet as a tool for political engagement, by analyzing some of the many points of connection between local concerns, global political issues, and transnational communications technologies. In particular, this chapter is intended to challenge the notion—widely accepted in academic and policy circles—that Internet politics are separate from other more traditional forms of protest, that they are "new" and "different." This argument is pursued through the use of examples that demonstrate how traditional political practices influence protests against the missile defense system.

While some forms of online protest may be novel, the basis for action generally is not. In this respect, it is important to focus on *national* politics relating to missile defense in order to understand *international* activism; the actions of missile defense activists are specific to the immediate contexts and conditions of their own lives, although the framework in which the actions take place is much wider than this. It may be that this argument can be extrapolated for application to other activist concerns, as many of the actions undertaken by those labeled "transnational" activists are directed toward local policies and national initiatives, rather than to the intangible machinery of international politics. Even the "global" protests against the WTO, NAFTA, and the WEF emerge from the tangible effects of policy, rather than from a purely abstract ideology. It is necessary, therefore, to address how extensive the international dimension of this form of protest really is. While the constituency of concerned activists is frequently transnational, the forms of protest and the targets thereof are often less so.

This chapter outlines the background to the missile defense program, a central pillar of U.S. defense strategy under the Bush Junior adminis-tration. The history of the program serves to illustrate its long-term significance for national security policy in the United States. It also demonstrates how an international security network is being established under its auspices. Details of protests against missile defense in a number of countries participating in the project are also presented in detail. Information from the protest websites and the campaigning methods thereon serve to contextualize the concerns of activists, raising the issue of how distinctions between national and international interactions via an inherently transnational technology can be understood. Finally, the chapter examines what the case of missile defense may mean for analysis of online activism. The emphasis on social movements in the literature has left little room for attention to specifically *political* movements (the case of the Zapatistas being the notable exception). Whereas missile defense activism is clearly part of a broader social movement, its objectives are focused on conventional politics, its concerns and its structures.

There is now a vast, and ever-increasing literature on the impact that the Internet is or may be having on political processes and practices and on the ways that activists use the Internet to further their causes.[4] There is, however, still a tendency to treat activism as separate from or only tangentially related to policy. The emphasis noted above on global civil society and social movements in the literatures on activism has focused attention on the normative dimensions of their activities. Speaking of the activities of nongovernmental organizations, Warkheim suggests that "thinking of NGOs as facilitators of attitudinal changes, and as shapers of norms and values in their own right, makes sense particularly given an understanding of global civil society as socially constructed."[5] This is a reasonable comment, of course, but it underplays—as does much of the work in this area—the realities of activism, particularly with regard to the policies, organizations, and institutions toward which their actions are directed.

Global civil society is not just socially constructed; it is necessary to be more literal and specific with the term, by considering how it is also expressly *politically* and *economically* constructed. The normative dimensions of activism are clearly important and much of the research on global civil society serves to enlighten us on how the transnationalization of political activities, and particularly the exposure of normative values, is being effected and extended. This chapter takes a "classic" concern in international relations—national security—and considers how activists pose challenges to the policies of both their own and other governments. Their actions are normative, certainly: the overarching aims of these networks are the abandonment of the missile defense program, the de-weaponization of space and, ultimately, world peace. The forms their activism takes, however, are deeply embedded in local policy, culture, and economics. A good deal of the initial part of this chapter is given over to an outline of the policies against which missile defense protesters are pitted. The history of the project helps to make sense of the contexts in which protests take place and identifies transnational activism as only one, and frequently a relatively insignificant, element of protest against this transnational issue. The examples of activism used later in the chapter are not case study material but are intended simply for illustration of the local/global dynamics of missile defense activism. A more extensive study would allow an opportunity to explore these issues and actions in greater detail; this chapter serves only to raise them and to add some new questions to this growing area of research.

2. Missile Defense—A Mini-History

The idea of missile defense systems is nothing new. On the contrary, as long as there have been long-range missiles, there have been discussions about ways of intercepting them. Many histories have been written of the developmental trajectory of the missile defense project, mainly by policymakers, nonprofit think tanks, and protest groups. Whereas use is made of some of these sources, Joshua Handler's comprehensive analysis of the history of missile defense is noted as an invaluable resource for scholars of this topic and, for the sake of brevity, the selective history below owes much to his research.[6] In addition, Donald R. Baucom's research for the Missile Defense Agency, an arm of the U.S. Department of Defense, provides policy information and historical data.[7]

The idea of missile defense systems originated during World War II, when it was learned that the Nazi missile program included proposals for intercontinental ballistic missiles (ICBMs). Both U.S. and Soviet missile defense systems began to be developed around this time.[8] The projects were kept on the agenda but given low priority in both East and West until the late 1950s. As the cold war escalated, however, both superpowers began testing their own antiballistic missile (ABM) systems. It is believed that the first Soviet system was established around 1961, while the United States conducted its first successful intercept of a dummy ICBM warhead in 1962.[9] Both sides continued to develop both offensive and defensive nuclear weapons systems throughout the 1960s. Talks to restrict the number of weapons on either side—the Strategic Arms Limitation Talks (SALT)—began in 1969, with the two superpowers led by Richard Nixon and Nikolai Pordgorny. This resulted in the SALT I accords of 1972, which included the ABM Treaty, under which each side was to be limited to two missile defense sites, each containing no more than 100 interceptors. Nationwide defense systems were banned under the treaty, and the sites in both countries were centered on the capital and one missile facility. An amendment to the treaty in 1974 reduced this number to one site for each side.[10]

The issue of missile defense was somewhat sidelined by the ABM Treaty, and the subject did not surface again as a major policy initiative until the election of Ronald Reagan in 1980. In his now-famous "Star Wars" speech in 1983, Reagan repositioned missile defense as a central feature of U.S. policy, saying:

> I call upon the scientific community in our country, those who gave us nuclear weapons, to turn their great talents now to the cause of mankind and world peace, to give us the means of rendering these nuclear weapons impotent and obsolete.[11]

The Strategic Defense Initiative Organization (SDIO) was established to carry out research and development on a *national* missile defense system, contra the ABM Treaty. In 1987, emphasis shifted toward the development of a space-based system, known as "Brilliant Pebbles," in which hundreds of large satellites would hold small interceptor missiles (the idea of these "garages" was later abandoned and the project became focused instead on individual missiles in space).[12]

Another shift in direction came with the end of the cold war and the first Gulf War in 1991. Under George Bush Senior, the putative system, announced in February 1991, now came under the title "Global Protection Against Limited Strikes" (GPALS), with the expected sites of missile attacks being rogue states or an unauthorized launch from the Soviet Union.[13] GPALS was to be a three-way protection system, involving ground-based national protection (national missile defense—NMD), ground-based theater missile defense weapons (known as TMD, and designed to intercept longer-range, theater class weapons), and a space-based global defense structure.[14]

Following the election of Bill Clinton in 1993, there was yet another change in emphasis; his administration focused on the development of TMD and downplayed the need for NMD, perceiving the main threat to the United States and its troops to come from theater missiles. Note that the assumption at this stage, as throughout its history, was that any threat was likely to be directed toward military targets. SDIO now became known as the Ballistic Missile Defense Organization (BMDO, but now known as the Missile Defense Agency, MDA) and the "Brilliant Pebbles" scheme was abandoned.[15]

Republican control of Congress from 1994 led to increased pressure to pursue an NMD system, pressure under which the Clinton administration capitulated in 1996, when "3 + 3" (three years of development and three of testing) was agreed.[16] The testing of nuclear weapons by India and Pakistan in 1998, however, led to renewed concerns about nuclear proliferation and, later that year, a similar test by North Korea added impetus to the calls for systems development.

The National Missile Defense Act of 1999 was introduced, in which it was stated:

> It is the policy of the United States to deploy as soon as is technologically possible an effective National Missile Defense system capable of defending the territory of the United States against limited ballistic missile attack (whether accidental, unauthorized or deliberate) with funding subject to the annual authorization of appropriations and the annual appropriation of funds for National Missile Defense.[17]

While the administration allowed the BMDO to work on the ground-based system, talks were also opened on revising the ABM Treaty to accommodate any changes that the new system might bring about. Discussions with Presidents Yeltsin and then Putin were held, although no agreement was reached. The Clinton government also backed off somewhat from the NMD system and, following two failed tests in 2000, decided to leave the decision on deployment to the next administration.

The current U.S. defense secretary, Donald Rumsfeld, told reporters in March 2000, that he had dropped the word "national" when talking about the project, saying "because what's national depends on where you live."[18] The removal of "national" also made the project appear more of a cooperative, international effort, rather than an exclusively U.S. concern. When George Bush Junior came to office in 2001, his administration took a different approach. The nature of the September 11, 2001 attacks notwithstanding:

> President Bush and members of his administration have been firm believers in the imminent danger posed by the proliferation of long-range missiles. They have been and are strong supporters of NMD development and the deployment of an effective NMD system.[19]

Their faith in the system is so strong, in fact, that the budget was increased by 3 billion U.S. dollars in 2002 (to 8.3 billion from 5.3 the previous year) and has grown year by year since.[20]

The administration also abandoned plans to modify the ABM Treaty and instead announced in December 2001 its intention to withdraw from it, while at the same time revisiting the possibilities for sea- and space-based, as well as ground-based, systems, effectively returning to the conceptualization of missile defense proposed during Bush Senior's presidency. In September 2002, President Bush stated:

> The deployment of missile defenses is an essential element of our broader efforts to transform our defense and deterrence policies and capabilities to meet the new threats we face. Defending the American people against these new threats is my highest priority as Commander-in-Chief, and the highest priority of my administration.[21]

The U.S. missile defense system doesn't operate in isolation, of course; although the architecture of the scheme is designed by the United States, its allies are both affected by its presence and have their own policies potentially influenced by its existence. The evolving system, in its current manifestation, is designed to operate from a series of ballistic missile early warning sites around the world, including bases in Alaska, California, the United Kingdom, Greenland, and Australia. In addition, discussions began in 2004 between U.S. defense department officials and Poland, Hungary, and the Czech Republic—all recent NATO members—about the possibility of positioning silos for interceptors on their territory. Polish foreign ministry spokesman, Boguslaw Majewski, is quoted as saying "We're very interested in becoming part of this arrangement. We have been debating this with the Americans since the end of last year."[22] Talks with South Korea, Japan, and a number of other countries are ongoing.

The British government, under Prime Minister Tony Blair, signaled toward agreement on cooperation with the United States, when in January 2003 Defense Secretary Geoff Hoon made a statement in the House of Commons in which he said:

> Missile defence is a defensive system that threatens no one. We see no reason to believe fears that the development of defences will be strategically destabilising. Reactions from Russia and China have been measured. And missile defence would only need to be used if a ballistic missile has actually been fired.[23]

He went on to note that agreement to cooperate with the United States in the development of the system would be a low-cost, high-gain policy for the United Kingdom:

> From the UK's national perspective, this specific decision is one that has real potential benefits at essentially no financial cost. But it will ensure

that if, in the coming years we find that a potentially devastating threat is becoming a reality, we have the opportunity to defend against it.[24]

Two sites are linked to the U.S. proposals for missile defense in the United Kingdom: Menwith Hill and Fylingdales, both located in North Yorkshire. Menwith Hill is a global "listening post" for the U.S. government and its allies (known as a "spy base" by local people), part of the Echelon system that purportedly sifts through some three billion communications, including up to 90 percent of Internet traffic, each day.[25] Fylingdales already exists as a ground-based early warning radar site, and would act as a tracking center for incoming missiles under the missile defense system. Following on from Hoon's January speech to the House of Commons, the British government granted permission in February 2003 to the United States to upgrade soft- and hardware systems at both sites.

February 2003 was a busy month for advocates of missile defense; the Japanese government agreed to participate in U.S. testing of the system in Hawaii.[26] Following the decision of North Korea to reveal its nuclear capabilities and to commence testing, Japan also announced that it would include some 1.26 billion U.S. dollars in its 2004 budget for a separate U.S.-made missile defense system.[27]

The Canadian government, which was long resistant to the idea of missile defense, exchanged letters with the United States in January 2004, agreeing to expand cooperation on the project.[28] The Danish government, which has administrative control over foreign and defense policies in Greenland, reached agreement in May 2004 for upgrade of the Thule base.[29] And, although previously voicing concern that its close trading relationship with China could be damaged by its cooperation with the project, in July 2004 Australia signed an agreement to participate with the United States in developing, testing, and possibly operating missiles for the system.[30] Prerequisites for the system—the cooperation of host governments and agreements on systems upgrades—are now in place and the United States is, at the time of writing, on track for the proposed first phase of the new system prior to the November 2004 general election.

3. Protesting Missile Defense—The Why and the How

The multiple locations of missile defense bases reveal different ways of, and rationales behind, protests against the system. All fall within the now-standard parameters of "online activism," a category that has only recently been subject to serious academic scrutiny. Since the introduction of the Internet, a good deal of research has been undertaken into its virtues as a political tool, with much of this work focusing on the new opportunities the technology presents for non-state actors to both access and share information. Early research in this area tended to take a largely idealistic view of the potential of the Internet to promote political change, effectively decontextualizing the technology from the real lives of the people using it. Access to, or the ability to exchange, information is only one part of the political process and some of the writings on the Internet during the 1990s were inclined to overplay the role that the mere ability to connect online might have in altering the landscape of politics.[31]

With the passage of time, as the Internet has become deeply embedded in the lives of many in developed regions, research on online activism has become more sophisticated. Interdisciplinary research has made an important contribution to this intellectual evolution: work across communications and media studies, international relations, sociology and other social sciences, and humanities areas has been linked with computer science and electronics, to develop analytical approaches that acknowledge the functions of the technology, its virtues and limitations, and the contexts in which it is used. Work in this area is now considerably less speculative, and there is a large and growing body of literature, and a significant amount of data, to work with.

On an empirical level, evidence of activist practices—from organizations and loose coalitions such as the anticapitalist, environmentalist, stop the war, independent media and human rights movements—has provided a solid foundation for analysis of the real and imagined impact of the Internet as a mechanism for dissent. At the same time, the increasing use of the Internet by governments to provide information, including press releases and policy documents, and to seek feedback from citizens online, provides opportunities for analysts to assess the potential impact of activist practices on policymaking. Similar approaches by major economic actors also contribute to our growing evidence-base on the Internet and its role in shaping the nature of societal interactions.

At the level of ontology and epistemology, there is also an expanding literature on the ways that we can analyze and understand the Internet. Drawing from research in communications studies, analysts of social and political use of the Internet have moved beyond the notion that access to information equates with impetus for action. Instead, focus has shifted toward developing frameworks for understanding what once seemed a rather diffuse and mysterious form of communication. Typologies of Internet practices and, most pertinent to this chapter, of online activism, have started to emerge, supplying mechanisms for interpreting practices by actors who may be geographically, culturally, socially, economically, and politically diverse, yet who may have previously unanticipated forms of contact around common interests.

In the developed world at least, the Internet is now a fairly standard tool in the armory of political activists and scholars have some reasonably efficient tools for interpreting the efficacy of its use. Vegh's classification, based on traditional social movement analysis, pins down the key types of online activism well:

> Awareness/advocacy; organization/mobilization; and action/reaction. This typology emphasizes the direction of initiative—whether one sends out information or receives it, calls for action or is called upon, or initiates an action or reacts to one.[32]

All these types of activism are common to social movement actors. What differs in the case of the Internet is that the strategies used to pursue these ends can reach wider and/or more targeted audiences than previously and, with the increasing sophistication of online graphics and audiovisual technologies, innovations in the presentation of material can be offered.

The use of literatures on social movement activities has been valuable for those who analyze Internet use. Expanding upon predeveloped interpretations of the nature of political engagement by non-state actors—whether in formal movements or as part of looser collectives—has helped to demystify some of the ways contemporary activism is effected. In particular, social movement literatures have helped to distinguish "new" forms of activism from "old" ones. Indeed, there is a clear sense that much of what happens in online activism is much like more conventional forms of political engagement, albeit technologically enhanced and capable of crossing greater distances and reaching wider audiences. As McCaughey and Ayers note:

> Technology is hardly new to activists. Social-movement groups have historically incorporated new technologies into their social-change struggles. Whether newspaper, radio, TV, or film, activists have embraced new communications media to circulate information, make statements, raise consciousness, raise hell.[33]

Political engagement across borders is also nothing new but the Internet has made a massive difference in the scale of transnational activism. Governments, of course, are not transnational and often appear as a secondary concern in the quest for change that is central to activism of any kind. For many activists, "their vision of politics is . . . based on normative concerns; they often see their concerns as shifting between global, local, and other arenas; and their image of politics is not necessarily focused on states or governments."[34] Unlike many other forms of contemporary political protest (such as anticapitalist protests where policy change is subsumed to broader concerns about societal change), activism against missile defense is specifically designed to have an impact on governmental policy. In an ideal world, halting the development of the project would be the central goal. Related to that aim is the desire to raise awareness, among both other potential activists and policymakers. The consciousness-raising role of missile defense activism certainly exists, as the examples below show. However, a significant amount of on- and offline activism around this issue centers on seeking influence over policymakers, both those local to the sites where the system will be based and at the level of national government.

Silver points out that analyzing activist websites isn't particularly straightforward. When approached as "texts" such environments prove tricky; they are most often decentered, fluid, temporary, and subject to constant change brought about by historical, economic, political, and technological developments.[35]

The discussion of activism against missile defense, then, is focused on the ways the websites demonstrate or diverge from the types of advocacy that Vegh identified earlier in the chapter. Whether awareness/advocacy, organization/mobilization, and action/reaction are the aims of online campaigning materials is considered. In doing this, the analysis suggests that the various campaigning organizations do not comprise a single social movement but should be seen as linked but distinct movement activists. This is a key consideration for Internet analysts, as we move toward a more detailed understanding of the impact of the Internet on policy. For policymakers, responding to localized actions, often with specialist knowledge of regional conditions and government policy, presents different challenges in dealing with the actions of international mobilization.

4. Missile Defense Protests

Activism is hardly a generic category. Activist practices cover a wide catalogue of activities and operate across a vast range of variables. The introduction of the Internet to activist movements has complicated the concept still further. While the bases for action may differ little from those foundational to pre-Internet social movements—world peace, clean water, social justice, and so on—the opportunities for links between actors with shared perspectives and priorities have expanded dramatically. Activism against missile defense has joined a long list of transnational movements that share a common interest but that have particular local, regional, and national concerns to confront and contend with. The Internet offers a mechanism for accessing and constructing networks that can respond to these differing spatializations of activist priorities.

At the same time, activism around this issue is part of a campaigning network with much greater longevity, existing much earlier than the new networks of Internet connectivity. A pacifist movement, in myriad manifestations, existed as a visible challenge to military and security policies throughout the cold war and has continued beyond. Despite few "successes" in changing governmental policies, the pacifist movement has persisted and grown in recent decades, signaling a commitment on the part of many to pursue the goal of social change in the face of rather extreme adversity. This adversity—seen in the continuation of civil and international conflict, heavy investment in military hard- and software, the development of projects like missile defense—may be viewed as an insurmountable obstacle for non-movement activists. For those committed to the cause of peace, however:

> The more open a society is to structural change, the more activists are likely to believe such change is possible, and thus to persist in movement work. Where they exist together, opportunity and hope can help to keep activists involved over the long term. . . . threat, such as that of nuclear war, can also be a crucial determinant to activist commitment.[36]

The restructuring of political engagement wrought by the Internet, through the increased availability of information, the chance to share resources, and so on, increases the sense that broader structural change may be possible. It is much easier to conceive of local action as being part of a much wider normative network when direct links between distant groups are made.

Missile defense activism links the two areas mentioned earlier: social movements with a significant online presence and pacifist sensibilities. Downton and Wehr suggest that there are now diverse groups that "form a loose global network of non-violence organizations working for change, largely in a Gandhian spirit. One could say that a permanent peace and justice lobby is now active in most nations."[37] Activism against the missile defense project operates within this Gandhian ideal and links activists with a broader network of similar movements, while also reflecting the specific localized concerns and practices that the project creates. It is these differences, as well as the broad similarities, which are identified in the examination of activism in different countries that is given in detail later. A brief overview of missile defense protests in three countries—the United Kingdom, Greenland, and the United States (specifically Alaska)—is given, along with an analysis of the Global Network site, which links protest sites from around the world. There is a strong tendency toward information provision regarding what activists see as the key issues relating to missile defense, issues which, of course, differ markedly from those outlined by the program's proponents. The examples used here are fairly eclectic and are intended to be illustrative rather than to provide a definitive analysis of missile defense activism.

All the sites considered provide a historical context for the project and for the origins of protest against it. There are some common themes (common to liberal social movements generally and to missile defense protests in particular) and some similar practices and forms of action across the sites. There are also area-specific themes and practices that differ significantly from place to place. On a normative level, the obvious issue is one of peace and pacifism: missile defense activism in all countries takes this as its starting point. Most of the activist sites listed here hold regular peace demonstrations close to the U.S. Air Force bases that will host the missile defense system. This kind of on-the-ground, real life protesting plays a significant role in maintaining the motivation of campaigners. Downton and Wehr highlight bonding to a group's principles, to the organization itself, and to its leaders as important factors in the retention of activists.[38]

For campaigners, the dangers of missile defense are the extensions of threats to security and the environment into outer space. There is a broad acceptance that space has been militarized through the use of surveillance satellites, military (and now, of course, civilian) GPS systems, space-based weather predictions, and so on. While this militarization is accepted, the *weaponization* of space is seen to pose an enormous threat to the safety of the earth's population: for those opposed to the system, missile defense has "the very real ability to provoke instability and weapons proliferation both on Earth and in space."[39] The "Star Wars" epithet has been valuable for campaigners in this respect, as the notion of space as a public good helps to position missile defense as a threat to a relatively untainted environment. While it is no longer possible to portray space as pristine, it is easy to make bold statements about the dangers of weaponizing—and by extension contaminating—it. Consciousness-raising of this kind falls squarely within Vegh's awareness/advocacy category, that was mentioned earlier. Popular culture portrays space as vast, uncluttered, and outside of our everyday experience; discussion of the weaponization of space makes it a place as real as the missile defense bases outside which campaigners regularly meet.

Yorkshire CND in the United Kingdom has had a website on the missile defense issue since 1997—a relatively lengthy period in the history of online activism. The website has a vast archive of both policy and protest material. In this sense, it is perhaps one of the most informative of the websites considered here, in that it provides both pro- and antimissile defense material. The web managers for the site have also worked to avoid one of the common pitfalls of website provision—information overload—by providing a separate space specifically for missile defense materials.[40]

The issues outlined by Yorkshire CND are international in nature: the militarization of space, Bush's space policy, the continuing development of weapons by the United States and other governments, decisions made on security policy by British and U.S. governments, the European Union, and so on. The *actions* they advocate are, however, specific to national and local priorities. The website provides: (1) links to email address for Tony Blair and the U.K. ministry of defense; (2) petitions to the U.K. government; (3) a downloadable postcard to send to the prime minister; (4) email, fax, and postal addresses for all members of parliament in the United Kingdom; (5) action packs for campaigning; (6) information on demonstrations; (7) membership information; and (8) posters for sale. Many of these are now common on activist sites, making the most of the available technology to supply as many options as possible for engagement. It is virtually impossible *not* to engage in some form of action once links to such sites have been opened. Hyperlinks to an MP's email address, along with prewritten text outlining the concerns of campaigners, make "activism" easy and, while it was once possible for policymakers to dismiss email messages as less significant than more formal communications, this becomes less tenable as email becomes a standard feature of workplace practice (in Western societies, at least) and the hierarchies of communications forms break down.

Another campaigning organization in the United Kingdom, closely associated with but separate to Yorkshire CND, takes a different stance altogether. Instead of the wider campaigning materials that the latter provides, the Campaign for the Accountability of American Bases (CAAB), engages in nonviolent, targeted actions against the U.S. bases in Yorkshire. In particular, the organization focuses on challenging local bylaws that allow the continued presence of—CAAB would argue "occupation by"—U.S. military personnel on British soil. While their actions cover a wide range of issues, the main actions undertaken by the group center on posing legal challenges to the legal decisions that allow the bases to effectively act as sovereign U.S. territory within the United Kingdom. The use of British courts to prosecute trespass on these U.S. bases is repeatedly challenged by the organization (mainly by engaging in repeated trespassing to provoke prosecution), as are the planning applications for both major and minor changes to the bases. Whereas on one level these actions are aimed at undermining the legal structures that support the U.S. bases in Britain, on another they also serve to raise awareness of the activities of U.S. security forces in the United Kingdom; by law, applications for changes to bylaws and planning permissions must be published in the local press, as must any challenges to them. This type of action is useful in both highlighting the support legal structures provide for U.S. bases and, given the media coverage that more innovative trespasses generate, brings the issue to mass media audiences.

Protesters in Greenland see the territory as caught in a continuation of a form of strategic colonization:

> Due to the strategic importance of Greenland during the Cold War, Greenlanders have again and again experienced that decisions affecting their lives were taken in Washington and Copenhagen were taken without even consulting them.[41]

Examples of these external threats to Greenland's stability listed by Greenpeace include the forced resettlement of the Inughuit community of Thule in 1953, the radioactive legacy of a B-52 accident in 1968, using the Thule base as a site for nuclear weapons during the cold war and, as in the case of Alaska, the environmental impact of the presence of U.S. military in the country.[42]

The greatest opportunity to influence policy in Greenland, and to raise public awareness of the issue, centers on the displacement of the Inughuit community. Application was made to the European Court of Human Rights in May 2004, in which a group named Hingitaq 53[43] is claiming its right to regain territory ceded by the Danish government to the Americans. The BBC suggests that "this localised struggle reflects the wider desire of Greenlanders to gain greater autonomy from Denmark and to have a greater say on American presence on its soil."[44]

Greenpeace sent its ship MV Arctic Sunrise to Greenland in 2001 on an awareness-raising mission, designed to provide information about the role of the Thule base in the missile defense program and to promote debate in Greenland, Denmark, and beyond. Interviews with Greenlanders, provided as MP3 audio files in the vernacular and as English-language transcripts on the website, are designed to give local people an opportunity to comment about the base and to provide a local context on the issue for an international audience.

Protesters in Alaska have similar concerns about colonization, albeit—rather confusingly—by their own government. Overseas allowances are paid to service women and men posted in Alaska and there is a long history of campaigning against environmental damage caused by activities near the U.S. bases in the state. At the same time, the presence of the U.S. forces provides the forms of primary and secondary employment relating to construction, service industries, and so on typically associated with military bases. In a remote territory like Alaska, protesters against missile defense are fighting not only to make their case to their state representatives, but are also required to convince many in the local population that the removal of the bases would be of benefit to the region. The tangibility of the income generated by the bases is therefore counterposed with the abstract notion of global peace.

The war on terrorism has given a major boost to missile defense activists; their online archives of information on military activity and spending have proven a useful resource for activists joining the Stop the War Coalition and other peace movements protesting against military campaigns in Iraq and elsewhere. When the media visibility of the missile defense program was low, protests against it operated far outside the mainstream. With the increase in peace activism since the war on terrorism began, there has been a concomitant rise in the links between activist sites and attempts by campaigners to ensure that these issues are not conceived of as being unrelated. No Nukes North, the main Alaska-based protest site, includes a link to the Cost of War website, with the now-familiar dollar counter clocking up military spending under the Bush administration.[45] The No Nukes North site also contains a link to the Iraq body count site, a website that aims to identify the numbers of civilians and military personnel killed since 2003.[46]

The Global Network Against Weapons and Nuclear Power in Space (otherwise known as the Global Network) acts as a form of umbrella NGO, addressing the issues raised by local campaigning organizations, supplying links to many of them, and providing current and archived documents on the history of the militarization of space. It also provides speakers for international events and a surprising array of merchandizing (including books written for the network, videos, audio CDs, t-shirts, music CDs, bumper stickers, and organizing packs). Founded in 1992 from a coalition of peace organizations, the Global Network focuses on the dangers of allowing the United States, or any other country, to dominate space:

> Now is our brief chance in history to prevent a great wrong from occurring. Now is the time that we must organize a global call to resist the nuclearization and the weaponization of space. We must make space for peace.[47]

As a rallying cry for all antimissile defense protesters, this acts as a central focus for action. The Internet provides a tool for the sharing of information that supports the activities of local activists. The forms local activism takes draw upon this material and frequently add to it. They also, however, reflect local concerns and conditions, highlighting the multilayering of "internet activism."

5. Conclusion

A number of common themes emerge from this examination of missile defense activism. One of the strongest is the links made to other social movements, positioning missile defense within broader global civil society movements. Environmental damage, particularly in Greenland and Alaska, plays a prominent role in portrayal of the program. This gives the movement both a general starting position that would kindle the interest of environmental activists, and a specific regional angle, which identifies local concerns, such as the potential for nuclear contamination.

In Greenland and Alaska there is also a sensibility suggestive of colonization, with activists in both territories expressing a strong sense of occupation, rather than shared control of the land and its resources. In the United Kingdom, a similar resentment of U.S. presence is occasionally expressed. While CAAB activists claim largely friendly relations with the troops at the bases where they regularly hold protests, the work of the organization in challenging the local bylaws to make the United States accountable for its actions within the United Kingdom, indicates a similar sense of injustice about perceived occupation.

Legal challenges to the U.S. presence take place in all three countries, at local, national, and regional levels. Taking cases beyond local regulators to national and transnational authorities gives activists an opportunity to establish legal precedents against which future U.S. actions can be regulated. While these challenges may differ (centering, e.g., on land rights in Greenland) they conform to a pattern of increasing awareness of the bylaws and broader legislation that permits the continued existence of the bases outside the U.S. mainland. Although the battles that have been won have been few, the small battles won contribute toward the bigger war and help to maintain motivation and momentum.

Missile defense activists, in common with most others who use the Internet for networking and information exchange, also participate in local actions—meetings, leafleting, town center stands, and so on. All the sites considered here highlight the significance of local meetings and the relevance of raising awareness among local communities. Social movement networks thrive on local connections and, whereas the Internet plays a significant role in creating global awareness, it is the local actions that act as the glue for the movement. The bonds between local campaigners are much easier to maintain in the offline world than over the Internet. Planned events and the "cups of tea" networks that provide opportunities for informal, face-to-face contact play a crucial role in both the sharing of campaign information and in building relationships between activists. In addition, the Internet is not a particularly efficient mechanism for organizing local events; telephone trees and personal contact tend to be much more effective when planning actions such as Saturday morning meetings, leaflet distribution, and fundraising campaigns.

The introduction of some form of missile defense system has been on the agenda of every U.S. president since Roosevelt and protesters are therefore challenging a long-established defense initiative of the world's leading power. They are also challenging their own governments and subjecting their own governments' relations with the world's leading superpower to scrutiny. Despite the obstacles that this would appear to bring, activism against missile defense has grown in recent years, both in terms of the number of people involved and in its public and media profiles.

There is one problem for transnational activists in claiming world peace as the goal for abandonment of missile defense: this is precisely what its supporters claim too. In posing challenges to the program at local, national, and international levels, missile defense protests make this an issue of transnational concern. At the same time, though, it is the local campaigns (often using transnationally exchanged information) that form the foundation of the movement worldwide. Missile defense activism demonstrates the ways, specifically, political protest (in the traditional political science sense of the term) operates at multiple levels, both spatially and conceptually. The Internet provides new tools for activism and campaigning—such as sound and video files, cheap synchronous communication worldwide, links to apparently increasingly accessible politicians—but doesn't change the basic design of political engagement. The movement may encompass broader social concerns but it is still a political movement, making use of available technologies to promote its cause as effectively as possible. In some cases, this will mean using the Internet to share information and coordinate large-scale actions. In many important senses, though, local meetings, events, and communications form the mainstay of global protest movements.

Notes

1. The American English spelling of this word—"defense"—is used in this chapter. Quotes and citations are made in the vernacular, though, and the spelling "defence" may occasionally appear. Similarly, "theater" and "theatre" are used depending on sources.

2. Vancouver Island Public Information Research Group, http://vipirg.ca/samd/dumb_and_dumber_poster.pdf [accessed June 30, 2004].

3. As ref. 1, http://vipirg.ca/samd/postcards.pdf [accessed June 30, 2004].

4. Barry Axford and Richard Huggins, eds., *New Media and Politics* (London, Thousand Oaks, New Delhi: Sage, 2001); Martha McCaughey and Michael D. Ayers, eds., *Cyberactivism—Online Activism in Theory and Practice* (New York, London: Routledge, 2003); Wim van de Donk, Brian D. Loader, Paul G. Nixon, and Dieter Rucht, eds., *Cyberprotest—New Media, Citizens and Social Movements* (London, New York: Routledge, 2004).

5. Craig Wartenkin, *Reshaping World Politics—NGOs, the Internet, and Global Civil Society* (Lanham, Oxford: Rowman and Littlefield, 2001), p. 23.

6. See Joshua Handler (2003), "National Missile Defense, Proliferation, Arms Control, Russia, and the United States," *Columbia International Affairs Online*, http://www.ciaonet.org/wps/haj06.html [accessed June 29, 2004].

7. Donald R. Baucom (2000), "Ballistic Missile Defense: A Brief History," *Missile Defense Agency*, http://www.acq.osd.mil/bmdo/bmdolink/html/briefhis.html [accessed June 20, 2004].

8. Ibid.

9. Handler, "National Missile Defense."

10. Baucom, "Ballistic Defense."

11. Video, Department of Defense, Missile Defense Agency, http://www.acq.osd.mil/mda/mdalink/html/mdalink.html [accessed July 06, 2004].

12. Handler, "National Missile Defense."

13. Robert Burns (2000), "GPALS: Bush's Missile Defense Proposal," *The Associated Press*, April 28, 2000, http://www.infoimagination.org/ps/election_2000/bush_action/gpals.html [accessed July 08, 2004].

14. Ibid.

15. Baucom, "Ballistic Missile Defense."

16. Handler, "National Missile Defense."

17. U.S. Department of Defense, National Missile Defense Act 1999 (Sec. 2, H.R. 4), http://www.acq.osd.mil/mda/mdalink/html/mdalink.html [accessed July 04, 2004].

18. Burns, "GPALS: Bush's Missile Defense Proposal."

19. Handler, "National Missile Defense."

20. For a breakdown of current and projected budgets through to 2007, see U.S. Department of Defense, Missile Defense Agency, "Fiscal Year (FY) 2005 Budget Estimates—Press Release," February 18, 2004, http://ww.acq.osd.mil/mda/mdalink/pdf/budget05.pdf [accessed June 30, 2004].

21. Missile Defense Agency, http://www.acq.osd.mil/mda/mdalink/html/mdalink.html [accessed July 04, 2004].

22. Ian Traynor, "US in talks over biggest missile defense site in Europe," *The Guardian*, Tuesday, July 13, 2004, http://www.guardian.co.uk/usa/story/0,12271,1260037,00.html [accessed July 16, 2004].

23. The full text of this speech can be found on the website of the U.S. Diplomatic Mission to Pakistan, entitled "Text: UK's Hoon Calls U.S. Missile Defense Proposal 'Invaluable'," http://usembassy.state.gov/islamabad/wwwh03011603.html [accessed July 09, 2004].

24. Ibid.

25. As the U.S. government is disinclined to discuss the nature of the Echelon project and its capabilities, much of the debate on its potential is speculative. The information here comes from UNESCO and so is probably as reliable as any: "Echelon: Legal, Ethical, Political, and Economic Issues of International Surveillance," UNESCO 2002, http://www.unesco.org/webworld/observatory/in_focus/290302_echelon.html [accessed July 04, 2004].

26. Alan Dowd (2004), "Missile Defense—Not 'Star Wars' Anymore," *The American Enterprise*, http://www.findarticles.com/p/articles/mi_m2185/is_2_15/ai_113456945 [accessed July 02, 2004].

27. Defense-Aerospace (2004), "Japan's Recent Step-up in Missile Defense," *Defence-Aerospace* http://www.defense-aerospace.com/cgibin/client/modele.pl?prod=27104&session=dae.4234443.1089071584.QOnp4MOa9dUAAEQyRYo&modele=jdc_1 [accessed June 01, 2004].

28. Department of Defence/Defense Nationale, "Letters Exchanged on Missile Defence," January 15, 2004, http://www.forces.gc.ca/site/Focus/Canada-us/letter_e.asp [accessed July 08, 2004].

29. Stephen Fottrell, "Inuit Survival Battle Against US Base," BBC News Online, May 27, 2004, http://news.bbc.co.uk/2/hi/europe/3753677.stm [accessed July 01, 2004].

30. Department of Defense (U.S.) (2004), "US and Australia Sign Missile Defense Agreement," http://www.defenselink.mil/releases/2004/ nr20040707-0991.html [accessed July 08, 2004].

31. I am deliberately not providing references to such works here. There is much of merit in early work on the Internet; authors were exploring new intellectual territories by attempting to examine the social, political, economic, and

cultural impact of the Internet in its formative years. The idea that the impact of the Internet on political processes was overplayed in some research is a personal opinion and I do not wish, therefore, to highlight particular works for criticism. It's probably also worth pointing out that I may also have engaged in some idealistic thinking on this matter.

32. Sandor Vegh, "Classifying Forms of Online Activism—The Case of Cyberprotests Against the World Bank," in Martha McCaughey and Michael D. Ayers, eds., *Cyberactivism—Online Activism in Theory and Practice* (New York, London: Routledge, 2003), p. 72.

33. Martha McCaughey and Michael D. Ayers, eds., *Cyberactivism*, p. 4.

34. Jayne Rodgers, *Spatializing International Politics—Analysing Activism on the Internet* (London, New York: Routledge, 2003), p. 73.

35. David Silver, "Current Directions and Future Questions," in Martha McCaughey and Michael D. Ayers, eds., *Cyberactivism—Online Activism in Theory and Practice* (New York, London: Routledge, 2003), p. 280.

36. James Downton Jr. and Paul Wehr, "Persistent Pacifism: How Activist Commitment is Developed and Sustained," *Journal of Peace Research*, Vol. 35, No. 5 (1998), p. 539.

37. Ibid., p. 531.

38. Downton and Wehr, "Persistent Pacifism," p. 541.

39. Yorkshire CND, "Fighting for Space—The Developing Threat of Space Warfare" (2004), http://cndyorks.gn.apc.org/yspace/overview.htm#status [accessed July 13, 2004].

40. The main site can be found at http://www.cndyorks.gn.apc.org/ while the missile defense site is at http://cndyorks.gn.apc.org/yspace/index.htm [both accessed July 12, 2004].

41. Greenpeace, "Star Wars and Thule—Bringing the Cold War Back to Greenland," http://www.stopstarwars.org/html/thulebrief.pdf [accessed July 16, 2004].

42. Ibid.

43. Hingitaq means "the deported."

44. Fottrell, "Inuit Survival Battle Against US Base," BBC News Online.

45. No Nukes North, http://www.nonukesnorth.net/ [accessed July 12, 2004].

46. Ibid.

47. Global Network Against Weapons and Nuclear Power in Space, http://www.globenet.free-online.co.uk/index.htm [accessed July 12, 2004].

CHAPTER 5

The Missing Public in U.S. Public Diplomacy

Exploring the News Media's Role in Developing an American Constituency

Kathy Fitzpatrick and Tamara Kosic

1. Introduction

In 1968, Stephen H. Miller lost his life in Vietnam. His service to his country was recognized when his name was inscribed on a memorial in Washington, D.C., that recognizes those who gave their lives for their country in the line of duty. But Miller's name is not on a wall of the Vietnam Memorial visited by millions every year. It is located on a wall in the lobby of the State Department seldom seen by visitors to the nation's capital.

In fact, there are two walls that display the names of 215 foreign service officers who died while serving America abroad.[1] Twenty-five of the names—including Miller's—are those of former officials in the United States Information Agency (USIA), for years the key institution responsible for U.S. public diplomacy, or the government's efforts to influence foreign publics' attitudes and opinions of the United States.[2]

The work of these and other public diplomacy specialists is an "untold story," according to former U.S. ambassador Christopher Ross, who serves as a special adviser to the undersecretary of state for public diplomacy and public affairs. While acknowledging that "we haven't done as thorough a job of informing the United States of what we do as we might," he said there needs to be greater understanding of both the importance and function of public diplomacy. Many people, he said, view diplomats simply as "striped-pants cookie pushers."[3]

The truth is that thousands of Americans work hard every day to develop and sustain good relations with the people of other countries. They staff more than 200 U.S. embassies and consulates abroad; they plan and implement international information programs; they carry out the functions of cultural and educational exchanges; they run Foreign Press Centers in the United States; they provide broadcasting services that reach worldwide audiences daily. And they have done all this for years with a fraction of the international affairs budget and relatively little support from the Congress, the president or the public.[4]

As Hans Tuchs, retired foreign services officer and author of *Communicating with the World: U.S. Public Diplomacy Overseas*, wrote, there is widespread public ignorance of the nation's diplomatic efforts. Although U.S. public diplomacy is widely recognized and appreciated abroad, he said, "among the [U.S.] public and even among Washington policy makers and politicians—there is little knowledge of what it is, what it can and cannot do, how it is practiced and by whom."[5]

This chapter addresses the growing importance of U.S. public diplomacy and the need for increased public understanding of this vital government function. The focus is on the news media's role in developing an informed citizenry and the potential impact of news coverage of public diplomacy on U.S. citizens' knowledge and understanding of the government's efforts in this area. The chapter analyzes a review of the *New York Times* coverage of U.S. public diplomacy over a ten-year period.

2. The Importance of Public Diplomacy

The rise of global anti-Americanism has revitalized interest in the U.S. international public relations efforts. Since the terrorist attacks of September 11, 2001, U.S. government leaders have focused unprecedented attention on the function called public diplomacy, or "the cultural, educational, and information programs, citizen exchanges, [and] broadcasts used to promote the national interest of the United States through understanding, informing and influencing foreign audiences."[6]

Although ineffective public diplomacy was not the direct cause of the terrorist attacks, the events raised considerable concern that the U.S. government had not done an adequate job monitoring Middle East opinion and addressing increasing hostility toward the United States. Soon after 9/11, members of Congress called for the revitalization of international informational efforts.[7] A new undersecretary for public diplomacy and public affairs was rushed through Senate confirmation to begin the task of repairing the image of the United States in the Middle East.[8] And new government public relations campaigns (e.g., "Branding America" and "Shared Values") were launched to combat anti-American sentiment in the region.[9]

Although people in other parts of the world expressed unity with Americans in the aftermath of 9/11, favorable views of the United States soon plummeted. Public opinion polls continue to show precipitous declines in foreign citizens' attitudes toward America, suggesting that the United States is losing what many have called the "war for the hearts and minds" of foreign publics.[10]

In response, government officials, academics, and others have proposed changes to bolster U.S. public diplomacy efforts. News and talk show participants have debated how to improve America's reputation in the world. Businesses—fearful that American brands are losing value—have banded together in an effort to come up with private solutions to America's image problem.[11] Although no consensus has emerged on the specific solutions needed, there is widespread agreement that public diplomacy needs to be "fixed."[12]

The urgency of such efforts was captured in the 2003 report of an Independent Task Force sponsored by the U.S. Council on Foreign Relations: "The problem of growing anti-Americanism is enormous, and America's response must be urgent, substantial and sustained."[13] In fact, national security, foreign policy, and national and local economies all are affected by the status of international relations—the purview of public diplomacy.

Public diplomacy specialists interpret the international environment, helping the United States better understand foreign publics' attitudes and opinions and the potential implications of those views. In turn, they explain to foreign audiences U.S. positions and perspectives. The goal is increased understanding of and respect for diverse points of view on issues that affect world citizens.

Breakdowns in international relations—whether caused by misunderstandings, a lack of information, or differences in opinions—can be costly, as the Bush administration learned in the invasion of Iraq. The views of *citizens* of other countries—in addition to those of national leaders—are important in the successful implementation of foreign policy, as this episode in American history showed.

Positive views of the United States also help shape an international environment in which American economic interests can flourish. Good international relations have become increasingly important as competition for trade and investments and qualified workers intensifies. The United States seeks a world in which policies related to such matters as immigration, environmental standards, and intellectual property are conducive to the growth and development of American enterprises.

At the same time, other nations have similar goals. Only through public discussion and debate can fair and equitable agreements be reached. Public diplomacy contributes to the development and maintenance of relationships that support both profitable trade and democratic ideals.

3. Lack of an American Constituency

Despite the obvious importance of public diplomacy to U.S. citizens, however, there seemingly is little public interest in public diplomacy outside government-related circles. Although Americans may wonder why foreign publics think ill of their nation, and may applaud a name change from "French fries" to "freedom fries" in support of nationalistic pride, there appears to be little understanding of the philosophical or practical issues associated with the process of developing relationships with the people of other nations. In other words, there is no domestic constituency for U.S. public diplomacy.

"If people don't know what public diplomacy is, they don't care," observed Matt J. Lauer, executive director of the U.S. Advisory Commission on Public Diplomacy, a bipartisan panel created by Congress in 1948 and appointed by the president to provide oversight of U.S. public diplomacy efforts.[14] Before early 2002, Lauer said, no more than two people showed up at annual commission meetings at which current initiatives in public diplomacy were reviewed and the commission presented its recommendations for improving public diplomacy efforts to the president, the Congress, the secretary of state, and the American people.

Notwithstanding the fact that the "American people" is a congressionally mandated audience for commission reports, few of the American people seem to care. Thomas Switzer, director of communication for the Foreign Service Association and a career foreign service officer, acknowledged, "It's amazing how little—if anything—people know about diplomacy generally, or public diplomacy specifically."[15]

Officially, it is the responsibility of the State Department's Office of Public Affairs "to help Americans understand the importance of foreign affairs" and "to feed their concerns and comments back to the policymakers."[16] However, limited efforts have been dedicated to educating U.S. citizens about the role of public diplomacy in foreign relations, according to State Department Public Affairs officer Price Floyd. Although some attempts have been made to increase local news media coverage that shows links between foreign affairs and domestic issues, he said, U.S. audiences have taken a backseat to foreign publics in a post–September 11 environment.[17]

At the same time, there seems to be a sense of futility among at least some State Department officials regarding the responsiveness of the American public to information regarding U.S. public diplomacy. When asked about citizen support for initiatives in this area, Floyd responded, "We don't have a U.S. constituency . . . It's hard to do." In blunt explanation, he added, "Who would give a shit?"[18]

Certainly, there is some truth to the fact that many Americans don't seem particularly interested in matters related to foreign policy or international relations. Perhaps they would care more, however, if they better understood the links between public diplomacy and national security, as well as the potential impact of foreign attitudes and opinions on national and local economies.

At the very least, U.S. citizens have a right to know how their taxpayer dollars are being used by Congress and the president to create international support for the nation's policies and interests. While a domestic constituency could provide support for—or against—existing or proposed public diplomacy initiatives, an uninformed citizenry has no chance to have its voice heard.

4. The Role of the News Media in Developing an Informed Public

In 1997, Claude Moisy, former chairman and general manager of Agence France-Presse, questioned the need for public involvement in international affairs. He asked, "Does it really matter for the United States foreign relations if the mass media and the general public become less interested in international affairs?"[19]

This question—posed in a pre–September 11 world—has become increasingly significant. The answer, many would argue, is yes. An informed electorate can help ensure that appropriate choices and actions are made in regard to public policy and foreign relations. Toward that end, the media are both important sources of information and significant influencers on policy.

President Harry S. Truman addressed the role of the media in developing an informed public in a 1950 speech to members of the American Society of Newspaper Editors. He began by noting the shared responsibility of the news media and the president "in helping to make the foreign policy of the United States of America."[20] No group in the country, he said, was of greater importance to foreign policy than newspaper editors:

> One vital function of a free press is to present the facts on which the citizens of a democracy can base their decisions. You are a link between the American people and world affairs. If you inform the people well and completely, their decisions will be good. If you misinform them, their decisions will be bad; our country will suffer and the world will suffer.[21]

At times, news coverage alone forces policymakers to consider—or reconsider—the public implications of their decisions and actions. In other situations, news reports serve to mobilize public opinion in ways that influence policy formation. Media scholar Maxwell McCombs, coauthor of the seminal work on news media agenda setting, explained:

> Through their day-by-day selection and display of the news, the editors of our newspapers and the news directors of our television stations exert a powerful influence on public attention to the issues, problems, and opportunities that confront each community. Over time, the priorities reflected in the patterns of news coverage become to a considerable degree the priorities of the public agenda.[22]

Although there is some debate about the full impact of news coverage on public attitudes and opinions, media scholars and professionals agree that journalists serve a critical role in the functioning of a democratic state. According to the Statement of Principles of the American Society of Newspaper Editors, "The primary purpose of gathering and distributing news and opinion is to serve the general welfare by informing the people and enabling them to make judgments on the issues of the time."[23]

Without question, defining the "issues of the time" in a "reality-TV" world may be difficult for media leaders forced to consider the commercial impact of the news menu. These government "watchdogs" must be careful, however, not to simply provide fare that pleases viewers' and readers' news palates but holds little informational value. As Professor Philip Seib observed in *Harvard International Review*, a decline in foreign news coverage driven by economic factors and a perceived lack of public interest "may prove to be a serious lapse of professional responsibility."[24]

Of course, it is not the job of the news media to *create* an American constituency for public diplomacy. It is, however, part of the journalistic mandate to cover policy matters in ways that allow news consumers to make up their own minds about how the government is functioning. Michael Shifter, writing for the *New York Times*, offered an example of what he perceived as a recent breakdown in the media's fulfillment of that charge. "Relations between Latin America and the United States are increasingly marked by irritation and distrust," he said. "Yet this tension has passed almost unnoticed by the United States press and unaddressed by the United States government."[25]

Such criticism is not surprising. News reporting of international affairs has been the target of media critics for years. British journalist and professor Ian Hargreaves bemoaned the fact that in both British and U.S. news media, the proportion of foreign news to domestic news dropped dramatically in the past 20 years. He asked, "Are we drifting into a state of dazed ignorance about other countries in which misunderstandings will take hold, fostering the re-nurturing of tribal passions?"[26]

In the wake of September 11, the U.S. media were compelled to consider such questions as they pondered the need to keep Americans better informed about issues in the world. For example, in addressing the danger posed to the United States by global terrorism, former *Los Angeles Times* editor and veteran foreign correspondent Michael Parks wrote, "News organizations were guilty of the same lack of judgment and neglected duty for which editorial writers have rebuked the Central Intelligence Agency and other governmental institutions."[27]

Former president of the American Society of Newspaper Editors and editor-in-chief of the *Manhattan (Kansas) Mercury* Edward Seaton told the *Columbia Journalism Review*, "We did not examine the country's anti-terrorism efforts adequately, our intelligence capabilities, our immigration policies, or the reasons for anti-Americanism." He said, "While we can debate whether this failure played a role in our national lack of preparedness, there is no question that we failed our readers."[28]

In contemplating the changes required to adequately cover foreign affairs, some media leaders pointed to the broadcast networks and "chains" as those in greatest need of a heightened commitment to international reporting. Leading national newspapers historically have done a better job in the international arena, they suggested. According to Leonard Downie, executive editor of *The Washington Post*, "The test is not what we or the *New York Times* or *The Wall Street Journal* or the *Los Angeles Times* does. We are committed to national and foreign coverage and will remain so."[29]

The next section considers Downie's assertion that leading national newspapers have done an adequate job reporting international news by examining one area of foreign affairs coverage during the past ten years. The authors review *New York Times* reports on U.S. public diplomacy—one of the "issues of our time" linked directly to possible "reasons for anti-Americanism" throughout the world.

5. The New York Times Coverage

The *New York Times* is a recognized leader in the national news media, viewed as a credible source of international news. The reach of the paper is significant, as is the potential impact on the public agenda. Although the *New York Times* and other elite newspapers are not the only influences on U.S. public opinion, they play key roles in helping American citizens determine the relevance of international issues and events. Because of their status, these papers also influence subsequent coverage of foreign news by other national newspapers, as well as regional and broadcast outlets.[30] The tone or angle of the initial coverage also may be evident in subsequent reports that contribute to public opinion formation.[31]

The *New York Times* coverage of public diplomacy, then, could be critical in shaping U.S. citizens' views regarding U.S. public diplomacy efforts. At the least, reporting on public diplomacy by the *New York Times* could help Americans better understand this important government function.

Methodology

Using the LEXIS/NEXIS database, the authors conducted a "guided news search" for "general news" in the "major papers" category for reports including the term "public diplomacy." In order to ensure accuracy, a search of the *New York Times* online archives, also using the search term "public diplomacy," was conducted and the results compared to the LEXIS–NEXIS findings. Opinion pieces—editorials and letters to the editor—were included because of the significant role such commentary plays in shaping public discourse and influencing the attitudes of opinion leaders and policymakers.

The dates chosen for analysis were "all dates" between August 2, 1993, and August 2, 2003. This ten-year period included the most significant modern events related to U.S. public diplomacy. The period provided a look at post–cold war coverage of issues related to public diplomacy; it included years during which the United States Information Agency was operating, as well as the period following the dissolution of the agency and the integration of public diplomacy into the State Department; and it included pre– and post–September 11, 2001, reports.

Using both quantitative and qualitative methods, the authors attempted to answer the following research questions:

(1) Did the *New York Times* view U.S. public diplomacy as an important news subject?
(2) What was the focus and tone of the *New York Times* coverage of issues and events related to U.S. public diplomacy?
(3) Was the *New York Times* coverage sufficient to educate and inform American citizens about U.S. public diplomacy?

To answer these questions, the authors conducted detailed content analyses of *New York Times* reports that included the term "public diplomacy." They examined the number and length of reports, publication dates, authors/bylines, page placements, and mentions of public diplomacy in headlines and leads. They then reviewed each report to identify topics of coverage and to evaluate the affective dimensions, or tone, of reports related to public diplomacy.

This inductive "framing" approach was chosen to allow themes to emerge rather than attempt to place reports in preselected categories of coverage. The media frame illustrates "the process by which a communication source . . . defines and constructs a political issue or public controversy."[32] Put another way, the news media provide the lens through which readers view and make sense of information.

Finally, the authors evaluated the sufficiency of the *New York Times* contribution to U.S. citizens' knowledge and understanding of public diplomacy on the basis of the quantity and nature of news coverage.

Results

The database search produced a total of 105 articles during the ten-year period studied. Fifteen reports were deleted because they were not directly related to the subject of public diplomacy.[33] Reports that did not reference U.S. public diplomacy, but were related to the diplomatic efforts of other nations, were included to illustrate the newspaper's use of the term "public diplomacy."

A total of 90 reports were included in the study. The authors reviewed 61 news articles, 1 news brief, 20 editorials, and 8 letters to the editor.

Forty-four reports mentioning public diplomacy appeared in the period before September 11, 2001, with 46 reports appearing after the terrorist attacks. Thus, the number of reports published during the almost eight-year period prior to September 11 was about equal to the number of reports appearing nearly two years after the event (see table 5.1).[34] Pre–September 11 coverage included 32 news articles, 7 editorials, 1 news brief, and 4 letters to the editor. Post–September 11 coverage included 29 news articles, 13 editorials, and 4 letters to the editor.

The average length of reports was 913 words overall, with an average of 713 words before September 11 and 1,122 words after September 11.

The majority of news articles published during the ten-year period were written by staff writers. However, more than half of the pre–September 11 news stories included what appeared to be freelance or stringer reports designated as "Special to *The New York Times*." No "special" submissions were included after September 11, with all but one of the news stories including the bylines of staff writers. The one exception was a brief Reuters wire service report. Editorials and letters to the editor during the ten-year period were written by government and other officials, academics, journalists, and citizen observers.

Of the total reports, 19 appeared on page 1 of the news section, with 2 reports published on page 1 of internal sections. Pre–September 11 coverage included eight reports on page 1 of the news section, no reports on the first pages of internal sections, and 36 other placements. Post–September 11 coverage included 11 reports on page 1 of the news section, 2 reports on the first pages of internal sections, and 33 other placements.

Table 5.1   Overview of *New York Times* reports

	Pre 9/11	Post 9/11	Total
Number of reports	44	46	90
News	32	29	61
News briefs	1	0	1
Editorials	7	13	20
Letters to the editor	4	4	8
Average length of reports (words)	713	1,122	913
Page one placements			
News	8	11	19
Internal sections	0	2	2
Mentions of "public diplomacy" in headlines	0	2	2
Mentions of "public diplomacy" in leads/introductions	6	5	11

The term "public diplomacy" appeared twice in headlines in post–September 11 coverage, with no headline coverage in the pre–September 11 period. In total coverage, "public diplomacy" appeared four times in the lead paragraphs of news stories, three times in the first paragraphs of editorials and four times in the first paragraphs of letters to the editor. Pre–September 11 coverage included two mentions of the term in news leads, one early mention in an editorial and three early mentions in letters, while post–September 11 coverage included two mentions in news leads, two early uses in editorials and one early use in letters to the editor.

Use of the Term "Public Diplomacy"

Perhaps the most compelling finding of this study was that public diplomacy seemed to be misunderstood by many of the journalists and commentators writing about it. Various uses of the term indicated considerable confusion regarding the role and function of public diplomacy.

In several cases, the term "public diplomacy" was used in reference to communication and/or relations with *domestic*—rather than foreign—audiences, and primarily with regard to influencing American public opinion on issues of war. For example, a September 10, 1994, report stated: "To try to persuade a skeptical American public that an invasion [of Haiti] is warranted, the Administration is stepping up its '**public diplomacy**'" [emphasis added].

In other reports, the meaning of the term "public diplomacy" was unclear, particularly in pre–September 11 coverage. Several references indicated that public diplomacy might be the same as foreign diplomacy. Consider the following confusing example from a June 25, 1996, editorial: "And it doesn't involve the sort of midnight diplomacy Israel used with the leaders of Egypt, Jordan and the P.L.O. to work their grand peace bargains in advance, in private, so they could leave only the details to **public diplomacy**" [emphasis added].

One of the few reports in which public diplomacy was both used and explained accurately was a 1994 "special" report by Steven Greenhouse, who wrote on October 16, 1994: "American diplomats tell Mr. Assad that **public diplomacy** can speed a peace accord and even strengthen his hand in the behind-the-scenes negotiations. The quicker he builds trust with the Israelis, the easier it could be to persuade Mr. Rabin to accept full withdrawal from the Golan Heights" [emphasis added].

Topics of Coverage

The primary subjects of *New York Times* reports in which public diplomacy was mentioned, along with the number of stories focusing on each topic, are presented in table 5.2. Although these topics emerged as subjects of apparent interest to journalists and commentators, there was no clear rationale for overall coverage. Perhaps the best description of reports would be that the coverage seemed "event-driven," primarily tied to conflicts in the Middle East before September 11 and the terrorist attacks and subsequent related actions on the part of the government after September 11. Most of the reports were reactive, or generated from government announcements, reports, and actions.

At the same time, the choice of topics seemed to reflect a keen sense of issues that should be of interest to U.S. citizens. Certainly, U.S. relations with the Middle East are important to the health and security of American citizens (although one could argue that media focus on one region of the world left others unattended). Effective leadership of the public diplomacy function is critical in ensuring its success in combating increased anti-Americanism throughout the world. The appropriateness of various public diplomacy techniques, such as U.S. broadcasting, cultural exchanges, and communication campaigns, employed by the government—and funded by citizen taxpayers—is vital if positive relationships with foreign publics are to be established.

Table 5.2 Categories of *New York Times* coverage

Topics of reports	Number of reports	
	Pre-9/11	Post-9/11
Middle East conflicts/peace negotiations	20	0
Anti-Americanism	0	6
Leadership of U.S. public diplomacy	6	6
U.S. public diplomacy agencies/structure	0	6
Foreign policy/relations	5	1
U.S. broadcasting	2	5
Reorganization of U.S. State Department	3	0
Function of U.S. public diplomacy	2	3
Legislation related to public diplomacy	2	0
U.S. wartime communication campaigns	2	4
U.S. public diplomacy techniques	1	4
Cultural exchange	1	4
National security	0	4
Foreign service	2	0
Al-Jazeera	0	1

Additionally, enhanced understanding of the function of public diplomacy, including its role and structure within the State Department and the various agencies involved in public diplomacy work, is significant in helping citizens reach informed decisions regarding government actions in this area. And reports addressing the links between public diplomacy and national interests could contribute to public and policymakers' understanding of U.S. national security initiatives and the need for qualified foreign service workers.

While the newspaper's natural instinct for *topics* of public interest seemed intact, however, the overall depth of reporting was lacking. The treatment of subjects was mostly superficial. For example, a report on Charlotte Beers' appointment as undersecretary for public diplomacy and public affairs, which fell into the "leadership" subject category, focused on her previous work on Madison Avenue and provided little insight into the government's public diplomacy function. A report on the secretary of state's interest in public diplomacy—also a "leadership" issue—failed to explain the function or provide insight into the nature or significance of public diplomacy. A piece on the debate over whether Voice of America should play more of an advocacy role in wartime—a topic related to "U.S. broadcasting"—provided little history or context that explained the intended function of the agency or its relationship to foreign policy objectives.

Overall, the *New York Times* provided little substantive news coverage of U.S. public diplomacy before September 11, with only seven reports addressing matters directly related to the function. Most of these reports focused on Middle East conflicts, with peace negotiations between Israel and Palestinian leaders receiving the greatest attention. In most cases, the term "public diplomacy" was simply used in reference to the actions of national leaders who were the subjects of news reports.

Even in the few stories that were directly related to U.S. public diplomacy, the function itself received secondary attention. For example, although the proposed dissolution of the USIA was addressed in three articles, the issue was reported in the context of a proposed reorganization of the State Department. The implications of such a move for U.S. public diplomacy were not addressed.

During the pre–September 11 period, three editorials and three brief letters to the editor addressed such topics as the possible consequences of U.S. administration officials making "undiplomatic" public statements about U.S. relations with other nations; efforts to fold the United States Information Agency and other agencies into the State Department; the proposed consolidation of the Voice of America and Radio Free

Europe/Radio Liberty; and a perceived need for U.S. foreign policymakers to "listen rather than simply dictate to their foreign partners." Most of these "opinion" pieces provided more insight into U.S. public diplomacy efforts than did the news stories.

Following the September 11 attacks, public diplomacy received considerably more attention in the news pages of the *New York Times*. While there were fewer news stories overall during this period, there was significantly more coverage of issues linked directly to U.S. public diplomacy. The post–September 11 reports focused almost exclusively on matters related to the terrorist attacks and the wars in Afghanistan and Iraq. U.S. efforts in public diplomacy were portrayed as part of a reactive, wartime "propaganda" effort. The paper provided mostly critical perspectives of the government's public diplomacy initiatives.

The *Times* ran several special war-related series during the post–September 11 period in which the U.S. government's public diplomacy efforts received considerable attention. The paper covered the president's attempts to handle "wartime public relations" and profiled the four women primarily responsible for U.S. global communications, who, according to the paper, all came from "the world of image making" and shared "a background in selling images and ideas."

According to the *Times*, the administration's "highly orchestrated" effort to combat the Taliban's daily denunciations of the American bombing campaign in Afghanistan was a "21st-century version of the muscular propaganda war that the United States waged in the 1940's." The "communication war," the paper said, was "an acknowledgment that propaganda is back in fashion after the Clinton administration and Congress tried to cash in on the end of the cold war by cutting back public diplomacy overseas."

Other reports covered private sector involvement in the development of campaigns to "bolster America's image abroad"; the establishment of a new Pentagon effort "to provide news items, possibly even false ones, to foreign media organizations as part of a new effort to influence public sentiment and policy makers in both friendly and unfriendly countries"; the hiring of a former advertising executive "to sell the American war to the Islamic world"; the creation by the White House of a new "public information 'war room' to coordinate the administration's daily message domestically and abroad"; and the President's decision "to transform the administration's temporary wartime communications effort into a permanent office of global diplomacy to spread a positive image of the United States around the world and combat anti-Americanism."

In the year after the terrorist attacks, *The New York Times* reported on a number of new State Department public diplomacy initiatives, reportedly designed "to get the upper hand in the propaganda war [in the Arab world] through broadcast, exchange programs and the Internet." According to the *Times*, the government was "putting a new spin on old-fashioned American propaganda." The State Department's public diplomacy strategies—"propaganda leaflets," Pentagon briefings and foreign language broadcasts—were part of U.S. "psychological warfare," the paper reported.

According to the *New York Times*, the United States' "multimillion-dollar public diplomacy campaign, complete with academic exchange programs and slick public service advertisements" was designed "to soften anti-American feelings." But, despite the efforts of the Bush administration's "message masters," the paper later reported, the administration's "public relations drive" had "floundered" because the message did not address "what the Arab media view as the main story: the invasion of Iraq by American troops."

Post–September 11 editorial coverage also focused on issues raised by the terrorist attacks and the government's response. The writers were mostly critical of U.S. efforts in public diplomacy, citing the need for improved relations with other nations. They expressed concern regarding rising anti-Americanism and offered suggestions for improving U.S. public diplomacy.

For example, William Safire chastised administration officials for wavering on the need for Voice of America to serve an advocacy role in the war in Afghanistan. Thomas Friedman called for a "much bigger investment in public diplomacy in the Muslim world." Nicholas D. Kristof cautioned U.S. officials that the belief that "many Iraqis will dance in the street to welcome American troops" may be a "potentially catastrophic misreading of Iraq."

Discussion of Results

According to the findings of this study, U.S. public diplomacy may have been among the most underreported international news stories of the past decade. Certainly, in the pre–September 11 period, the function was rarely mentioned and never discussed in any detail. While post–September 11 coverage indicated increased interest in public diplomacy as a news subject, in-depth coverage of the function itself was still lacking. Overall, the event-driven reports created somewhat of a hodgepodge of pieces that likely had little influence on either the public diplomacy agenda or public understanding of the function.

The usage of the term "public diplomacy"—particularly in the pre–September 11 period—provided clear evidence that many writers were unfamiliar with the specific function of U.S. public diplomacy, possibly creating confusion on the part of readers about what public diplomacy is.

At the same time, it should be recognized that public diplomacy is a complex function not easily defined or described. Even State Department officials have trouble explaining it. In commenting on the expanded media interest in public diplomacy after September 11, State Department deputy spokesperson Philip T. Reeker said that although former "USIA people had always bemoaned the fact that nobody knew what we were doing . . . suddenly there was this great interest and we were sort of stymied on how to describe what we were doing."[35]

Language could also have been important in shaping readers' impressions of the U.S. government's work in the area of public diplomacy. The frequent use of the word "propaganda," for example, could have created the impression that the United States was using questionable means to influence foreign audiences. Phrases such as "putting a new spin on old-fashioned American propaganda" and "get the upper hand in the propaganda war," along with references to "the Bush administration's message masters," "selling images and ideas" and "slick" advertisements, could have contributed to public views that the government's communication efforts were designed to create false images rather than present an accurate picture of the United States and its policies.

This potentially biased coverage might be partially attributed to journalists' negative views of "public relations." For example, while only two report headlines included the term "public diplomacy," five reports used "public relations" as a subhead in post–September 11 coverage. Journalists who historically have viewed public relations as simply "spin" might view public diplomacy with the same skepticism afforded the public relations function in business or politics.

The presentation of public diplomacy in the post–September 11 period as a reactive, wartime communication effort also may have skewed readers' views of the function. The terms chosen to describe U.S. public diplomacy functions—"psychological warfare," "war propaganda machine," "propaganda war"—collectively suggested that public diplomacy was more of a weapon of war than a strategy for peace. The reports did a poor job helping readers understand the significance of public diplomacy outside the context of war.

Additionally, *The Times* injected a sense of cynicism in its reports of State Department public diplomacy initiatives during the post–September 11 period. In most cases, criticism of the new initiatives received more attention than did explanations of them. Notwithstanding the facts that the efforts *were* the target of significant criticism among Washington observers and that healthy skepticism on the part of journalists covering government affairs is a good thing, the critical nature of the reports raise questions of balance.

Finally, some gaps in news coverage of important policy matters related to U.S. public diplomacy were noted. For example, the funding of public diplomacy initiatives was not covered in any detail although financial resources had been a constant concern in annual reports by the U.S. Advisory Commission on Public Diplomacy. Additionally, important legislative initiatives related to public diplomacy, including bills introduced in both the House and the Senate after the events of September 11, received sparse attention by the *New York Times*.[36]

According to Reeker, one reason for the apparent lack of media attention to such matters could be that some editors and reporters don't fully understand the links between foreign affairs and domestic agendas. Reeker noted that because of the provincial nature of most media—U.S. and foreign—they sometimes fail to look at the big picture. Some journalists, he said, are "almost naïve in their approach to things, like looking at context." What you often find, he said, is an "understandable parochialism."[37]

The inclusion of opinion pieces in the review of coverage was helpful in developing a full picture of the "conversation" about public diplomacy that took place in the pages of the *New York Times* during the ten-year period studied. The editorials, particularly, demonstrated the potential importance of such commentary in the development of public and policy agendas. For example, the picture collectively painted by editorial writers in the post–September 11 period was that U.S. public diplomacy needed some attention. A number of respected commentators called for an increased investment in the public diplomacy function, a message that could have had some influence on the views of the American public and policymakers.

Notwithstanding the *potential* impact of both news and editorial coverage on the public and policy agendas, however, it is unlikely that the limited quantity and nature of the *New York Times* reports on U.S. public diplomacy over the ten-year period influenced either the U.S. public or policymakers in significant ways. The topics addressed were important, yet the breadth and consistency of coverage needed to build public interest in and understanding of public diplomacy were lacking. Although increased coverage during the post–September 11 period was encouraging, the reports overall were insufficient to educate and inform American citizens about U.S. public diplomacy.

6. Looking Ahead

This study represents only a first step in gauging national media perspectives on U.S. public diplomacy. Future efforts are needed to better understand the links between news media coverage and an informed citizenry on public diplomacy.

The study had a number of limitations. Certainly, the choice of "public diplomacy" as the sole search term may have limited the number of reports identified in this study—particularly if writers shied away from using it in their reports. Future research should be expanded to include topics related to public diplomacy—but not called "public diplomacy"—to draw a clearer picture of the news media's potential influence on the public diplomacy agenda.

Future studies should also include other national and regional newspapers, as well as broadcast outlets. Comparative studies could provide additional clues regarding media treatment of matters related to public diplomacy and the potential impact of media reports on U.S. citizens' understanding of the function.

Finally, it is important to note that news media attention to public diplomacy is only one possible reason for the U.S. public's ignorance of the nation's diplomatic efforts abroad. Long-term Congressional and presidential neglect of public diplomacy, combined with limited oversight of the function and outdated legislation limiting the distribution of public diplomacy materials in the United States, are significant concerns, too.[38] If public diplomacy is to be recognized as a vital instrument in successful foreign relations, then all these issues must be addressed.

Within the next century, the United States will face a barrage of challenges and conflicts. Whether it is religious fundamentalism, human rights violations, or other matters, the government cannot possibly know every challenge to come. Yet, modern nation-states possess the capabilities to prepare for such events by building strong relationships with other governments and peoples throughout the world. Understanding and respecting other cultures and providing for the free flow of information makes respect for and greater understanding of—if not always agreement with—U.S. policies and ideals more likely.

The importance of such support cannot be overestimated in a world in which terrorist threats are everyday concerns. As the twenty-first century unfolds, public diplomacy could be one of America's most effective tools in defending and protecting its citizens from future conflicts.

Notes

1. Retrieved from http://www.afsa.org/plaques.cfm on July 12, 2003.
2. "United States Information Agency, A Commemoration," 1999.
3. Personal interview with Christopher Ross, June 26, 2002.
4. See U.S. Advisory Commission on Public Diplomacy, "Building America's Public Diplomacy Through a Reformed Structure and Additional Resources," 2002. See also Kathy R. Fitzpatrick, "U.S. Public Diplomacy: Telling America's Story," *Vital Speeches of the Day*, Vol. 70, No. 13 (May 1, 2004), pp. 412–417.
5. Hans N. Tuchs, "Why American Don't Appreciate Public Diplomacy," *Foreign Service Journal* (January 1991), pp. 11–16, at 11.
6. U.S. Advisory Commission on Public Diplomacy, "Building America's Public Diplomacy Through a Reformed Structure and Additional Resources," 2002, p. 1.
7. In 2002, House International Relations Committee chairman Henry J. Hyde introduced the Freedom Promotion Act of 2002 to form U.S. public diplomacy operations, but the bill later died in Senate.
8. See Marci McDonald, "Branding America," *U.S. News & World Report* Vol. 131, No. 22 (November 26, 2001), p. 46.
9. See Report of the Advisory Group on Public Diplomacy for the Arab and Muslim World, Changing Minds Winning Peace, 2003, Appendix A: The Shared Values Initiative. See also Kathy R. Fitzpatrick, "U.S. Public Diplomacy: Telling America's Story," *Vital Speeches of the Day*, Vol. 70, No. 13 (May 1, 2004), pp. 412–417, in which the lead author also cites these efforts.
10. See, e.g., The Pew Research Center for the People and the Press, Views of a Changing World 2003, June 3, 2003.
11. See Kathy R. Fitzpatrick, "U.S. Public Diplomacy: Telling America's Story," *Vital Speeches of the Day*, Vol. 70, No. 13 (May 1, 2004), pp. 412–417.
12. See, e.g., U.S. Advisory Commission on Public Diplomacy, "Building America's Public Diplomacy Through a Reformed Structure and Additional Resources," 2002; and Stephen Johnson and Helle Dale, "How to Reinvigorate U.S. Public Diplomacy," The Heritage Foundation Backgrounder, April 23, 2003.
13. Report of an Independent Task Force sponsored by the Council on Foreign Relations, Finding America's. Voice: A Strategy for Reinvigorating U.S. Public Diplomacy, 2003, p. 5.
14. Personal interview with Matt J. Lauer, June 13, 2003.
15. Personal interview with Thomas Switzer, July 16, 2003.
16. http://www.state.gov/www/outreach/reorg_n_oview.html. Retrieved on June 17, 2003.

17. Personal interview with Price Floyd, June 24, 2003.
18. Ibid.
19. Claude Moisy, "Myths of the global information village," *Foreign Policy*, No. 107 (Summer 1997), pp. 78–87, at 86.
20. Harry S. Truman, speech delivered at the annual convention of the American Society of Newspaper Editors, Washington, D.C., April 20, 1950.
21. Ibid.
22. Maxwell McCombs, "Building Consensus: The News Media's Agenda-Setting Roles," *Political Communication*, Vol. 14, No. 4 (1997), pp. 433–443, at 433.
23. John L. Hulteng, *Playing It Straight: A Practical Discussion of the Ethical Principles of the American Society of Newspaper Editors* (Chester, CT: The Globe Pequot Press, 1981), p. 5.
24. Philip Seib, "Politics of the Fourth Estate," *Harvard International Review*, Vol. 22, No. 3 (Fall 2000), pp. 60–63, at 63.
25. Michael Shifter, "A Policy for the Neighbors," the *New York Times*, July 17, 2003, p. A27.
26. Ian Hargreaves, "Is There a Future for Foreign News?" *Historical Journal of Film, Radio and Television* (March 2000), pp. 55–62.
27. Michael Parks, "Foreign News: What's Next?" *Columbia Journalism Review*, Vol. 40, No. 5 (January–February 2002), pp. 52–53, at 52.
28. Michael Parks, "Foreign News: What's Next?" *Columbia Journalism Review*, Vol. 40, No. 5 (January–February 2002), pp. 52–53, at 53.
29. Ibid., p. 53.
30. See Bernard Cohen, *The Press and Foreign Policy* (Princeton, NJ: Princeton University Press, 1963), p. 299; Maxwell McCombs, Edna Episode, and David Weaver, *Contemporary Public Opinion: Issues and the News* (Hillsdale, NJ: Lawrence Erbium Associates, 1991), p. 47; James P. Winter and Chain H. Eye, "Agenda Setting for the Civil Rights Issue," in David L. Protests and Maxwell McCombs, eds., *Agenda Setting: Readings on Media, Public Opinion, and Policymaking* (Hillsdale, NJ: Lawrence Erlbaum Associates, 1991), pp. 101–107.
31. See Benjamin I. Page and Robert Y. Shapiro, "Presidents as Opinion Leaders: Some New Evidence," *Policy Studies Journal*, Vol. 12 (1984), p. 651, finding that prestige newspapers "may not be a bad indicator of the general thrust of news" read by U.S. citizens.
32. Thomas E. Nelson, Rosalee Clawson, and Zoe M. Oxley, and, "Media Framing of a Civil Rights Conflict and Its Effect on Tolerance," *American Political Science Review*, Vol. 91 (1997), pp. 567–583, at 567.
33. For example, several articles were obituaries of individuals who were associated with U.S. public diplomacy.
34. These and the following figures include reports that mentioned public diplomacy but did not necessarily focus on topics specifically related to U.S. public diplomacy.
35. Personal interview with Philip T. Reeker, June 26, 2002.

36. See, e.g., HR 3969, "Foreign Relations Authorization Act, Fiscal Years 2004 and 2005," also known as the Freedom Promotion Act of 2002, introduced by Henry J. Hyde, chairman of the U.S. House of Representatives Committee on International Relations.
37. Personal interview with Philip T. Reeker, June 26, 2002.
38. The Smith–Mundt Act (CITE), e.g., passed in 1948 and still in effect today, prohibits the distribution of public diplomacy materials in the United States and limits access by the U.S. media to information targeted for dissemination outside American borders. See Kathy R. Fitzpatrick, *Vital Speeches of the Day*, May 1, 2004.

CHAPTER 6

Characteristics of War Coverage by Female Correspondents

Cinny Kennard and Sheila T. Murphy

As we enter the twenty-first century, television continues to be the dominant communication technology for war coverage. In an age of globalization, television is the tool whereby most of the world's citizens and world governments obtain information. Television coverage plays a pivotal role in determining a story's salience and shelf life that, in turn, can drive public opinion and can even compel an administration to act. Often, as the television coverage of an international crisis builds, the pressure to do something, anything, about it becomes overwhelming. Consequently, accurate, fair, and balanced coverage of a news event on television—especially war—is critical.

But what constitutes balanced news coverage? Past research has paid a great deal of attention to whether news coverage is "balanced" with respect to the political ideologies expressed. In contrast, substantially less attention has been paid to the issue of gender balance in television news coverage in general and war coverage in particular.[1] Do war stories filed by female correspondents differ from those of their male counterparts not only in terms of their frequency and prominence in the newscast but also in terms of content? This chapter will explore the importance of gender in televised war coverage by presenting a brief historical overview followed by the results of a content analysis of actual war coverage. This content analysis will compare war-related stories filed by female and male correspondents during the first 100 days of three different wars—the Persian Gulf War, the war in the former Yugoslavia, and the war in Afghanistan. Finally, the personal experiences of female war correspondents are used to supplement and provide context to the results of the content analysis.

1. Women and War Coverage

Today's female war correspondents are following a trail blazed two centuries ago by pioneers such as Margaret Fuller who reported the bloody Italian revolution of 1848 for the New York Herald Tribune, Jane Swisshelm who reported on the conditions in Union military hospitals during the American Civil War, and Anna Benjamin who went to Cuba and the Philippines to cover the Spanish–American War.[2] In the intervening years much has changed regarding the coverage of war and women's role in that coverage. Perhaps the most dramatic changes have simply been the direct result of technological advances. For example, during the Vietnam War there was only the anonymous wire service reporter and a small amount of TV coverage, mostly film, was sent out of the war zone often days after a conflict. But now videophones and the Internet allow images to be transmitted instantaneously from the front lines. These constant images are needed to fill the ever-expanding news hole created by the advent of cable news channels and continuous 24-hour coverage.

The relationship between the media and the government with respect to war coverage has also shifted dramatically over time. For years the U.S. government blamed the vivid images of the casualties from Vietnam broadcast on the nightly news for forcing an end to the Vietnam War. This is in stark contrast to the 2003 war in Iraq where the U.S. military invited hundreds of reporters to become "embedded" with the troops, from the deployment stage all the way to the front lines. Prior to the actual battle, the U.S. government also provided combat safety training for reporters. Nearly 800 reporters were approved for slots as embeds—reporters approved by the Pentagon to be firmly fixed among the troops to cover movements on the battlefield. While this was not the first time the concept of embeds was used, it was the first time the system was used by the Pentagon to such an extent. According to U.S. Army Major Tim Blair who organized the embed mission, reporters were assigned to units after being selected by their news organizations. This embedded news arrangement provided an unprecedented view from the battlefield with reporters broadcasting live with combat underway immediately behind them. But this arrangement came with a price. Television networks had to abide by strict government guidelines in exchange for the extraordinary access.

Another important dimension to the change in war coverage is the increase in the number of female correspondents covering the battlefield, particularly for American television networks. Women did cover Vietnam as war correspondents in unprecedented numbers in the 1960s and early 1970s. For example, Liz Trotta covered the Vietnam War for NBC and Marlene Sanders reported for ABC news in the spring of 1966. Available records indicate that just over 300 women, mostly print reporters, were accredited to cover the wars in the decade between 1965 and 1975.[3] Of those 300, a total of about 70 women are identifiable as correspondents by their published or broadcast war reports. During the decades following America's withdrawal from Vietnam women have taken an increasingly prominent role in covering wars. Women have been routinely assigned to cover conflicts in Central America, the Persian Gulf, Yugoslavia, Albania, and countries throughout Africa, among others.

Hillary Brown, originally trained on Canadian radio, has been an ABC News battlefield correspondent for years, but she remembers when there were few if any women working with American Network television covering the front lines. In 1973, while in Israel covering the Yom Kippur war as a freelancer for ABC, correspondent Lou Cioffi told Brown that ABC wanted to hire women full-time as on-air reporters to cover the battlefield and fulfill an equal opportunity requirement for hiring that was way out of date. "You should apply sweetie pie," Cioffi told her. She did and got the job becoming the first female foreign correspondent for ABC News. Brown also was among the first in what has become a long list of female correspondents hired from the Canadian Broadcasting Company to cover foreign news and the battlefields for American television networks. American network news operations (AMNETS as they are known at the CBC) were not necessarily the spawning grounds that the Canadian Broadcasting Company television was for female war correspondents. In the United States, it was a slow climb with only a few women like Martha Teichner (CBS), Liz Trotta (NBC), and Betsy Aaron (CBS) who managed by sheer talent and persistence to land the war assignments. But their presence in America's living rooms, broadcasting from the front lines was sporadic and fleeting. For American viewers it took Iranian born CNN war correspondent Christiane Amanpour to crash through the glass ceiling as the senior female correspondent covering the battlefield in the 1990s.

Currently, there is the widespread perception that the number of women reporting for American television news networks on war both from home and abroad has increased substantially in the past decade. As the number of women covering war increased, so too did speculation about the content of their coverage. It has been suggested that when females report from war zones their coverage tends to focus on victims and families, filing reports that may put a more human face on war coverage, whereas male reporters more often file stories on military strategy, bombs, and bullets.

As a former television war correspondent for CBS News in London and Moscow, and having years of experience in local television in the United States, Cinny Kennard, the first author of this chapter, can offer unique insight into this issue. "From my own experience and watching many of my female colleagues, many of us seemed to possess a missionary zeal while covering the battlefield—a desire to expose the horrors of war as opposed to detailing the weapons, strategy, and deployment." In January 2002, Kennard, along with Sheila Murphy, at the time both professors at the University of Southern California's Annenberg School for Communication, received a grant for the Women and War Project from the Ethics and Excellence in Journalism Foundation to document the relative frequency of female war correspondents in the Persian Gulf War, the war in Bosnia and the war in Afghanistan as well as examine whether the content of the stories differed from those of their male counterparts. What follows is a brief description of the project and its key findings.

2. The Women and War Project

In March 2002, a USC Annenberg School research team began to comb the Vanderbilt University Television News Archives in search of all stories filed by female correspondents from ABC, CBS, NBC, and CNN (MSNBC and Fox were not included because they were not operational during the first Persian Gulf War). The team identified stories filed from the home front and from the battlefront in the first Persian Gulf War, the nearly four-year-war in the 1990s in former Yugoslavia, and the 2001 war in Afghanistan. The sampling frame focused on the first 100 days of each conflict. It is during this peak period that American television news networks expend the most time and money squarely on conflict coverage. In the last two decades, American network news and the 24-hour cable news stations tended to invest in war coverage largely when American troop movements were deployed for a combat or a peacekeeping mission. Day-to-day coverage of international conflict like the protracted war in former Yugoslavia is rare unless there is a distinct American government or military role. Even with enormous involvement of the American military, networks often pull back resources once the fierce battles and dramatic footage wind down.

The first Persian Gulf War began on January 17, 1991. Thus, the content analysis included all war-related stories with female correspondents on ABC, CBS, NBC nightly news and the comparable newscast on CNN for the 100 days between January 17 and April 20, 1991 as well as an equal number of war stories covered by their male counterparts during the same time frame. The sampling frame for the war in Afghanistan involved nightly newscasts between October 7, 2001 and January 15, 2002. Because the mission was peacekeeping as opposed to combat, the appropriate time frame for the war in former Yugoslavia was more difficult to determine. For example, the mortar attacks on Sarajevo markets—particularly deadly in August 1995—generated a very brief concentration of coverage because of the audacity and tragedy of the assault. Four months later, America sent 10,000 troops into former Yugoslavia as part of its agreement in the Dayton Peace Accord and news networks and CNN flooded the region with coverage. Millions of dollars were invested. Each network leased and then remodeled homes owned by the locals to set up news headquarters outside the air base in Tuzla, northern Bosnia. CNN even rented a huge restaurant and set up a newsroom. American Network anchormen were flown in. It was the largest concentrated commitment of resources by American news networks during the nearly four-year conflict. Ultimately, December 11, 1995–March 19, 1996 was selected as the "peak period" of news coverage for the Bosnian conflict because of this extraordinary peacekeeping troop deployment by the United States. Interestingly, the three wars selected for analysis in the Women and War research project occurred approximately five years apart—1991, 1995–1996, and 2001.

Once the relevant war stories were identified, videotape copies of each story were coded on a variety of dimensions. During the coding period the team actually viewed and content-analyzed 526 war stories filed by the female correspondents for ABC, CBS, NBC, and CNN. The team then drew a random sample of an equal number of war-related news stories with male correspondents from the same period with the same news channels.

The coverage was analyzed on a variety of dimensions such as the following:

(1) The relative percentage of stories filed by female reporters as compared to their male colleagues;

(2) Whether war stories filed by women were given equal prominence (i.e., length of time, placement in newscast);

(3) Whether the content of the female coverage was qualitatively different from that of their male counterparts (content, hard-edged or

soft-edged, patriotic or critical of the U.S. government, exclusive and so on);

(4) Whether female correspondents were filing their stories from domestic or foreign locations.

3. Results

Relative Percentage of War-Related News Stories Covered by Women

There is a widespread perception that television news has spawned an entire new generation of female war correspondents. However, the Women and War Project content analysis of the first 100 days of three major wars occurring between 1990 and 2001 revealed that this is not necessarily the case. As shown in table 6.1, the percentage of war stories filed by women did not grow steadily during this ten-year period. Just 13 percent of the 1710 stories filed during the 1990 Persian Gulf War I study period were filed by women. This percentage improved dramatically during the Bosnian conflict with 30 percent of the 320 war stories being filed by female correspondents. But this shift does not appear to be stable as in 2001 during the war in Afghanistan; the ratio was once again down to 20 percent of the 1033 war stories being filed by women.

Prominence

Gender differences also emerged when considering placement of the story in the newscast. As shown in table 6.2, just 15 percent of the stories

Table 6.1 Percentage of war-related stories covered by female correspondents

	Gulf War %	Bosnia %	Afghanistan %	Overall %
ABC	13	35	12	15
	(59/471)	(25/71)	(30/245)	(114/787)
CBS	11	20	16	14
	(49/432)	(18/91)	(46/280)	(113/803)
NBC	6	2	32	16
	(26/438)	(1/47)	(94/297)	(121/782)
CNN	23	49	19	26
	(85/369)	(54/111)	(39/211)	(178/691)
Total	13	30	20	17
	(219/1710)	(98/320)	(209/1033)	(526/3063)

Source: Women and War Coverage, USC Annenberg School Study, 2003.

Table 6.2   Percentage of lead stories by a female correspondent

	Gulf War %	Bosnia %	Afghanistan %
ABC	14.3	20	27.6
CBS	10	33	6.9
NBC	12	0	10.6
CNN	14.8	18.9	19.6
Overall	14.8		

Source: *Women and War Coverage*, USC Annenberg School Study, 2003.

Table 6.3   Average length of war-related stories in seconds

	Gulf War	Bosnia	Afghanistan	Total
Female	105	159	142	127
Male	182	229	248	208

Source: *Women and War Coverage*, USC Annenberg School Study, 2003.

Table 6.4   Primary content of war stories

	Men %	Women %
Human interest		
Victims	8.6	14.2
Human rights abuses	1	3.6
Soldier profiles	2.2	5.3
Military families	2	2.6
Hard-edged		
Mission strategy	24.2	12.2
Weapons and deployment	6.8	7.9
Politics	20	21.5

Source: *Women and War Coverage*, USC Annenberg School Study, 2003.

filed by women in the study were the lead story in the newscast versus 26 percent of stories filed by male correspondents. In addition, the male stories are significantly longer (see table 6.3). War stories in the study filed by male correspondents averaged 208 seconds each while stories filed by women were on an average of 127 seconds, or a little over half that length.

Content

One of the primary objectives of the content analysis was to to determine if gender differences emerge with respect to the content of the story. Do women report wars differently from men, giving more attention to victim-based stories than more hard-edged coverage about weapons, strategy, and politics? Our analysis does reveal a systematic difference in the way women and men cover wars. As shown in table 6.4, the female correspondents filed many more stories involving victims of war, military families, U.S. children's reaction to war, the cost of war, profiteering, and stories of rallies and protests than their male counterparts. Females also reported more frequently on subjects like rape and human rights.

When it came to the hard-edged war story with strategy and weapons, the results indicate that the vast majority of war stories filed by both men and women were hard-edged dealing with topics such as weapons and deployment, politics, and the battlefield. Across all three wars, 67 percent of stories filed by women were considered hard-edged compared to 74 percent of stories filed by men.

Location

Nearly 59 percent of the male correspondents filed stories from foreign locations such as the battlefield, an overseas military base, and the combat frontlines, compared to just 45 percent of women filing stories from foreign locations. Conversely, female correspondents' stories were significantly more likely to be filed from domestic locations such as Washington D.C., Allied command, or cities across America. There may be several reasons for the differences in filing location.

4. Discussion

The primary goal of the Women and War Project was to explore whether the war-related news stories filed by female correspondents differed from those of their male counterparts either quantitatively (in terms of relative frequency, length, and prominence) or qualitatively (in terms of content). We address each of the four research questions posed earlier below.

Are the Relative Numbers of Female War Correspondents Increasing on American Television Networks?

Overall the answer is no. The Women and War content analysis of the first 100 days of the three major wars occurring between 1990 and 2001 refutes the widespread perception that television news has spawned an entire new and rapidly growing generation of female war correspondents. Whereas the overall percentage of female-filed stories more than doubled between the 1990 Persian Gulf War and the Bosnia conflict in 1995 from 13 to 30 percent, there are several reasons to be suspicious of this trend. First, as our data show, the Bosnian conflict received substantially less concentrated coverage than either the Persian Gulf War or the war in Afghanistan. This suggests that even relatively small shifts could result in large changes in the percentage of female stories. Second, this dramatic shift does not appear to be stable. By 2001, during the war in Afghanistan, the ratio was once again down to 20 percent of war stories being filed by women—only a 7 percent increase from the 1990 Gulf War.

These findings should also be placed in a historical context. During the 1990 Persian Gulf War at least three out of the four news channels built a stable of female war correspondents (CNN correspondent Christiane Amanpour and CBS London based correspondent Sheila MacVicker, among others). Several of those same female correspondents covered much of the war in former Yugoslavia particularly the U.S.-led military deployment known as IFOR, which fell within the peak period under consideration in this study. By the time the war in former Yugoslavia was at its peak, five years later, the television news networks had a more experienced pool of female television correspondents to assign to the war zone. Some had honed their skills in Saudi Arabia, Kuwait, and Israel during the 1991 war in the Gulf (i.e., CNN's Christiane Amanpour, CBS's Sheila MacVickar, ABC's Hillary Brown, CBS's Martha Teichner and myself for CBS News, ABC's Linda Pattillo, CBS's Susan Spencer) and seeing the success of their television news colleagues, even more women expressed a willingness to be assigned to cover the Bosnia story (CNN's Jacki Shamansky, CNN's Siobhan Darrow, CNN's Eileen O'Connor, CBS's Vicki Mabrey). But the war in former Yugoslavia was deadly and dragged on for nearly four years. The BBC's Kate Adie, a longtime war correspondent, says of all the places she had worked before, Yugoslavia was by far the worst: "It's a nightmare, beats anything in terms of danger." Adie readily admits to having often experienced real fear. "There were mortars, rockets, and shells every second and I found myself unable to breathe properly." Most journalists agree that Yugoslavia was more dangerous to them than almost any previous conflict with no protection offered effectively for a civilian reporter.[4]

When the Afghanistan war began in October 2001, many of the women who had covered the earlier Gulf War and Bosnia deployments were no longer covering the battlefield and some had quit journalism altogether. In addition, during the late 1990s some of the networks underwent cutbacks and staff reductions that may have affected the number of female correspondents on staff available to cover the war in Afghanistan. The exception to this overall pattern was NBC who showed an increase in the percentage of female stories in 2001. This seeming anomaly might be explained by the fact that prior to the war in Afghanistan the NBC news division had bolstered its staff with the hiring of more female correspondents, some of whom were subsequently assigned to cover the war. But even the NBC data does not significantly change the overall picture that by the time of the war in Afghanistan five years later, many of the same female correspondents had either changed assignments or dropped out of the business altogether or scaled back on their work schedule to have children or marry.

Longtime war reporter Edith (Edie) M. Lederer of Associated Press believes the demanding lifestyle belonging to a war correspondent makes marriage and domestic responsibilities impossible. "What man would put up with that sort of schedule. . . . I've seen a lot of men traveling around the world whose wives are foreign correspondents, but I have yet to meet women traveling with foreign correspondent husbands."[5] A preferred change in lifestyle may be one reason the numbers of females covering the war in Afghanistan dipped but certainly decisions by television newsroom assignment managers regarding who is assigned to cover the war story is also a factor and more research is needed here to determine the impact of the assignment manager's decisions.

One must be careful, however, not to attribute the low proportion of women to the rigors of war because, as revealed by the 2002 Network TV Correspondent Visibility Report, the percentage of women on network newscasts decreased for the third consecutive year from a high of 33 percent in 1998 to 29 percent in 2001. As Joe Foote, the author of the report points out, "It is discouraging to see three years of backward movement for women and hardly any forward movement for minorities after such impressive double-digit gains during the nineties. Three consecutive years of either flat or declining visibility is clearly a setback."[6]

Are War Stories Covered by Females Given Equal Prominence?

Whereas war stories covered by male correspondents were placed in the lead story position 26 percent of the time, only 15 percent of those covered by women were given this prominent placement. Moreover, the male stories in our sample were significantly longer, lasting an average of

208 seconds or 61 percent longer than those of their female counterparts. Taken together with the disproportionately low incidence of war stories covered by females, the fact that stories of female correspondents tend to receive less airtime and less prominent placement adds to the gender imbalance of war coverage.

It is important to note, however, that length and placement may be directly related to content. For instance, the lead story is chosen as being the most important "news of the day" (i.e.,—the latest from the frontlines, the latest deployment of weapons and troops, the latest political developments from the White House). A "hard-edged" type of story may be deemed more suitable for consideration as the lead. It is also typical that a lead story from the frontlines of battle tends to run longer because of the multidimensional nature of the piece. The reporter must include the news of the day, updating troop movements, casualties, the political landscape, and the forecast for the immediate future.

Is the Content of Female Coverage Qualitatively Different?

The gender disparities in frequency, placement, and length are even more relevant if male and female correspondents tend to cover war differently. Our study did reveal a systematic difference in the reports filed by women and men during the war coverage study period. When considering coverage of victim-based stories, women consistently file more stories in that category than men. More specifically, female correspondents filed stories involving victims of war and soldiers' profiles at a rate almost double that of men. The contrast in the percentage of human rights stories is even starker, with women filing almost three times as many stories as men.

Female correspondents like ABC's Brown acknowledge reporting stories to show the horror of the Bosnia conflict. Brown was determined to do human-interest stories to show how people withstood the siege of Sarajevo early in the war. One night she filed a story for ABC that showed the members of the Sarajevo string quartet who kept playing, performing for an audience though the city was under siege and mortar shells were slamming into nearby apartment buildings. According to our study, some male correspondents also felt it important to look at the human face of war but not in the same numbers as women.

Many female correspondents feel reporting on victim-based issues brings a sensibility to the coverage. People and passions are central to the story rather than tactics and troop movements. Former Boston Globe war correspondent Elizabeth Neuffer, killed in an auto accident in Iraq in 2003, credited female reporting with being partly responsible for bringing attention to the rapes in Bosnia and wrote about it in her book, *The Keys to My Neighbors House* written a year before her death. From her unique vantage point as a reporter covering the reality and aftermath of genocide and rape in Bosnia and Rwanda, the award-winning journalist tells the story of two parallel journeys toward justice in each country—one involving the international war crimes tribunals, and one of those left behind. Neuffer argues that most of the reporting on human rights violations in Bosnia, especially the rapes of an estimated 20,000 Muslim women in Bosnia, was done by female correspondents. Our study substantiates her claim by showing that the majority of these stories made it to the television screen because of reporting by female television correspondents in Bosnia. Neuffer further credits these news stories as playing a pivotal role in the decision by the International Tribunal at The Hague to formally designate rape as a crime against humanity and an element of genocide.[7]

When it came to the hard-edged war story with strategy and weapons, the results indicate that the vast majority of war stories filed by both men and women were hard-edged dealing with topics such as weapons and deployment, politics, and the battlefield. Across all three wars, 67 percent of stories filed by women were considered hard-edged compared to 74 percent of stories filed by men. One significant difference did emerge, demonstrating that the percentage of stories filed by men about mission strategy was double that of women—24 percent for men and 12 percent for women.

Susan Spencer, a longtime CBS News correspondent admits to wanting to be assigned to cover the first Persian Gulf War because she felt in some way that the war coverage needed a woman's perspective. Spencer felt that the American television viewer was being inundated with what she calls "boys with their toys" stories in the lead up to the Gulf War. Spencer describes the news audience as being flooded with information on the M1A1 tank and the F-16 and the F-15.

> Maybe it is because we as women, most of us, whether we were tomboys or not, were not really brought up with that kind of frame of reference. And whether it is an advantage or a disadvantage, it is a difference, and since half the population of this country is female, I felt it important that the difference should be reflected in the war coverage.[8]

Are Female Correspondents Filing Reports From the War Zone in Foreign Locations or Domestic Locations Such as the Pentagon, Allied Command, and Military Bases Back Home?

The higher percentage of males reporting on mission strategy and troop deployments could also be related to the location from which the story is filed. Nearly 59 percent of the male correspondents filed stories from foreign locations—the battlefield, an overseas military base, and the combat frontlines—whereas just 45 percent of women filed stories from foreign locations. Women's war-related stories were more likely to be domestic in origin, coming from Washington D.C., Allied command, or the "homefront." There may be several reasons for this difference in filing location. First, the personnel decisions are typically made by the news manager or the assignment manager. Experience and knowledge of the story are often key considerations. It cannot be determined from our data whether a correspondent requested or was simply assigned a story. More research is needed to determine the reasons. Still a correspondent's desire to be deployed must be entered into the equation. Many correspondents simply elect not to go to the battlefield where safety is always a risk. Whatever the reason, our data clearly show that female correspondents are significantly less well-represented than their male counterparts in reporting from foreign war zones.

5. Conclusions

Our findings clearly show both a quantitative and qualitative difference between war stories filed by male and female correspondents across three major conflicts. As is often the case with research, these findings raise a host of other questions. For example, if women do bring a different perspective with respect to human rights that, in some cases, has resulted in pressuring officials to take actions to punish human rights violators, is not deploying women to cover the battlefield a missed opportunity for American television news? To what extent is the relative low percentage of female war correspondents due to self-selection? Are there also gender differences in the way war coverage is perceived by viewers? These are a just a few of the many issues to be resolved by future research.

Notes

1. J. Foote, *2002 Network TV Correspondent Visibility Report*, Walter Cronkite School of Mass Communication, Arizona State University.
2. Penny Colman, *Where the Action Was, Women War Correspondents in World War II* (New York: Crown Publishers, 2002), p. vii.
3. Tad Bartimus, Denby Fawcett, Jurate Kazickas, Edith Lederer, Ann Bryan, Mariano, *War Torn, Stories of War from the Women Reporters Who Covered Vietnam* (New York: Random House, 2002), pp. xviii, xix. Anne Morrissy Merick, Laura Palmer, Kate Webb, and Tracy Wood.

4. Anne Sebba, *Battling for News: The Rise of the Woman Reporter* (London: Hodder and Stoughton, 1994), p. 271.
5. Anne Sebba, *Battling for News*, p. 256.
6. J. Foote, *2002 Network TV Correspondent Visibility Report*, Walter Cronkite School of Mass Communication, Arizona State University.
7. Elizabeth Neuffer, *The Keys to My Neighbor's House: Seeking Justice in Bosnia and Rwanda* (New York: Picador, 2002).
8. Susan Spencer, *"Women Covering the War."* A Panel discussion, The National Press Club (Washington, D.C.: March 26, 1991).

CHAPTER 7

The Real War Will Never Get on Television

An Analysis of Casualty Imagery in American Television Coverage of the Iraq War

Sean Aday

In 1862, photographer Alexander Gardner visited the battlefield at Antietam and shot several dozen pictures for the New York gallery run by his employer, Matthew Brady. Most of the images he captured were landscapes and group portraits, reflecting the tastes of the limited but enthusiastic contemporary market for photographs, which had only begun to be in mass circulation for about two decades. About a third of his exposures, however, were of dead Confederate soldiers who had not yet been removed from the field.[1] At the time, Gardner had no reason to think these shots would be of any commercial interest; they were, after all, the first images of battlefield death scenes circulated in America. As it turned out, the pictures were a sensation, stimulating a highly profitable frenzy of interest in similar scenes from other battles. When Gardner went to Gettysburg a year later, having set off on his own business, three-quarters of his pictures were graphic depictions of the dead, albeit often rearranged into romanticized poses.[2]

Today, our historical memory of the gruesomeness (and romanticism) of the Civil War is illustrated by the pictures of dead soldiers taken by Gardner, Brady, and others. Several factors made it possible to capture these images, notably the wet plate processing method that made outdoor photography easier, and the proximity of many important battles like Antietam and Gettysburg to population centers and roads, especially in the north. Despite these factors, though, the rapid mobility of the armies and the still cumbersome technical requirements of the medium meant that only six battles yielded pictures of dead soldiers.[3] In all, probably no more than 100 such photographs were taken during the entire war.[4]

Yet the history of war photography in the Civil War offers several interesting points of departure for understanding the images transmitted through television coverage of the recent Iraq war. First, as in the 1860s, important technological advances in the visual medium, most notably mobile satellite video, allowed reporters to get closer to the fighting and, if they chose to, show the gory reality of modern warfare to their audiences back home. Second, changes in military policy allowed journalists to be embedded with military units and have even better battlefield access than their civil war counterparts. Indeed, journalists covering the last several American military engagements before Iraq were intentionally kept from the front by the military. The question is whether American journalists chose to take advantage of these technological advances and increased battlefield access to show audiences not only the exciting whiz bang nature of American military power, but also the grim ramifications of its use.

This chapter begins to answer this question through a detailed and comprehensive content analysis of battle and casualty coverage of the Iraq war on CNN, Fox News Channel (FNC), and ABC.[5] At its most basic level, this study asks: given that broadcast news had the ability to generate a complete portrait of the war, did it do so? Or did it instead reduce the war to a video game and shield viewers from the dead and wounded? This question takes on added significance in light of the criticism that the 1991 Persian Gulf War was covered in a sanitized fashion. In that case, though, much of the blame could fairly (if not wholly) be placed on the Pentagon for restricting press access to the front and censoring the broadcast of casualty visuals.[6] In the Iraq war, military censorship was not nearly as severe, meaning that reporters generally had the freedom, access, and technological means to accurately report on the war if they chose to.

1. Visualizing War

For millennia, war has been depicted through imagery, be it on a canvas, a plate, or a broadcast signal. Before photography, these images were invariably captured after the fact (often years later) by artists who were nowhere near the action being depicted, and were heavily romanticized even when they were quite graphic.[7] As mentioned already, these characteristics also describe the photographers and their pictures during the Civil War. Of course, there are important differences between painters and journalists, most obviously that the former are artists and the latter are chroniclers. (Civil War photographers, and the medium itself in the 1860s, are perhaps best considered as a hybrid, or bridge, between the two.) And yet battlefield art and battlefield journalism share a basic function described by historian Francis Haskell:

> Closely related to the faith placed in images of the past was the concept (which has proved so influential ever since) that great or extraordinary events will necessarily be recorded as much through the medium of the visual arts as they are in written histories, and that if they are not so recorded they not only lose some of their power to move later generations, but also some of their actuality.[8]

Importantly, the recording of these events has historically been done in a way that glorifies the protagonists (typically the victors, but more generally the countrymen of the artists or culturally similar participants). Hence, these images are more artful in every sense of the word than they are literal. One might even refer to them as propagandistic. At the least, they have often been driven by and reflected marketplace demands, be it from sponsors in the case of pre–twentieth-century painters or collectors and readers of illustrated weeklies in the case of Civil War era photography and woodcuts.[9]

In other words, the imagery of war and battle has historically been intended to do two things: rally the public consciousness around the righteousness of the conflict (even, and perhaps especially, as the event itself drifts back in time and memory), and please a commercial audience.

Critiques of contemporary war coverage in the American press, particularly in broadcast news, often make the same case against the media, with coverage of the 1991 Persian Gulf War being a prime example. In that conflict, the Pentagon enforced strict censorship of the press and instituted a system of pool reporting that virtually eliminated the potential for independent journalistic observers and allowed the military to exercise near total control of the portrait of the war fed to American audiences. Although media organizations and reporters complained about the restrictions, at the same time they dutifully saturated their coverage with Pentagon press briefings that included dramatic visuals of bombs mounted with cameras striking targets in Iraq, and effusive claims of technical wizardry and precision, many of which turned out to be gross exaggerations at best and outright falsehoods at worst.

The result was imagery that made the war look, to use a popular metaphor, like a video game.[10] Daniel Hallin wrote that coverage defined the Persian Gulf conflict as "patriotic celebration and technological triumph."[11] He also showed how coverage mirrored that during the early years of the Vietnam War in many ways, with the war seen as: (1) a national endeavor, complete with use of the first person plural, such as "our troops," a trait of some Iraq war coverage, too;[12] (2) an American tradition, signified by references to World War II and other iconic moments and images in American history; and (3) necessitating a win at all costs commitment.[13] Others showed how these tendencies were particularly pronounced at CNN, whose need to fill a 24-hour news cycle led them to be less analytical and more focused on event-driven, flashy imagery than the network newscast.[14]

In addition to a focus on the alleged technical perfection of the American war effort and the Pentagon-produced images purporting to demonstrate it, a key component of the media's sanitization (and indeed romanticization) of the Persian Gulf War was their near total lack of casualty visuals. Hallin's analysis showed that American audiences were shown an essentially "clean" war,[15] despite the loss of an estimated 100,000 Iraqi soldiers and perhaps the same number of civilians (not to mention more than 100 American troops). Although much of the explanation for the lack of casualty visuals can be explained by the fact that reporters were kept from the front lines and Baghdad where casualties would occur, others have pointed out that press norms and even ideology were also at play. Cheney for instance, pointed out that the avoidance of casualties extended to the definition of what constituted a story in the first place, with the press largely ignoring coverage of American troops burying Iraqis in mass graves and the massive scale of civilian casualties.[16] Instead, Cheney and others argue, coverage essentially parroted the White House and Pentagon talking points on the war, complete with visuals that seemed to reinforce them.

That the press largely followed the lead of official Washington in the Persian Gulf War is in many ways to be expected. Between Vietnam and the recent Iraq war, the main finding of scholars looking at war and foreign policy coverage is that the news tends to privilege official sources, especially those from the White House. Most notably, Bennett has shown that news coverage of war and foreign policy is indexed to the limited range of elite opinions, at least in the short run.[17] Dickson, for example, found that government sources defined the range of debate in *New York*

Times coverage of the U.S. invasion of Panama.[18] Entman and Page found similar results in coverage leading up to the beginning of the Persian Gulf War, showing that dissenters received less coverage than did officials who exercised some control over war policy, and that even when the press did air criticisms of the administration's policy, those critiques were procedural rather than fundamental in nature.[19]

Although Althaus[20] has recently questioned these assumptions by showing various ways in which dissenting opinions appeared in the press during the Persian Gulf War period, the prevailing finding of scholars to date is that officials exercise a great deal of control over the content and framing of international news, even in the contemporary era of technological advances in news gathering that might theoretically allow for more media independence.[21]

The tendency of modern war reportage, especially on television, to reflect establishment sentiment could be seen as extending to the hesitancy to show images of casualties. As mentioned above, broadcast coverage of the Persian Gulf War fit well with the administration's view that it was waging a moral and relatively painless war. Hallin's seminal study of coverage of the Vietnam War—a conflict conventionally perceived as bringing death and destruction into American living rooms on a nightly basis—showed that in fact casualties of any type were rarely shown before the Tet Offensive in 1968, after which reporters became skeptical as it became clear the war was going much worse for the United States than Washington would admit. But even after Tet, Hallin's analysis showed that there was virtually no quantifiable change in the coverage of Vietnamese civilian or military casualties (North or South).[22] The implication of Hallin's research was echoed by Patterson's study of Persian Gulf War coverage and Livingston's analysis of the CNN effect on America's Balkan policy, both of which argued in different ways that the news media would not air challenging stories and images as long as a war remained short and relatively free of U.S. casualties.[23]

At the same time, coverage of the Persian Gulf War in other countries, especially Arab ones, showed the gory results of American "smart" bombs, further suggesting that American coverage reflected the biases of its indigenous culture and official point of view in the same way foreign coverage did.[24] Although this chapter reports the results of the first thorough examination of the scale and nature of casualty imagery in American broadcast coverage of the Iraq war, an earlier study looking just at the nightly news across five U.S. networks and two Arabian-based news channels (Al Jazeera and Egypt's Esc-1) also found cultural differences in the overall tone of coverage and in the depiction of casualties.[25] In addition, an exhaustive analysis of British Broadcasting Company coverage of the Iraq war by Cardiff University found casualty coverage largely absent.[26] In that case, researchers noted that British laws forbidding the airing of graphic imagery prevented the press from showing them, but they expressed apprehension that the resulting bloodless war shown on television might inure citizens from the grave consequences of military action.

2. The Iraq War

American broadcast reporters often candidly admit that the norms of their medium prevent them from showing the same shots of bodily carnage aired in other parts of the world. Discussing his time covering the recent Iraq war as a reporter embedded with the Second Light Armored Recognizance Battalion, CBS's John Roberts said bluntly, "In terms of what kind of images we could air, there are certain pictures that you just can't show on television. *We saw plenty of those*, so you had to sanitize your coverage to some degree."[27]

Other reporters embedded in Iraq pointed out that most of the casualties were inflicted at long range, limiting their ability to capture them on film. But they also implied that even if they did shoot the gore, their superiors at the network back in America often edited the images out of the final story. For instance, CBS correspondent Jim Axelrod said,

> There was never any opportunity, or attempt to limit the pictures we took and fed to New York or to London. If we found bodies we would photograph them. . . . I saw a couple of burned bodies, just a rib cage. I wrote the script, and referenced bodies in it. . . . (B)ut I never saw the final report. I don't know what was cut and what wasn't.[28]

CNN's Martin Savidge made a similar point, but unlike some of his brethren was not so accepting of the norm discouraging graphic visuals. His comments are worth citing at length:

> As someone who covers war, I believe you should show every single aspect of it, because otherwise you give people the misimpression that war is a very sanitary, very clean, relatively painless type of campaign, and it's not. I mean, you see the smart bombs in the Pentagon video. What you never see is what happens after the nose camera goes to hash. What was the explosion like afterwards? What was the suffering of the people on the ground? Did they linger for hours, maybe days? You don't know any of that.

We didn't allow human suffering to be seen in America. There is a tendency on the part of domestic networks not to show that, because they know that the American public is revolted by it, and they don't want to make the American public uncomfortable. It's censorship, and I've seen it many times before, so I'm not surprised by it.

Let me give you an example. . . . [Describes capturing the killing of an Iraqi soldier at close range on camera.] I called (CNN) ahead of time and said, "Look, at the end of this feed, there's some pretty graphic stuff, an Iraqi being killed, and you have to make a determination." I've heard talk that it will air someday, but it has not yet. . . .[29]

Yet especially since the terrorist attacks on September 11, many, including several prominent journalists, have argued that to show casualties, especially civilians, is unpatriotic. Indeed, everything from whether anchors should wear patriotic lapel pins to how much a network should show civilian casualties has been at issue,[30] with some suggesting that there is no place for detachment in wartime.[31] As FNC lead anchor Brit Hume said in defending his network's reluctance to show images of civilian casualties during the U.S.–Afghanistan war in 2001–02: "Look, neutrality as a general principle is an appropriate concept for journalists who are covering institutions of some comparable quality. This is a conflict between the United States and murdering barbarians."[32]

This raises the question of what effect showing, or ignoring, casualty imagery might have on shaping public opinion about a given war. Several scholars have explored the role of media coverage in general on generating support or opposition to war. But while these studies might reference trends in casualty coverage as an explanation for their findings, they do not parse its specific effects or can only infer them imprecisely from time series analyses.[33] In an unpublished doctoral dissertation using student subjects, Fuller performed an experiment manipulating visuals of casualties and found that exposure to such imagery led to decreased support for war. That study, however, also varied the narratives used in the experimental conditions and employed a documentary rather than news format, making it difficult to extrapolate to the effects of broadcast news images of dead and wounded.[34]

If the central critique of recent war coverage has been that it sanitized conflicts and reduced them visually and emotionally to the level of a video game, the war in Iraq offered the press an opportunity to provide a more comprehensive portrait of battle. The Pentagon's policy of embedding reporters with military units gave the media access to the front lines they hadn't had during an American war since Vietnam. Granted, the killing still occurred at long range, but the human aftereffects of that combat were seen in the hours and days that followed as forces moved past the remnants of vanquished Iraqi units and toward Baghdad. First-person accounts of embedded reporters after the war describing the carnage they saw make this clear. Second, unlike in the Persian Gulf War, all American networks had correspondents based in Baghdad, where much of the civilian casualties were inflicted. Finally, advances in technology theoretically made it possible for reporters to show viewers exactly what they saw, even live. If a legitimate defense of the press coverage of the first Gulf War was that they were preventing from seeing, much less airing images of casualties, the war in Iraq rendered that excuse moot.

3. The Study

A team of three graduate students and two professors coded 600 hours of coverage on CNN, FNC, and ABC aired during the period of "major combat operations," as President George W. Bush would famously refer to it, from March 20 through April 9. March 20 was the first day of hostilities and April 9 was the day the government of Saddam Hussein was deposed, as symbolized in the media by the fall of his statue in Baghdad's Firdos Square. Prior research shows that coverage of the statue had a significant impact on the news framing the war as being over.[35]

In order to capture both the highly rated morning news shows and the evening newscasts, coders analyzed coverage broadcast from 7:00 A.M. to 10:00 A.M., and from 1:00 P.M. to 8:00 P.M. Because the overall research question is whether the media were more likely to show the reality of war or to depict it as a video game, all stories that included an audio or visual illustration of battle or casualties (or both) were coded, with the unit of analysis being individual shots within a story that included those images. Hence, if a story did not have any shots of battle or casualties, it was not included in the analysis. If it did, shots that did not depict these occurrences were not coded, but those that did were. So, a battle story might have ten shots but of those, five showed the reporter doing a standup after the battle was fought and five showed the battle in progress. In that case, only the latter five shots would be included, and would be numbered one through five. A "Shot" can best be understood as beginning and ending with an edit. Finally, a shot was counted every time it was aired, so the N in this case is not unique shots. In fact, all channels, especially the 24-hour networks, replayed the same handful of images in a loop throughout the day and even within an individual story. A total of 5,087 shots are included in the dataset.

4. Findings

Despite their presence at the front lines of the war and in the heart of Baghdad, and despite a largely passive censorship of their stories by military officials, reporters at the networks analyzed, still presented a largely bloodless—but action-packed—view of the Iraq war to American audiences. More than five times as many shots of firefights[36] and battles were aired than images of casualties (table 7.1).[37] ABC showed the highest ratio of casualty to firefight images (22 percent–77 percent), while FNC had the lowest (10 percent–90 percent) (table 7.2). As with the 1991 Persian Gulf conflict, visually speaking television reduced the war in Iraq to a fireworks display.

Interestingly, in the few instances where casualties were shown, at FNC and CNN they were most likely to be civilians. Only at ABC were American (and a few British) casualties shown more than Iraqis (table 7.3). As seen in table 7.4, however, the dead were virtually never shown, especially on FNC where only about 2 percent of shots showed people killed in the war. Even more rare (only 4 shots in 600 hours of coverage) were pictures taken in close enough proximity or with an angle that allowed the audience to see the victim's face. Instead, the dead were seen at a distance, covered by a sheet, or through a surrogate (most commonly a coffin and very rarely anything as graphic as a pool of blood). Compare this, for example, to the haunting images of dead Confederate soldiers with their mouths agape and bodies bloated and stiff from rigormortis.

It is also interesting to note that, although we did not code for it, a significant number of the civilian casualty visuals came from Arab language

Table 7.1 Total shots of casualties and firefights, all networks

Shots containing imagery of casualty (N = 5,087)	Shots containing imagery of firefights (N = 5,087)
15% (N = 763)	85% (N = 4,323)

Table 7.2 Ratio of casualty–firefight shots by network

	ABC (N = 596)	CNN (N = 2,126)	FNC (N = 2,365)	Total (N = 5,087)
Casualty	22% (N = 134)	18% (N = 386)	10% (N = 243)	15% (N = 763)
Firefight	77% (N = 459)	82% (N = 1,741)	90% (N = 2,123)	85% (N = 4,323)

Table 7.3   Percentage of shots showing different types of casualty by network

	ABC (N = 596)	CNN (N = 2,126)	FNC (N = 2,365)	Total (N = 5,087)
Civilian	8.4% (N = 50)	10% (N = 212)	5.5% (N = 131)	7.7% (N = 393)
Iraqi	1.2% (N = 7)	1.9% (N = 41)	0.2% (N = 5)	1% (N = 53)
Coalition	12.6% (N = 75)	6.1% (N = 130)	4.4% (N = 104)	6.1% (N = 309)

Table 7.4   Type of gore visual by network

	ABC (N = 596)	CNN (N = 2,126)	FNC (N = 2,365)	Total (N = 5,087)
Dead bodies, faces not visible	4.9% (N = 29)	5.2% (N = 110)	1.9% (N = 45)	3.6% (N = 184)
Dead bodies, faces shown			0.2% (N = 4)	0.1% (N = 4)
Wounded	17.6% (N = 105)	13% (N = 276)	8% (N = 190)	11.2 % (N = 571)

media, as evidenced by the network logo or other signifying device on the screen. The vast majority of these images were of people recovering from their wounds in Baghdad hospitals, but these did not approach the kind of lurid and lingering pictures one would have seen had they been watching the source network rather than the relatively sanitized images picked up by American broadcasters.[38]

Embedded reporters might have been expected to show more visuals of Iraqi military and Coalition casualties than unilateral reporters (i.e., reporters independently trailing the American and British troops or reporting from Baghdad before the fall of Saddam Hussein) for the obvious reason that they were in closer proximity to them. In fact, however, they were about as likely to show shots of the dead, and unilaterals were more than three times as likely to show the wounded (table 7.5). The latter is due primarily to the fact that stories about civilian casualties mostly originated in Baghdad. And again, our impression is that most of these visuals were taken off Arabic language media, not the result of independent news work by the American networks.

Finally, not only did embedding, access to Baghdad, and a more laissez-faire policy of military censorship not lead to a more realistic portrait of war, neither did the advanced technology of satellite videophones.

Table 7.5 Type of gore visual, embed versus unilateral reporter

	Embed (N = 1,250)	Unilateral (N = 788)
Dead bodies, faces not visible	4.7% (N = 59)	4.3% (N = 34)
Dead bodies, faces shown	0.3% (N = 4)	
Wounded	5.8% (N = 72)	20.5% (N = 161)

Table 7.6 Shots of firefight and casualties using satellite videophones

	Videophone (N = 838)
Firefight	89% (N = 748)
Casualty	11% (N = 90)

Despite the greater mobility and, theoretically, independence that this technology offered reporters, the ratio of firefight to casualty shots using these cameras was 89 : 11 (table 7.6). Although our coding scheme did not allow us to quantify it, our impression was that satellite videophones were used mainly for reporter stand-ups, interviews with military personnel in the field or air base, and much less even for shots of artillery fire or combat. In addition to the impression given by reporters' comments (and confirmed in our data) that journalistic norms and cultural standards discourage the airing of casualty coverage, the image transmitted using this technology is not clear, especially when trying to capture motion. Hence, more stationary uses like interviews and stand-ups look better.

5. Conclusions

Following the Persian Gulf War, the press came under considerable attack both from outside and inside its ranks for presenting a sanitized version of events to American audiences. Many, again outside and inside the media, blamed the Pentagon for its heavy-handed policy of precensorship, the implication being that freed from their kennels the press would be aggressive and reliable watchdogs.

In 2003, the Pentagon loosened censorship restrictions and embedded reporters with coalition units at the front lines of the Iraq war. Yet the resulting imagery broadcast by American networks did not differ discernibly from those 12 years earlier. Television transformed a war with hundreds of coalition and tens of thousands of Iraqi civilian and military casualties into something closer to a defense contractor's training video: a lot of action, but no consequences, as if shells simply disappeared into the air and an invisible enemy magically ceased to exist.

That those shells end up tearing apart people is clear to anyone who gives it some thought, and certainly to the soldiers embroiled in the fighting. But more to the point, it is obvious to the reporters covering the war because they see it right in front of them. As CBS's John Roberts described of his experience embedded in Iraq:

> It was pretty horrible to see all those guys lying around. There was this one guy whose feet were facing me; he's lying out of the back, his feet were facing me, he was sort of spread-eagled on the ground. As I walked up, his body was in perfect shape, but when I got right up on top of him, his head was missing, like it had been removed. Then there was another guy whose head was blown into three pieces and part of his body had been ripped off by a shell.[39]

Reading the accounts of reporters in Iraq, this was not an uncommon sight. And yet, as this study shows, they rarely turned on their camera and showed even a relatively less gruesome angle to their audiences. The proportion of firefight to casualty images was overwhelmingly in favor of the former, and the dead were rarely shown at all, even by reporters embedded on the front lines who saw hundreds if not thousands of corpses. As Walt Whitman wrote of the Civil War, "The real war will never get in the books."

Indeed, a great irony can be found in comparing the defining images from the Persian Gulf and Iraq wars—the smart bomb hitting its target in the former and artillery firing in the latter: the dominant image of war actually became *more* distanced in Iraq as reporters got closer to the front.

Critics of past war coverage, especially in the Gulf War, worry that such a sanitized portrait dehumanizes an enemy and its citizenry, helps perpetuate (or, if one is so inclined, manufacture) consent for war and any policies an administration might try and link to it, and risks numbing the moral revulsion that leads societies to see war as a last resort. When Roberts saw the broken bodies of the Iraqi soldiers described above, his reaction was compassion: "I said to myself, 'Gosh, this is tragic. These poor people,' regardless of the fact that they're enemy

soldiers. You have to have some sort of human pity for the
does not, of course, have to lead journalists to stop doing their
tively, or even to change their personal opinion on the valid
war. As Savidge commented:

> You have to realize that people die in war. I'm not saying all wars are bad.
> I am saying all wars are awful. There is no such thing as a pleasant war. I've
> been in enough of them to know that. War can be justified. There could
> be reasons why, as a last resort, you go to war. You must know that once it
> starts, it's a horrible, terrible thing. People die gruesome, terrible deaths.
> But in America we'll edit that down. Especially anything that deals with
> U.S. service personnel.[41]

What is remarkable given the data presented in this study is that war
correspondents think this way precisely *because* they have seen the
gruesome reality of war, and yet they, or at least their network superiors
(themselves often veteran reporters), insist on shielding audiences from
that same knowledge.

Reporters—and policymakers—have typically justified this self-
censorship by arguing that viewers would be repelled by a more accurate
portrait of war. Presumably, the fear here is at one level a commercial
one: they might lose their audience to a network presenting a more
upbeat story. And indeed, there is research suggesting that they may be
right.[42] There is also the perception that such imagery might damage
public support for a just war, that Americans don't have the stomach for
casualties. Although these are considered part of conventional wisdom,
in fact they are testable hypotheses that scholars should spend more time
exploring.

Also worth investigating further is the role of new technologies in
press–government relations. Livingston and Bennett have shown that
contrary to what one might expect, the dominance of news norms privi-
leging official sources overwhelms the potential of these new technologies
to create a more independent press in international coverage.[43] Cameras
may be mobile, but the news it seems is still tethered to bureaucrats and
policymakers.

Finally, it is interesting to note that in the time since the birth of realistic visual media in the form of photography, American popular images
of war have become less, not more, authentic. For all the posing and aes-
thetic manipulations of the dead in photographs of the Civil War, the fact
remains that people were able to see contemporary pictures of the true cost
of war. Historian John Keegan makes the point that the paradox of modern

warfare is that as Western society has become more humane—mostly banning the death penalty, making remarkable advances in medicine and healing, and expressing great concern for the sick and dying—it has simultaneously become increasingly innovative in devising weaponry that destroys human beings in progressively more creative ways.[44] He might have added that this societal cognitive dissonance—or hypocrisy, in his words—is amplified through the images of war we see on television.

Notes

1. Granted, the audiences for their work were northerners and all the dead pictured were Confederates. But this was due to the requisite delays in reaching the battlefield and setting up the camera. By the time that had happened, Union soldiers had already buried their own dead (always the priority) and the only bodies left on the field were those of the enemy.
2. Earl Hess, "A Terrible Fascination: The Portrayal of Combat in the Civil War Media," in P.A. Cimbala and R.M. Miller, eds., *An Uncommon Time: The Civil War and the Northern Home Font* (New York: Fordham, 2002), pp. 1–26.
3. Antietam, Corinth, Marye's Heights during Chancellorsville, Gettysburg, Alsop's Farm during Spotsylvania, and the capture of Fort Mahone on the Petersburg lines. Hess, "A Terrible Fascination," pp. 1–26.
4. Ibid.
5. Only network news on ABC was analyzed, not news on its local affiliate. "Network" news included Good Morning America, World News Tonight, and, when it occurred, national break-ins and extended coverage at other times of day that fell during our sample period.
6. Daniel C. Hallin, "Images of the Vietnam and the Persian Gulf Wars in U.S. Television," in Rabinovitz and S. Jeffords, eds., *Seeing Through the Media: The Persian Gulf War* (New Brunswick, NJ: Rutgers, 1991), pp. 45–58; Margot Norris, "Only the Guns Have Eyes: Military Censorship and the Body Count," in Rabinovitz and S. Jeffords, eds., *Seeing Through the Media: The Persian Gulf War* (New Brunswick, NJ: Rutgers, 1991), pp. 285–300; George Cheney, "We're Talking War: Symbols, Strategies, and Images," in Bradley S. Greenberg and Walter Gantz, eds., *Desert Storm and the Mass Media* (Cresskill, NJ: Hampton Press, 1993), pp. 61–73; Oscar Patterson III, "If the Vietnam War had been Reported Under Gulf War Rules," *Journal of Broadcasting & Electronic Media*, Vol. 39, No. 1 (1995), pp. 20–29.
7. H. Bruce Franklin, "From Realism to Virtual Reality: Images of America's Wars," in Rabinovitz and S. Jeffords, eds., *Seeing Through the Media: The Persian Gulf War* (New Brunswick, NJ: Rutgers, 1991), pp. 25–44; Francis Haskell, *History and its Images: Art and the Interpretation of the Past* (New Haven: Yale, 1993).
8. Haskell, *History and Its Images*, p. 86.

9. Ibid.; Hess, "A Terrible Fascination."
10. Franklin, "From Realism to Virtual Reality" Cheney, "We're Talking War."
11. Hallin, "Images," p. 52.
12. Sean Aday, Steve Livingston, and Maeve Hebert, "Embedding the Truth: A Cross-Cultural Analysis of Objectivity and Television Coverage of the Iraq War." Paper presented at the annual meeting of the International Communication Association in New Orleans (May 29, 2004).
13. Hallin, "Images," pp. 53–54.
14. R.H. Wicks and D.C. Walker, "Differences Between CNN and the Broadcast Networks in Live War Coverage," in Bradley S. Greenberg and Walter Gantz, eds., *Desert Storm and the Mass Media* (Cresskill, NJ: Hampton Press, 1993), pp. 99–112.
15. Hallin, "Images," p. 55.
16. Cheney, "We're Talking War."
17. W. Lance Bennett, "The News About Foreign Policy," in W.L. Bennett and D.L. Paletz, eds., *Taken by Storm: The Media, Public Opinion, and U.S. Foreign Policy in the Gulf War* (Chicago: The University of Chicago Press, 1994), pp. 12–42.
18. Sandra H. Dickson, "Understanding Media Bias: The Press and the U.S. Invasion of Panama," *Journalism Quarterly*, Vol. 71, No. 4 (1995), pp. 809–819.
19. Robert M. Entman and Benjamin I. Page, "The News Before the Storm: The Iraq War Debate and the Limits to Media Independence," in W.L. Bennett and D.L. Paletz, eds., *Taken by Storm: The Media, Public Opinion, and U.S. Foreign Policy in the Gulf War* (Chicago: The University of Chicago Press, 1994), pp. 82–104.
20. Scott L. Althaus, "When News Norms Collide, Follow the Lead: New Evidence for Press Independence," *Political Communication*, Vol. 20, No. 4 (2003), pp. 381–414.
21. Steven Livingston and W. Lance Bennett, "Gatekeeping, Indexing, and Live-Event News: Is Technology Altering the Construction of News?" *Political Communication* (October–December, 2003), pp. 363–380.
22. Daniel C. Hallin, "The Media, the War in Vietnam, and Political Support: A Critique of the Thesis of Oppositional Media," *The Journal of Politics*, Vol. 46, No. 1 (1984), pp. 2–24.
23. Patterson, "If the Vietnam War had been Reported"; Steven Livingston, "Media Coverage of the War: An Empirical Assessment," in A. Schabnel, ed., *Kosovo and the Challenge of Humanitarian Intervention: Selective Indignation, Collective Action, and Individual Citizenship* (New York: United Nations University Press, 2000), pp. 360–384.
24. David L. Swanson and Larry D. Smith, "War in the Global Village: A Seven-Country Comparison of Television News Coverage of the Beginning of the Gulf War," in R.E. Denton, Jr., ed., *The Media and the Persian Gulf War* (Westport, CT: Praeger, 1993).
25. Aday, Livingston, and Hebert, "Embedding the Truth."

26. Cardiff School of Journalism, Media and Cultural Studies, "The Role of Embedded Reporting During the 2003 Iraq War." Report commissioned by the British Broadcasting Company (2003).

27. Bill Katovsky and Timothy Carlson, *Embedded: The Media at War in Iraq* (Guilford, CT: The Lyons Press, 2003), p. 173 (emphasis added).

28. Ibid., p. 27.

29. Ibid., p. 276.

30. Bill Carter and Felicity Barringer, "At U.S. Request, Networks Agree to Edit Future bin Laden Tapes," *New York Times*, October 11, 2001; Paul Farhi, "For Broadcast Media, Patriotism Pays," *Washington Post* (March 28, 2003, p. C1); Howard Kurtz, "CNN Chief Order 'Balance' in War News," *Washington Post* (October 31, 2001, p. C1).

31. Tim Graham, "No Honest Eyewitnesses: There's Little Truth Coming Out of Baghdad," *National Review Online* (April 4, 2003); Morton Kondracke, "Memo to U.S. Media: Stop Spreading Negativism Over War," *Roll Call* (November 8, 2001); Dorothy Rabinowitz, "Neutral in the Newsroom," *Opinionjournal.com* (November 6, 2001).

32. Jim Rutenberg and Bill Carter, "Network Coverage a Target of Fire from Conservatives," *New York Times* (November 7, 2001), p. B2.

33. John Mueller, *War, Presidents, and Public Opinion* (New York: John Wiley and Sons, 1973); M.B. Oliver, M. Mares, and J. Cantor. "New Viewing, Authoritarianism, and Attitudes Toward the Gulf War," in R.E. Denton, Jr., ed., *The Media and the Persian Gulf War* (Westport, CT: Praeger, 1993); Scott S. Gartner and Gary M. Segura, "War, Casualties, and Public Opinion," *Journal of Conflict Resolution*, Vol. 42, No. 3 (1998), pp. 278–300.

34. Tony Fuller, "Video War in the Persian Gulf: Experimental Effects of Visuals on Individual Political Opinion and Feeling." Unpublished doctoral dissertation, University of Houston (1996).

35. Sean Aday, John Cluverius, and Steven Livingston, "As Goes the Statue, So Goes the War: The Evolution and Effects of the Victory Frame in Television Coverage of the Iraq War." Paper presented at the annual meeting of the Broadcast Educators Association in Las Vegas, April 19, 2004.

36. A firefight was defined as any armed attack. Examples include soldiers firing their weapons, artillery firing, and bombs exploding in Baghdad.

37. Although technically these categories are not mutually exclusive—the camera could capture a soldier getting shot, for instance—this was never the case in the period we studied.

38. Aday, Livingston, and Hebert, *Embedding the Truth*.

39. Katovsky and Carlson, *Embedded*, p. 173.

40. Ibid., p. 174.

41. Ibid., p. 277.

42. Oliver et al., *The Media and the Persian Gulf War.*

43. Livingston and Bennett, "Gatekeeping, Indexing, and Live-Event-News," pp. 363–380.

44. John Keegan, *The Face of Battle* (New York: Penguin Books, 1976).

CHAPTER 8

News Coverage of the Bosnian War in Dutch Newspapers

Impact and Implications

Nel Ruigrok, Jan A. de Ridder, Otto Scholten

In April 1992 war in Bosnia broke out. Media coverage was initially modest, but eventually the war received full media attention after the discovery of detention camps in Bosnia. Images of emaciated men behind barbed wire shown worldwide on television provoked memories of pictures from the death camps of World War II and a public outcry to "do something" followed.

American and European policymakers and media struggled with the question of what to do: intervene or stand by. The four major Dutch newspapers published over twice as many articles about the situation in Bosnia during August 1992 than they would publish monthly on average during the whole year of 1993 (579 in August 1992, in 1993 on average 277). More important than the number of articles is the articles' tone of moral indignation about Serbian atrocities. Looking back we can conclude that the images from Tronopolje had a major impact. They didn't cause the immediate political decision to intervene, but formed the basis for such decisionmaking in the years to come. Moreover, they added an emotional dimension to the discussion about intervention. The moral indignation they produced was such that columnists and editorial boards considered military intervention inevitable.

Images can become icons of a conflict, as the photo of Tronopolje prisoner Filkret Alic became an icon of the Bosnian war. However, news coverage is not only about images. The larger scope of a conflict is found in the content of news articles. In this chapter we focus on the texts of articles about the Bosnian war as published by Dutch newspapers, and we discuss the framing of the Bosnian war in four major Dutch newspapers. We examine the coverage during the year 1993 and the period January–July 1995 and investigate the extent to which Dutch newspapers framed the Bosnian war in a specific way, by looking at seven different themes that occurred in the news.

1. Framing Literature

Framing can best be summarized as all factors used to determine *what* events are reported and *how* they are presented. Tuchman wrote that news frames "both produce and limit meaning." Like window frames, "characteristics of the window, its size and composition, limit what may be seen. So does its placement, that is, what aspect of the unfolding scene it makes accessible."[1] From this perspective, framing starts with the selection process. In our research we perceive this selection process as the most general level of framing, while the actual presentation of the story can be seen as a more refined or second level of framing.

The general level of framing shows its similarity with the agenda-setting theory devised by Maxwell McCombs and Donald Shaw in 1972[2]. The essence of the agenda-setting theory is that by selecting and reporting the news the press influences not so much what we think, but it tells us what to think *about*. Through their daily selection and coverage of news, media exert an influence on public attention to the issues, problems, and opportunities in society. The second, more refined, level of framing can be seen as an extension of the agenda-setting theory. Framing analysis "expands beyond agenda-setting research into what people talk or think about by examining how they think and talk about issues in the news."[3] This relationship between framing and the agenda-setting theory is also recognized by other researchers. McCombs, Shaw, and Weaver[4] use the term "second-level agenda-setting" to describe the effects of the framing process on audiences' interpretations of the news stories produced. McCombs and Ghanem state in this respect, "Beyond the agenda of objects there is another aspect to consider. Each of these objects has numerous attributes, those characteristics and properties that fill out the picture of each object."[5] The attributes connected to the objects form the central part of this second-level agenda-setting. According to the researchers "these attributes suggests that the media also tells us *how* to ık about some objects."[6]

Recent framing research ignores the most general level of framing and focuses on the second level dealing with factors influencing the production of the news by journalists, the presentation of the news, and its impact on the consumers. Looking at the selection process or, in other words, the general level of framing, we understand a media frame, according to Gitlin to be "persistent patterns of selection, emphasis, and exclusion which furnish an interpretation of events."[7] Entman also combines in his definition of framing the choices made by journalists and the outcome of these choices. He states: "Frames essentially involve *selection* and *salience*. To frame is to select some aspects of a perceived reality and make them more salient in a communicating text, in such a way as to promote a particular problem definition, causal interpretation, moral evaluation and/or treatment recommendation for the item described."[8] To make these aspects more salient means, in Entman's words, making the message "noticeable, meaningful or memorable."[9] According to Entman salience begins with the process of selection, which means omitting some pieces of the picture to emphasize others. "The exclusions are at least as important as the inclusions; they reinforce the inclusions by depriving the audience of the data they would need to forge an alternative interpretation of reality."[10]

2. The Selection of News

There is an overrepresentation of atypical events in the news: everyday realities are not news. News is not about long-term processes but about short-term events. It is not about decades of development, it is about sudden destruction by a natural disaster. The focus on action, "event orientation," leads to neglect of background circumstances. Reporters tend to be more interested in events than causes. Nevertheless, not all events are included, as Hartley concludes:

> Events don't get into the news simply by happening . . . they . . . must fit in with what is already there . . . be known and recognised . . . To win inclusion in any particular news, they must fulfil a certain number of criteria . . . Finally, newsworthy events themselves must jostle for inclusion in the limited number of slots available.[11]

Journalists depend on agreed upon professional news values in order to make their selection of news. According to McQuail news values are "the criteria applied by journalists and editors in news organizations to determine whether or not to carry particular items of news."[12] A wide range of research has been done about news values that journalists use in selecting the stories they cover. This kind of research can best be understood within the context of the social construction of reality approach to the news media. "People communicate to interpret events and to share those interpretations with others and reality is constructed socially through communication."[13] The social construction of reality approach emphasizes that there is no single "reality," rather a range of definitions of "reality." Reality as presented by the mass media is therefore a constructed interpretation of reality. The role of the media in this theory is to provide multiple portrayals of reality.[14] The question is which parts of the perceived reality are presented to us.

Chang, Shoemaker, and Bredlinger[15] divided the criteria used by journalists into either event-oriented or context-oriented. The former is related to the newsworthiness of the event itself, like the magnitude, the importance, the sensationalism, novelty, or impact of the event. Context-oriented criteria are related to the nature of the location where the event took place, such as the economic, political, and social position of the nation in the world. To determine in which way these factors influence news coverage two lines of research, which are partly overlapping, can be distinguished: the gatekeeper perspective and the logistical perspective.[16]

The first line of research focuses on the social psychology of the news professionals, or in other words, the factors that determine journalistic practices and the news output. "News is the end product of a complex process which begins with the systematic sorting and selecting of events and topics."[17] Decisions made in this newsgathering process determine what and how stories are covered. Both event-oriented and context-oriented criteria influence the decisions of the gatekeeper. Researchers concluded that out of the numerous events happening every day and the myriad ways of describing the chosen events, journalists tend to rely upon frames to select certain facts, make sense of the facts, and to structure the story line.[18] Research shows that institutional structures, routines as well as professional aspirations of journalists, and factors such as competition between them, influence to a great extent decisions of journalists while selecting news stories. Audience interest also plays an important role.[19] All these factors together determine the choices between events competing for space and prominence. Although the specific details of a day's event might be unique—a natural disaster, a political debate, or the shelling of a town in a war—the way journalists report the happenings has a lot to do with how similar events were covered in the past. "The construction of news is best thought of as a process in which journalists use established concepts and practices for 'routinizing the unexpected'."[20]

The second line of research, the logistics perspective, concentrates on the economic, social, political, and geographic characteristics of a nation that determine the amount of coverage the country receives in the press. In this respect, mostly context-oriented factors influence the decisions made by journalists in deciding what to cover.[21] There is a consensus of ideas held by analysts and researchers about the criteria that an event must fulfill to become viable news. Galtung and Ruge[22] defined in their classic research 12 criteria that media use to select news stories. The first criterion they found is the time span of the event; the event must fit in the time period between two consecutive issues of the medium. Murders, presidents' speeches, and plane crashes are of short duration and will therefore always fit in the medium's schedule. Such events are also unambiguous, a second criterion journalists use according to Galtung and Ruge. This characteristic of news is directly linked to the criteria of unexpectedness, the threshold an event has to pass—is the news "big" enough—and its meaningfulness. Discussing the latter criterion Hartley refers to "cultural proximity." Events happening in other cultures, geographically distant, are less likely to be covered than events happening in Europe or the United States. Moreover an event must show consonance with what the media expects of the event and it must fit in the total composition of the news. This is a question of balance. If one big event fills the foreign news page, other stories will be dropped so as not to infringe on the space/time allocated for coverage of domestic news.

Continuity of an event also influences journalists' choices. Once an event has been covered, journalists tend to cover it some more—the running story. Beside these general criteria, Galtung and Ruge added specific criteria that could be applied to Western media, which tend to focus primarily on powerful and important countries and persons—so-called elite nations and elite people. Finally negativism is an important criterion; the more negative the event is, the more likely it will be covered. In other words, "Bad news is good news."

Recent studies of the selection process of journalists reexamined these criteria. In the age of globalization, with news being produced by a limited number of corporations primarily seeking to maximize their profits, audience preferences determine to a great extent the content of the media. This is especially true for television news, as noted by Greg Philo who cited a Granada Television producer's observation that "We're past the days of giving audiences what they should have—now it's all about what they want."[23]

We focus on the decisions made by journalists in selecting the news. In this respect the criteria defined by Galtung and Ruge can serve as a starting point. However, they are open to question. A first shortcoming of this classic research is the focus on only three major international crises, ignoring the day-to-day coverage of domestic and less important news.[24] Moreover the focus on the crises meant a focus on events. "Many items of news are not 'events' at all, that is in the sense of occurrences in the real world which take place independently of the media."[25] According to Vasterman the assumption that journalists actually report events following a list of criteria falls short. They don't report news; they construct it. They reconstruct "a" reality.[26]

Tony Harcup and Deirdre O'Neill tested Galtung and Ruge's original criteria in an analysis of news published in three major daily U.K. newspapers. They first questioned the criteria of clarity and frequency. The former criterion is related to the profession of journalists who are trained to present news in an unambiguous way. "Interestingly, we noted many news stories that were written unambiguously about events and issues that were likely to have been highly ambiguous. NATO's bombing of Serbia, for example."[27] They argue that news also fulfills an entertainment function, and that perceived audience demand leads news media "to resort to packaging news in a new form of tabloidism that mixes information with entertainment."[28]

3. Media Processes and War Reporting

Wars fit well into the process of news story selection: they are episodic, emotional, and provide conflict, impressive images, and more. Conflict is underway somewhere every day, but is covered only selectively by the Western news media. In a recent study of media coverage of conflicts around the world, Virgil Hawkins[29] came to the conclusion that all media sources that were researched devoted by far the most attention to conflict in the Middle East. Neither the scale of the conflict nor the number of deaths and human suffering determine the amount of coverage. According to Hawkins, the reasons can be found in the influence of elites in the domestic political arenas, the geographical location, but most of all, the ability to cover the conflict at a low cost. Most media outlets have their own permanent reporters in the Middle East who can immediately cover a new outbreak of violence.

Besides the presence of reporters on the spot, the availability of footage determines if a conflict is covered: "the main principle is: no pictures, no serious coverage of a conflict."[30] Also, coverage of conflict is framed within a domestic perspective. For example, the presence of troops from the news organization's country can guarantee journalists' presence.[31]

News also focuses not on causes of the conflict, but on victims: "good people to whom bad things happen."[32] The media, according to Martin Bell, speaking from his own experience in former Yugoslavia, "personalized the conflict, so that people elsewhere could relate to it more easily, as if it were their homes and families being targeted, and not some foreign conflict of no consequence."[33] The tendency to focus on human suffering in a personalized way without looking at the causes of the crisis can cause "compassion fatigue"[34] as Susan Moeller calls it. The sameness of the news about far away victims makes the audience unable to feel "pity." "Compassion without understanding"[35] as Keane calls it is not likely to endure. Because of this compassion fatigue, not all conflicts are covered in the news. Patrick Poivre d'Arvor, of the evening news on TF1, said, "There is only room for one overwhelming emotion a day or week. There'll always be forgotten countries."[36] Danziger showed this in a cartoon in *The Christian Science Monitor* where an editor sitting on the Bosnia desk answers a telephone call saying: "Tajikistan? Sorry, we've already got an ethnic war story . . ."[37] The war in former Yugoslavia seemed to be an exception and was covered over a long period of time. Reasons for this were its geographical and cultural closeness to the heart of Europe, popular interest in the conflict because of the presence of soldiers from numerous countries serving as UN peacekeepers, and the fact that it was about "people who could have been us."[38]

However, critics have argued that coverage of conflict sometimes abandons objectivity. Peter Brock described American media coverage of the Bosnian war as follows:

> Readers and viewers received the most vivid reports of cruelty, tragedy, and barbarism . . . It was an unprecedented and unrelenting onslaught, combining modern media techniques with advocacy journalism . . . The media became a movement, co-belligerents no longer disguised as noncombatants and nonpartisan. News was outfitted in its full battle dress of bold headlines, multiple spreads of gory photographs, and gruesome . . . footage. The clear purpose was to force governments to intervene militarily.[39]

Sadkovich underlined the lack of background information in the press coverage:

> If early coverage tended to focus on violent or dramatic events, later coverage was similar, except that there was a lot more of it. Flurries of

diplomatic activity, reports of ethnic cleansing, and military operations were covered in detail. Even so, aside from sporadic human interest stories or op-ed pieces, there was little effort to follow up events and less to gain any real understanding of why they had occurred.[40]

Research about news coverage of the Bosnian war by two major French television channels found that the media tended to present the conflict according to three basic criteria that determined the coverage. First of all, proximity, which caused domestication of the news; second, the reliance on spectacle in the sense that emotional content could increase the audience; third, the researchers found an ideological criterion, when reporters focus on the suffering of the people and present them as close to us. They concluded that French television reports covered the events from a human interest angle, using spectacular images of human suffering while they didn't place the coverage in a wider political context.[41]

In order to determine the extent the aforementioned criteria were used by Dutch newspapers in their coverage about the Bosnian war, we divided the data in seven possible settings that cover the total content of the news coverage about the conflict. To decide on the themes, we used earlier research into the settings covered during a conflict. We also used a bottom-up method by looking at the UN Security Council resolutions about the situation in former Yugoslavia and the topics covered in the news.

Armed conflict. This theme concentrates on the actions between the belligerent parties as well as the military actions of internal parties against external and Dutch military actors, like the UN peacekeepers. Beside these actions, background issues such as the tactics used, general statements about the war, and the use of propaganda fall into this category.

Civil conflict. Beside the "battlefield" fighting against other armies, the belligerent parties also caused suffering to the civilian population. All military actions against civilians as well as war crimes are included in this category.

Diplomatic intervention. This theme includes all attempts to establish a peaceful solution for the conflict through cease-fire accords or peace accords, the positions of all actors involved as well as their expressed sympathy or antipathy toward various parties.

Military intervention. This theme deals with all questions around a possible military action in order to stop the conflict, and the expressed opinions of all parties involved, as well as statements of external diplomats about internal military parties.

Humanitarian intervention. This theme includes all statements concerning the humanitarian situation in former Yugoslavia and its civilian population, the humanitarian aid that was provided by aid organizations and that was obstructed by internal forces.

Legal intervention. This covers judicial measures taken by the international community in order to end the conflict, as well as the establishment of the International Criminal Tribunal for former Yugoslavia for the prosecution of war crimes.

Dutch issues. All issues that directly involved or affected Dutch actors.

4. Research Questions

Elaborating on the seven possible settings in which the Bosnian war can be described in the news, we address the following research questions:

(1) How did Dutch newspapers frame the Bosnian war?

(2) Does the way in which the Bosnian war is framed differ significantly over time?

(3) Does the way in which the Bosnian war is framed differ significantly in the four newspapers?

5. Methodology

Periods

As stated earlier, the study proceeded from a quantitative content analysis of the news coverage in four major Dutch newspapers during the year 1993 and the period January–July 1995. The war in Bosnia broke out in 1992 and ended in the autumn of 1995 with the Dayton accords. Because of money and time reasons, it was impossible to analyze the media content of this whole period. After careful consideration with the Netherlands Institute of War Documentation, the commissioner of the project, we decided to focus our research on these periods. From a Dutch perspective, 1993 was a crucial year. In retrospect the Dutch government decided step-by-step to send ground troops to Bosnia, although the decision to encamp the Dutch soldiers in Srebrenica was not made by the Dutch government. In July 1995 the Dutch protected Muslim enclave Srebrenica was run over by the Bosnian Serbs. It is self-evident that we included the period leading to the fall of Srebrenica as well as the aftermath of the drama in our research.

Newspapers

Despite the increasing importance of audio-visual media in Dutch society, newspapers continue to be of great significance in the process of forming a political opinion.[42] In 1995 around 4.5 million copies were distributed, 90 percent by subscription. This placed the Netherlands in the top ten of newspaper-reading countries. In 1995 the time spent reading newspapers was 120 minutes a week.[43]

In this study we use data from an extensive content analysis of newspaper articles about the Bosnian war executed by the Amsterdam School of Communication Research (ASCoR) for the Netherlands Institute for War Documentation as part of their research into the fall of Srebrenica in July 1995.[44] This research was based on the content of four newspapers: De Telegraaf, Trouw, NRC Handelsblad, and de Volkskrant. De Telegraaf is more popular whereas NRC Handelsblad, de Volkskrant, and Trouw are regarded as quality press.[45] The popular newspapers attend more to gossip, sensationalism, and entertainment, whereas the quality press is characterized by an unadorned layout, paying more attention to politics, economics, and science. De Telegraaf is an independent conservative newspaper with a daily circulation of about 800,000 and reaching over two million people. Based on education and social class, its readers constitute a perfect representation of the Dutch population.[46] De Telegraaf has no actual equivalent in other countries. It publishes numerous human-interest stories with slightly sensational aspects although it is more politically oriented than the British tabloids, for example.

Trouw was founded as an orthodox Protestant newspaper but can currently be seen as featuring a progressive Protestant outlook. Trouw is one of the smaller national newspapers with a circulation of 115,000 issues a day and reaching 250,000 readers. The readers are relatively highly educated (42 percent have a university degree) and belong to the higher classes of society.

NRC Handelsblad is an independent, moderately progressive evening paper with a circulation of 280,000 issues a day that reach 463,000 readers. The readers are relatively old (67 percent are older than 35), well educated (59 percent have a higher education), and rich (90 percent belong to the highest social classes).

de Volkskrant was originally founded as a Catholic newspaper but now has a readership of young and highly educated people. The newspaper is politically more left wing. The circulation of the newspaper is 450,000 issues a day and reaches almost 800,000 people.

5. Chronology: News Coverage as a Reflection of Reality

A study of news coverage of a certain event can be considered as a research into the relationship between the actual happenings and the parts of these happenings covered by the media. Or in other words, to what extent do journalists meet the ideal of objective news coverage? This is an important aspect since the audience, depending on the media for their information, consider the coverage they read as a reflection of reality. Report-oriented studies focus on differences among media reports about a certain event whereas event-oriented studies try to reconstruct the event and compare it with the coverage in the media. Our study is an event-oriented one.

Reconstruction of all events that happened during the Bosnian war is impossible. Reality can never be fully described. However, a chronology can serve as an objective reflection of the war reality to which the newspaper coverage can be compared. To achieve this comparison we coded the chronology as put together by the Netherlands Institute for War Documentation. The content of the chronology is based on about 30 chronologies prepared by international organizations like the UN, NATO, NGOs, universities, press agencies, private persons, and, to a limited extent, books. The chronologies are combined and edited in such a way as to give a general overview of the most important political and military developments in former Yugoslavia during the period 1990–95 and the involvement of both the international community and the Dutch government. Therefore we considered the NIOD chronology a good reflection of the actual happenings in former Yugoslavia and a useful standard to examine the extent to which the newspapers provide distorted images of the happenings during a conflict. We coded the enumerated events in accordance with the events that compose the seven themes of the news to make a comparison possible (see table 8.1).

Method

We selected all articles about the war in Bosnia appearing in the first section of the four newspapers: 3,197 articles from 1993 and 1,672 articles from 1995. These produced 59,298 coded statements for 1993 and 32,188 coded statements for 1995. For the content analysis of the articles we used the program Ceta2 (Computer evaluative text analysis) based on the Net-method (Network analysis of evaluative texts). This method is an elaboration and generalization of Osgood's evaluative assertion analysis and is based on the idea that the explicit or manifest content of

Table 8.1   Relative attention per day for the seven general news frames in total and for each year, divided into sources

	Relative attention		Daily average attention and difference with the news (1993)		Daily average attention and difference with the news (1995)	
	Chron	News	Average attention	Difference news	Average attention	Difference news
Armed conflict	31.9	20.9	119.7	41.2	144.9	42.0
Diplomatic intervention	30.5	31.2	114.3	−2.6	82.4	5.7
Military intervention	14.3	17	53.5	−10.3	51.0	−32.7
Humanitarian intervention	10.9	14.5	41.0	−13.4	35.8	1.4
Legal intervention	4.3	4.5	16.0	−1.0	12.7	−2.2
Dutch issues	2.0	4.4	7.4	−9.0	5.3	−16.2
Civil conflict	6.1	7.5	23.0	−5.0	27.6	1.9
Total	100	100				
Total sentences	8,214	18,2972				

a text can be depicted as a network consisting of relations between meaning objects.[47]

Results

The war in Bosnia received extensive media coverage in the Netherlands. Great differences in the amount of coverage can be seen, but during both years there was no week without attention to the conflict. During the first minor peak in 1993, February–March, the media was reporting the deteriorating situation for besieged Muslims in Srebrenica and other parts of eastern Bosnia. At the same time the Security Council adopted Resolution 816 that authorized the enforcement of a no-fly zone above Bosnia. Dutch F16 fighters participated in the operation. In April, events in Srebrenica caused another minor peak in the news. General Philippe Morillon accompanied a UN aid convoy to Srebrenica where he promised the population UN protection (see figure 8.1).

The first peak took place during the week of May 3–8, when the Bosnian-Serb parliament rejected the Vance–Owen peace plan. This rejection gave rise to public debate in the news about intensification of the sanctions against Serbia and Croatia and possible military intervention by the international community. Moreover, a new outbreak of fighting caused an increase in media coverage.

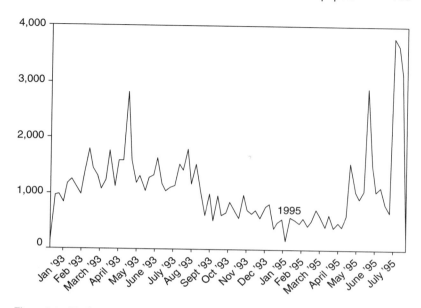

Figure 8.1 Total number of statements in the news per week

In June, fighting between Muslims and Croats in northern Bosnia triggered another small peak in the news coverage. The news mostly concerned the debate among Western diplomats whether or not to end the weapons embargo on Bosnia. The issue divided politicians sharply in both the Netherlands and the European Union. In August 1993, the story of 5-year-old Irma caused another surge in news coverage. The girl was severely wounded and would surely die if she stayed in Sarajevo. British prime minister John Major decided to evacuate the girl with other wounded civilians to England. After this, during the last months of 1993, newspapers still paid attention to the Bosnian war on a daily basis but at a lower scale.

During the first four months of 1995 the newspapers paid modest attention to the events in Bosnia. News coverage increased considerably in May when the general cease-fire expired and new fighting broke out. During this period reports about possible misbehavior of Dutch soldiers in Srebrenica entered the news. The second major peaking of news coverage came during the crisis between the international community and the Bosian Serbs, who had taken several hundred UN soldiers hostage after NATO bombed their weapons depots. In July 1995, coverage was the most extensive because the Muslim enclave at Srebrenica, protected by Dutch peacekeepers, was overrun by Bosnian Serb forces.

6. Armed Conflict and Diplomatic Intervention

"Fighting in Sarajevo, talking in Geneva" read a headline in *NRC Handelsblad* on July 28, 1993. This headline shows the relationship between the themes "armed conflict" and "diplomatic intervention" in the news about the Bosnian war. After a cease-fire was agreed upon during the negotiations, fighting temporarily died down, flaring up again when negotiations were interrupted because of continuous shelling of civilians by one of the parties. This relationship was even clearer in 1993 with the international community trying frantically to find a political solution to the conflict. This war with three principal belligerent parties—Croatia, Bosnia, and Serbia—often had no clear front line, locations of the battle-fields changed almost every week, and the belligerent parties repeatedly formed different coalitions to fight the (temporary) common enemy. The peace process was similarly unsettled. Mediators flew to former Yugoslavia to meet with the political leaders of the three countries or they invited delegations to Geneva or New York to discuss the latest peace plan. At the negotiation table, coalitions between the different leaders were formed to cut out the (temporary) common opponent.

During 1995 the news coverage was different. A cease-fire agreement of four months was agreed upon and its continuous violation by various parties led to increased news coverage. The moment the agreement expired, fighting increased considerably. Besides the continuous fighting between the belligerent parties, the peacekeepers became more and more involved in the conflict. After NATO bombed weapons depots near the headquarters of the Bosnian Serbs in Pale, Bosnian Serbs took several hundred peacekeepers hostage. This caused an enormous increase in Dutch newspaper coverage, and even more when Dutch peacekeepers became directly involved after the Bosnian Serb attack on Srebrenica. Peace negotiations continued but on a smaller scale. After numerous peace plans were rejected, *NRC Handelsblad* concluded that the diplomatic efforts were failing: "Discord about Western policy in Bosnia increases" (June 23, 1995).

In the continuous news coverage about the events in Bosnia the news about the battlefield represented 20.9 percent of the total. More attention, almost one-third of the total coverage, was given to the interrupted, canceled, and restarted peace negotiations (31.2 percent). Armed conflict received slightly more attention (31.9 percent) than diplomatic efforts (30.5 percent).

There is a great difference in the attention to the battlefield between the two periods we studied. In 1993 both the chronology as well as the news reporting focused on diplomatic activities to find a solution for the war, while the fighting itself received secondary attention (22.7 percent in the chronology versus 16.8 percent in the newspapers). In 1995, on the contrary, news about the fighting increased considerably, even more in the chronology than in the newspapers (40.3 percent versus 28.6 percent) whereas the attention to diplomatic intervention decreased in both chronology (22.9 percent) and newspapers (21.3 percent). In both periods, on a daily basis the average attention for the armed conflict in the chronology exceeded the one in the newspapers significantly (22.9 percent in 1993 and 42 percent in 1995) whereas the daily average attention to diplomatic intervention shows small differences between chronology and newspapers.

The differences between the four newspapers in their attention to the armed conflict are small. *De Telegraaf* covered the activities on the battlefield the most (23.2 percent) and *NRC Handelsblad* the least (20.1 percent). In comparison to 1993, the coverage about the armed conflict increased slightly in 1995 in all four newspapers, while the chronology paid almost twice as much attention to the activities on the battlefield in comparison with 1993. This caused a significant difference in the daily average attention between the chronology and all four newspapers.

The results show no significant difference between the daily average coverage of diplomatic issues in the chronology and the newspapers. Interesting, however, is the difference between the newspapers. Diplomatic issues tend to deal with more background issues of the war, such as reasons why parties refuse to sign a peace agreement and the preconditions each party puts forward. In both 1993 and 1995 the daily average attention to this theme in *De Telegraaf* was significantly less than in the chronology, whereas *NRC Handelsblad* and to a smaller extent *de Volkskrant* paid more attention to diplomatic intervention than to the chronology.

7. Military Intervention

This theme concerns a number of different military activities, such as the use of force by the UN forces in Bosnia, the expansion or reduction of the UN forces, the expansion or reduction of the mandate of the forces, the observance of a declared flight embargo, and so on. However, the actual military intervention in different forms (e.g., air strikes, deployment of ground troops) represents the greatest part in this theme. With the deteriorating situation in the enclave of Srebrenica and the negotiations dragging on, the call for a military intervention became louder. Mediator Lord Owen used the threat of military intervention to push the Bosnian Serbs to sign the Vance–Owen peace plan: "Owen threatens Serbia with air-strikes." (*de Volkskrant*, April 27, 1993.) After Bosnian Serbs rejected the peace plan, the discussion about military intervention became more prominent in the news, but again the international community was divided: "West not yet in line about action" (*Trouw*, May 7, 1993).

The same development was found in 1995, even stronger in the newspapers than in the chronology. Until May 1995, little attention was paid to military intervention in the newspapers, but after the peace efforts failed again and again and Bosnian Serbs threatened UN peacekeepers, the discussion about a military intervention increased. This discussion became even more vehement after the fall of Srebrenica.

Overall the military intervention issues received almost equal attention in both the chronology (14.3 percent) and the newspapers (17 percent). However, a big difference can be seen between the two periods. In 1993 the attention to these issues in the chronology exceeded the attention in the newspapers (14.4 percent versus 13.6 percent), but in 1995 the media coverage of military intervention represented almost a quarter of the total news coverage and exceeded even the attention to diplomatic issues (23.3 percent) while in the chronology the attention to military intervention stays more or less the same (14.2 percent). Looking at the daily average attention to this theme, all these newspapers in 1995 paid significantly more attention to military intervention than the chronology did. Differences between the four newspapers are marginal.

8. Legal Intervention

Legal intervention issues received just a small part of the coverage in both the chronology and the newspapers (4.3 percent and 4.5 percent). In 1993 both the chronology and the newspapers paid more attention to this theme than in 1995. This can be explained by the creation of the International Criminal Tribunal for former Yugoslavia (ICTY) in reaction to continuous violations of human rights during the war. The tribunal was established in May 1993 by Resolution 808 of the Security Council and began operations that autumn. In 1995 the ICTY received coverage when it issued the first indictments against Bosnian Serbs and the first trial began. There was little difference in the attention paid to legal intervention between the four newspapers. *de Volkskrant* paid most attention to the theme (4.9 percent) while *de Telegraaf* paid the least attention to it (4 percent).

9. Dutch Issues, the Domestication of the War

Newspapers tend to find a national angle in order to "domesticate" the news about foreign affairs. The moment national interests are at stake, news coverage increases considerably. This tendency is evident when looking at "Dutch issues." These issues represented only 2 percent of the total news in the chronology, whereas the relative attention given to Dutch issues in newspapers was more than twice as much (4.4 percent). The daily average attention to this theme in newspapers was significantly more (9 percent) than the daily average attention in the chronology. In 1993 the chronology paid more attention to Dutch issues (2.5 percent) than in 1995 (1.5 percent), whereas the newspapers paid much more attention to Dutch issues in 1995 (6 percent) than in 1993 (3.5 percent). The presence of Dutch soldiers in Bosnia received continued coverage; "Dutch UN soldier wounded in Bosnia" (*de Volkskrant*, January 23, 1993); "Our boys in Bosnia under fire" (*De Telegraaf*, September 3, 1993).

Besides the activities of Dutch actors involved in the conflict, this theme also includes discussion about military intervention and the role of the Netherlands. This discussion started in August 1992 after the discovery of detention camps in Bosnia and continued in the newspapers in 1993. In summary, it was a discussion between "moralists" and "realists." The moralists argued that "something needs to be done" in order to stop the cruelties against the civilians, whereas the realists argued that a military intervention would only worsen the situation, since there was no clear political goal to achieve. However, the governmental decision in autumn 1993 to send Dutch soldiers to Bosnia was supported by the moralists as well as the realists. Therefore little discussion about Dutch participation in the UN peace force was found in the newspapers.

In 1995 this was different. With the war receiving even more serious attention when UN peacekeepers (some of them Dutch) were taken hostage, the discussion about the importance of Dutch participation flared up in the news. Dutch issues received the most attention during the fall of Srebrenica and its aftermath. With the Dutch soldiers standing powerless against the Bosnian Serb forces, national prestige was at stake, increasing the news coverage immensely. After the fall of Srebrenica,

Dutch issues dominated the media agenda discussing in detail the failure of both UN forces and Dutch forces to protect the declared "safe area." During 1995 these discussions led to a daily average attention to Dutch issues in the newspapers that significantly exceeded the daily average attention to this theme in the chronology. *De Telegraaf* focused by far the most on Dutch issues, especially in 1995, when Bosnian Serbs cornered Dutch soldiers: "Attack on our boys" (*De Telegraaf*, June 6, 1995). In *Trouw*, much the same pattern can be seen. Both *NRC Handelsblad* and *de Volkskrant* focused less on Dutch issues in comparison to the other two newspapers.

10. Bosnia-Fatigue, the Human Aspects of the War

In her book *Compassion Fatigue* (1999), Susan Moeller describes the phenomenon that occurs after news consumers have been exposed to continuous coverage of complex international crises, with little or no explanation of causes and consequences. In Dutch newspapers this

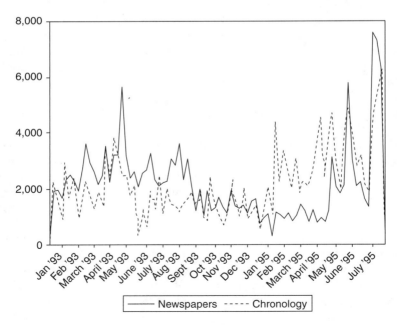

Figure 8.2 News coverage about the Bosnian war in the chronology and the newspapers

phenomenon, or more specifically a "Bosnia-fatigue," could be found as well, especially in 1995. This is shown in figure 8.2. The line "Chronology" represents the total attention to the Bosnian war in the chronology, standardized to the total news coverage, while the line "Newspapers" represents the total news coverage about the Bosnian war as found in the four newspapers.

The first signs of Bosnia-fatigue emerged in the news just during the summer, as was reflected in July by cartoonist Jos Collignon:

"It switches over automatically to another channel when the word Bosnia is mentioned."

In the summer of 1993 Serbian forces besieged Sarajevo, causing increased media coverage. By the end of 1993, however, the news lagged behind what might be expected. As the Croatian writer Slavenka Drakulic put it "There is nothing left to tell about Sarajevo" (*de Volkskrant*, December 22, 1993).

The international community made frantic attempts to find a political solution to the conflict, but was itself divided. The complexity of the conflict, the continuous reports of killings of innocent citizens, and the images of streams of refugees eventually decreased. Readers tend to pay less attention to what they have already seen many times. The sharp decrease of news coverage after a short peak was evidence of Bosnia-fatigue. The moment the crisis between the UN and the Bosnian Serbs was over and the hostages were liberated, attention to the conflict decreased significantly, again resulting in articles in newspapers discussing the phenomenon of compassion fatigue. ("Bosnia-fatigue," editorial *NRC Handelsblad*, July 4, 1995.) In this period the fatigue could also be seen in diminished enthusiasm among the Dutch population for a military mission in Bosnia: "Support for UN mission decreases" (*Trouw*, July 5, 1995).

11. Humanitarian Intervention and Civil Conflict

Compassion fatigue is mostly related to news coverage of human suffering during conflicts. The reports of personal grief and misery have great impact on people watching the news. Two themes deal with these aspects of the war, "humanitarian intervention" and "civil conflict." In the total coverage of both periods, newspapers paid relatively more attention to both themes than the chronology (14.5 percent versus 10.9 percent; 6.1 percent in the chronology versus 7.5 percent in newspapers). This was especially true in 1993, when the daily average attention to both humanitarian interventions and civil conflict significantly exceeded the attention to these themes in the chronology. In 1995, the relative attention to the themes was almost the same in the chronology and the newspapers. This development shows the "Bosnia-fatigue." The human suffering did not decrease in 1995, but the media became overloaded with personal reports of suffering. Only the fall of Srebrenica, with an immense outbreak of violence and cruelty, caused a temporary increase of media coverage about human suffering.

A first news flow occurred in March 1993 when the humanitarian situation in Eastern Europe deteriorated because of obstructions of UN aid convoys by Serbian forces. During this period the international community carried out airborne food drops to provide some relief to the civilians. In April 1993 this was followed with a news flow when the humanitarian situation in the enclave of Srebrenica deteriorated quickly with thousands of refugees packed together in the surrounded area and General Philippe Morillon personally declared the city a safe haven protected by the UN. The coverage as found in August 1993 is a striking example of personalized coverage of human suffering in newspapers. In the summer of 1993 the father of the five-year-old severely wounded Irma called for help in front of British cameras. Irma would surely die if she stayed in Sarajevo. As a reaction British prime minister John Major decided to evacuate the girl to England. Susan Moeller concludes in her book "The 'unfair' attention given to Irma among so many Bosnian victims replicated, in microcosm, television's elevation of only certain crises into global 'events'."[48] Irma's case was extensively discussed in Dutch newspapers as well, especially in *De Telegraaf.* In this newspaper both as front-page coverage "British Prime Minister saves Irma from Sarajevo" (*De Telegraaf,* August 10, 1993) and in analyses "Bosnia's Irma symbolises powerless West" (*De Telegraaf,* August 11, 1993). On August 13, *NRC Handelsblad* commented on the media hype around Irma: "History needs a face. Only on a human level can news about war and peace become really stirring."

In December 1993, the humanitarian situation in Bosnia received media attention after the start of a national action to collect money and goods to help the Bosnian people: "The Netherlands help Bosnia" (*De Telegraaf,* December 18, 1993). During the first four months in 1995, little attention was paid to the humanitarian situation and the civil conflict in the newspapers. Everything seemed to have been told already and nothing new about human suffering could be added. Only the immense violence accompanying the takeover of Srebrenica could cause renewed attention to the civil conflict in the newspapers: "Pronk: Serbs commit genocide in Srebrenica" (*de Volkskrant,* July 19, 1995).

12. Conclusions

In contrast to French television coverage as was found in earlier research and in contrast to the chronology that focuses on the activities on the battlefield, the Dutch newspapers paid attention mostly to diplomatic issues during the Bosnian war. The newspapers also paid more attention to military and legal issues than the chronology. These three themes together represent little more than half (50.2 percent) of the total newspaper coverage about the Bosnian war. In other words, newspapers did not only frame the Bosnian war as a civil war between the three belligerent parties, but also paid attention to the complex diplomatic and political aspects of the war. An explanation for the difference between the Dutch newspaper and the French television coverage is the nature of the two media: television news provides fewer possibilities for coverage of complex diplomatic matters, whereas in newspapers more space for these issues can be reserved.

The newspaper coverage about the armed conflict was significantly less than the chronology and appears to go hand-in-hand with news about human suffering. Dutch newspapers, like those elsewhere, frame armed conflict in a personalized way, presenting civilians as people "like us" who become victims of extreme violence.

The theory that news coverage increases when national interests are at stake is also borne out by this case study. The presence of Dutch soldiers in Bosnia guaranteed continuous attention to their activities. This tendency was even more apparent in May 1995 and July 1995, when UN peacekeepers, some of them Dutch soldiers, were taken hostage by the Bosnian Serbs. News coverage increased immediately. In early July, when Bosnia-fatigue seemed to be taking hold, the Dutch-protected enclave Srebrenica was overrun by Bosnian Serbs. This drama increased the newspaper coverage enormously.

This development proves that the framing of the Bosnian war changed over time. The fact that a Dutch soldier present in the conflict can die was generally accepted and prompted little coverage. But the moment Dutch soldiers were threatened collectively and became a more integral part of the war, the newspaper coverage increased sharply.

The presence of Bosnia-fatigue is the strongest proof of the changes in the framing of the Bosnian war over time. In 1993, newspaper coverage about the armed conflict was more often accompanied by stories about human suffering and the deteriorating humanitarian situation, while in 1995 the news about the battlefield was accompanied by news about military intervention, and the human aspects of the war received relatively less attention. Only when the gravity of human suffering reaches a level without recent precedent, as during the massacre accompanying the fall of Srebrenica, do newspapers pay attention to this theme. Despite this renewed media attention, the "Bosnia-fatigue" is still firmly rooted in readers' minds. Two days after the fall of Srebrenica Henri Beunders, professor of sociological history, noticed this compassion fatigue among the Dutch population. He wrote that the Dutch, enjoying their holiday and a real heat wave would rather spend their time at the beach instead of getting excited about the last events in a lingering conflict (*NRC Handelsblad*, July 13, 1995).

13. Differences Between the Newspapers

Both *de Volkskrant* and *NRC Handelsblad* framed the Bosnian war as a complex, diplomatic, military, and legal conflict, with *de Volkskrant* focusing especially on war crimes committed during the war and the measures taken against it by the international community. Both newspapers also paid extensive attention to the discussion about a possible military intervention by the international community, while themes dealing with the humanitarian situation during the war, as well as Dutch issues, received less attention than in the other newspapers.

De Telegraaf framed the war mostly from a personal point of view, with news coverage from the battlefield mostly focusing on the human suffering during the war. The case of Irma is a clear example of the way the newspaper framed the war. In *De Telegraaf*, Dutch soldiers were mostly called "our boys," and other Dutch issues received a lot of coverage. There was little attention to issues related to diplomatic, military, and legal intervention.

The way *Trouw* framed the Bosnian war can be positioned between the two extremes. *Trouw* focused more than *De Telegraaf*, but less than *NRC Handelsblad* and *de Volkskrant*, on the diplomatic, military, and legal aspects. On the other hand, *Trouw* focused more on the human aspects of the war and Dutch issues than *de Volkskrant* and *NRC Handelsblad*, but less than *De Telegraaf*.

14. Lessons to Learn

This study shows that news coverage in Dutch newspapers wasn't solely episodic, dramatized, and relying on a high level of human interest. A considerable amount of coverage dealt with complex diplomatic, military, and legal issues that were involved. A part of the military intervention theme, for example, addressed whether to intervene in Bosnia, a question which occurred often in relation to the humanitarian situation in Bosnia. These articles, as described in the introduction, were very often full of emotional references to atrocities committed during World War II and created an atmosphere in which being cautious about a military intervention was "not done." The basis for this was created in August 1992 when images of the Trnopolje camp shocked the world. And here is the main lesson of this study: no matter how much attention is paid to background issues and no matter how much effort journalists put into an explanation of the complexities of the conflict, the picture that remains was created in August 1992. The (Bosnian) Serbs were the bad guys and the Muslims their victims.

A striking example of the consequences of such an immense news flow depicting the good guys and bad guys is the research done by Findahl (2002). He followed the news audience in the Swedish town Umea and questioned them about their memory of news items. One of his findings was a rewriting of the history by the audience. A massacre committed by Croatian armed forces in autumn 1993 became front-page news for a couple of days. One year later, most people still remembered the vivid pictures of the massacre. However, their interpretation of the pictures changed. Where they said in 1993 that the Croatian forces committed the atrocities, one year later the Serbs replaced the Croats and the Croatian massacre had become a Serb massacre. The pictures remained the same, the context changed according to a general picture about the Bosnian war that was presented in the international media. The Serbs were the bad guys, the Muslims the victims. Findahl concludes, "In this way the history, or one's memory of the history, can be influenced by the news especially when the audience does not have relevant knowledge and experience of their own on which they can rely."

More recently, images from a Baghdad prison shocked the world and affected the continuing debate about the future of Iraq. The role of the media in this discussion can be crucial. An interesting aspect to consider is the news flow in which the news is presented. As we saw discussing the total coverage about Bosnia, most of the news coverage during peaks deals with human suffering of "people like us," as opposed to professional combatants. The impact on public opinion of these peaks or surges of coverage might be much greater than a steady but smaller flow of news that examines background issues.

Looking at the situation in Iraq today we can conclude that the images coming from the battlefield are providing a more complicated picture than at the time of the Bosnian war. Now we are dealing with shocking images from both sides. First we saw images from the Abu Ghraib prison, with American soldiers humiliating Iraqi prisoners, shocked the world. These pictures without a doubt were damaging the American prestige and political position in the world in general and especially the position of President Bush. At least the images throw doubt upon who actually is the bad guy and who is the good guy during the Iraqi war. Shortly afterward a video where five masked men behead the American businessman Nick Berg goes around the world and causes an even greater shock than the images from the Abu Ghraib prison.

Questions remain. Which images will be retained in the collective memory? How will the news coverage of these events shape lasting perceptions of the players in the Iraq war and its aftermath? Will coverage of postwar Iraq and future conflicts conform to patterns such as those seen in the Dutch newspapers' coverage of the war in Bosnia? What elements of coverage will shape global publics' judgments about justice and injustice?

Notes

1. G. Tuchman, *Making News: A Study in the Construction of Reality* (New York: Free Press, 1978) p. 209.
2. M.E. McCombs and D.L. Shaw, "The Agenda-Setting Function of the Mass Media," *Public Opinion Quarterly*, Vol. 36, No. 2 (1972), pp. 176–187.

3. Z. Pan and G.M. Kosicki, "Framing Analysis: An Approach to News Discourse," *Political Communication*, Vol. 10 (1993), p. 70.

4. Maxwell McCombs, Donald L. Shaw, and David Weaver, *Communication and Democracy: Exploring the Intellectual Frontiers in Agenda-Setting Theory* (Mahwah, NJ: Lawrence Erlbaum, 1997).

5. M. McCombs and S. Ghanem, "The Convergence of Agenda Setting and Framing," in S.D. Reese, O.H. Gandy, and A.E. Grant, eds., *Framing Public Life* (Mahwah, NJ: Lawrence Erlbaum, 2001), p. 68.

6. Ibid., p. 69.

7. T. Gitlin, *The Whole World is Watching: Mass Media in the Making and the Unmaking of the New Left* (Berkeley, CA: University of California Press, 1980); T. Gitlin, *Inside Prime Time* (London: Routledge, 1994).

8. R.M. Entman, "Framing: Towards Clarification of a Fractured Paradigm," *Journal of Communication*, Vol. 43, No.4 (1993), p. 52.

9. Ibid., 53.

10. Ibid., 54.

11. John Hartley, *Understanding News* (London: Routledge, 1982), p. 75.

12. D. McQuail, *McQuail's Mass Communication Theory*, 4th ed. (Thousand Oaks, CA: Sage, 2000), p. 500.

13. S.W. Littlejohn, *Theories of Human Communication* (Belmont: Wadsworth Publishing Company, 1996).

14. See also T. Chang, P. Shoemaker, and N. Bredlinger, "Determinants of International News Coverage in the U.S. Media," *Communication Research*, Vol. 14, No. 4 (1987), pp. 396–414; H.J. Gans, *Deciding What's News: A study of CBS Evening News, NBC Nightly News, Newsweek, and Time* (New York: Vintage Books, 1980); G. Tuchman, *Making News: A Study in the Construction of Reality* (New York: Free Press, 1978); C. Whitney and L. Becker, "Keeping the Gates for Gatekeepers: The Effects of Wire News," *Journalism Quarterly*, Vol. 59, No. 1 (1982), pp. 60–65.

15. T. Chang, P. Shoemaker, and N. Bredlinger, "Determinants of International News Coverage in the U.S. Media," *Communication Research*, Vol. 14, No. 4 (1987), pp. 396–414.

16. T.J. Ahern, Jr., "Determinants of Foreign Coverage in Newspapers," in R.L. Stevenson and D.L. Shaw, eds., *Foreign News and the New World Information Order* (Ames: Iowa State University Press, 1984).

17. S. Hall, C. Critcher, T. Jefferson, and J. Clarke, *Policing the Crisis: Mugging, the State and Law and Order* (London: MacMillan Education, 1978), p. 53; E. Bird and R.W. Dardenne, "Myth, Chronicle and Story: Exploring the Narrative Quality of News," in Dan Berkowitz, ed., *Social Meaning of News* (Thousand Oaks, CA: Sage, 1997).

18. See, e.g., S. Hall, C. Critcher, T. Jefferson, and J. Clarke, *Policing the Crisis: Mugging, the State, and Law and Order* (London: Macmillan Education, 1978); M. Schudson, "The Sociology of News Production Revisited," in J. Curran and M. Gurevitch, eds., *Mass Media and Society* (London: Edward Arnold, 1996).

19. See, e.g., S. Hall, C. Critcher, T. Jefferson, and J. Clarke, *Policing the Crisis: Mugging, the State, and Law and Order* (London: Macmillan Education, 1978); G. Tuchman, *Making News: A Study in the Construction of Reality* (New York: Free Press, 1978), p. 193.

20. G. Tuchman, *Making News: A Study in the Construction of Reality*, p. 193.

21. See, e.g., W. Bennett, *News: The Politics of Illusion*, 2nd ed. (New York: Longman, 1988); J. Galtung and M. Holmboe Ruge, "The Structure of Foreign News: The Presentation of the Congo, Cuba and Cyprus in Four Norwegian Newspapers," *Journal of Peace Research*, Vol. 2, No. 1 (1965), pp. 65–91; R. Stevenson, and D. Shaw, *Foreign News and the New World Information Order* (Ames, IA: Iowa State University Press, 1984).

22. J. Galtung and M. Holmboe Ruge, "The Structure of Foreign News: The presentation of the Congo, Cuba and Cyprus in Four Norwegian Newspapers," *Journal of Peace Research*, Vol. 2, No. 1 (1965), pp. 65–91.

23. G. Philo, "Television News and Audience Understanding of War, Conflict and Disaster," *Journalism Studies*, Vol. 3, No. 2 (2002), pp. 173–186.

24. J. Tunstall, *Journalists at Work* (London: Constable, 1971).

25. J. Curren and J. Seaton, *Power without Responsibility* (London: Routledge, 1997), p. 227.

26. P. Vasterman, *Media Hypes* (Amsterdam: Aksant, 2004).

27. T. Harcup and D. O'Neill, "What is News? Galtung and Ruge Revisited," *Journalism Studies*, Vol. 2, No. 2 (2001), pp. 261–280.

28. L. Minear, C. Scott, and T.G. Weiss, *The News Media, Civil War, and Humanitarian Action* (Boulder, CO: Lynne Rienner, 1994), p. 35.

29. V. Hawkins, "The Other Side of the CNN Factor: the Media and Conflict," *Journalism Studies*, Vol. 3, No. 2 (2002), pp. 225–240.

30. N. Gowing, "Real-Time TV Coverage from War: Does it Make or Break Government Policy," in James Gow, Richard Paterson, and Alison Preston, eds., *Bosnia by Television* (London: British Film Institute, 1996), p. 81.

31. See L. Minear, C. Scott, and T.G. Weiss, *The News Media, Civil War, and Humanitarian Action* (Boulder, CO: Lynne Rienner, 1996), pp. 59–62.

32. Minear, Scott, and Weiss, 1996, p. 64.

33. M. Bell, *In Harm's Way: Memories of a War Zone Thug* (London: Hamish Hamilton, 1995), p. 99.

34. S. Moeller, *Compassion Fatigue: How the Media Sell Disease, Famine, War, and Death* (London: Routledge, 1999).

35. F. Keane, *Season of Blood: A Rwandan Journey* (New York: Viking, 1996), p. 7.

36. J. Benthall, *Disasters, Relief and the Media* (London: Taurus, 1993), p. 28.

37. Reproduced in Minear, Scott, and Weise, *The News Media*, 1994, p. 39.

38. N. Gowing "Real-Time Television Coverage of Armed Conflicts and Diplomatic Crises: Does it Pressure or Distort Foreign Policy Decisions," working paper. Harvard: Joan Shorenstein Barone Center, 1994.

39. P. Brock, "Dateline Yugoslavia: The Partisan Press," *Foreign Policy*, No. 4 (1993).

40. J.J. Sadkovich, *The U.S. Media and Yugoslavia, 1991–1995* (Westport, CN: Praeger Pub Text, 1998), p. 117.

41. P. Charaudeau, *La Télévision et la Guerre : Déformation ou Construction de la Réalité?: le Conflit en Bosnie (1900–1994)* (Bruxelles: De Boeck Université; Paris : Institut national de l'audiovisuel, 2001).

42. K. Shoenbach, *Das unterschaetzte Medium: Politische Wirkungen von Presse und Fernsehen im Vergleich* [*The Underestimated Medium: Comparing Political Effects of Press and Television*] (Munich: Saur, 1983).

43. W. Knulst and G. Kraaykamp, *Leesgewoonten* (Rijswijk: Sociaal en cultureel planbureau. Sociale en culturele studies—23, 1996).

44. Nederlands Instituut voor Oorlogsdocumentatie, *Srebrenica: een "veilig" gebied* [Srebrenica: a "safe" area] (Amsterdam: Boom, 2002).

45. P. Bakker and O. Scholten, *Communicatiekaart van Nederland [Communicationcard of the Netherlands]* (Alphen aan den Rijn: Samsom, 1999).

46. Ibid., pp. 6–8.

47. J.J. van Cuilenburg, J. Kleinnijenhuis, and J.A. de Ridder, "A theory of evaluative discourse," *European Journal of Communciation*, Vol. 1, No.1 (1986), pp. 65–96; J.A. de Ridder and J. Kleinnijenhuis, "Time-Series analysis using CETA," in M. West, *Progress in Communication Science, Volume 17*: *Applications in Computer Content Analysis* (Norwood, NJ: Ablex, 2001), Vol. 17.

48. S. Moeller, *Compassion Fatigue: How The Media Sell Disease, Famine, War, and Death* (London: Routledge, 1999), p. 210.

CHAPTER 9

Terrorist Web Sites

Their Contents, Functioning, and Effectiveness

Maura Conway

1. Introduction

The majority of the literature dealing with terrorism and the Internet focuses on cyberterrorism. In particular, it focuses on the vulnerability of critical information infrastructure(s) to cyber attack. Consistently alarmist in nature, many of these texts focus on the potentially disastrous consequences of a successful future cyberterrorist attack[1] while skipping blithely over the proven role played by the Internet in a vast amount of current terrorist activity.[2] The fact remains that despite the presence of many terrorist organizations online worldwide, no act of cyberterrorism has ever yet occurred. The point is not that cyberterrorism cannot happen or will not happen, but that it has not happened yet. Given this fact, the state of research into terrorist groups' very real online presence is curious on two counts. First, only a small number of political scientists, international relations scholars, or even those whose exclusive focus is the study of terrorism, have researched terrorist Web sites.[3] As a cursory glance in any bookstore or library reveals, the majority of what passes for knowledge about the intersection of terrorism and the Internet is based on opinion and impression, not on social science theory or empirical investigation. Further, most of the research that is available is focused on specific groups and dispersed across space and time such that meaningful synthesis is next to impossible.

This chapter explores the primary materials provided by modern terrorists in the form of their Web sites, in an effort to map the virtual terrorist presence, with a view to highlighting the increasing role of soft power in our information society and the way in which Internet-savvy terrorist groups have wielded this.

Terrorist Web sites have not yet been the subject of any sustained academic investigation. A majority of the research and analysis pertaining to the Internet and Web sites as political tools, has focused on the power of transnational advocacy groups, such as Green Peace, Amnesty International, and other civil society actors, and their ability to harness the power of international communications technologies to forward their goals.[4] Much less attention has been paid to those groups that compose "uncivil society," particularly terrorist groups. This may be due to a number of factors, including the difficulty associated with fitting groups that employ violence into the various frameworks devised to categorize social movements, and a certain "feel good factor" that imbues the work of scholars concerned with issues of transnationalism and international advocacy.

An alternative reason why the academic community has essentially ignored Web sites maintained by terrorist organizations may be that scholars doubt the efficacy of the Internet as a political tool. Walter Laqueur, a respected figure in terrorism studies, made the following observation in 1999:

> No amount of e-mail sent from the Baka Valley to Tel Aviv, from Kurdistan to Turkey, from the Jaffna peninsula to Colombo, or from India to Pakistan will have the slightest political effect. Nor can one envisage how in these conditions virtual power will translate into real power.[5]

This statement is doubly startling when one considers that a few lines previously Laqueur admits that audiocassettes smuggled into Iran played a key role in the Khomeini revolution. In more recent times, numerous civil society actors have conducted successful campaigns via the Internet that have had significant political effects. For example, e-mail was credited with halting a U.S. banking plan aimed at combating money laundering; the Nobel Prize–winning International Campaign to Ban Landmines, which successfully lobbied for a treaty stopping the use, production, stockpiling, and transfer of antipersonnel mines, coordinated its activities via the Net; the Web site MoveOn.org, best known today for its efforts to mobilize opponents of both George W. Bush and the Iraq war, has attracted over two million subscribers to join its e-mail list and has instituted a U.S.-wide TV advertising campaign paid for by online donations. In each case "virtual" or "soft" power was translated into "real" power, whether financial, legal, or otherwise. These and similar successes have not gone unnoticed by terrorist groups and their supporters who realize that establishing a meaningful virtual power base is reliant on a well-designed Web site that performs effectively.

This chapter focuses on four core issues surrounding the functioning and effectiveness of terrorist Web sites:

(1) Which terrorist groups are online?
(2) What are the functions of terrorist Web sites?
(3) What are the contents of these Web sites?
(4) Are some terrorist sites more effective than others?

2. Which Terrorist Groups are Online?

In 1998, it was reported that approximately half of the 30 terrorist groups designated as "Foreign Terrorist Organizations" under the U.S. Antiterrorism and Effective Death Penalty Act of 1996 operated Web sites. Today, virtually every known terrorist group—there are approximately 70 operating worldwide—has an online presence, and many groups are the subjects of more than one site. Nationalist-separatist groups that maintain Web sites include the Irish Republican Army (IRA), *Armata Corsa* (the Corsican army), the Moro Islamic Liberation Front (MILF) in the Philippines, and various Chechen organizations. Islamist groups also maintain a prominent online presence with sites representing Al-Qaeda, Palestinian Islamic Jihad, *Ansar al Islam* (Supporters of Islam), the Kashmiri *Hizb-ul Mujehideen*, the Islamic Movement of Uzbekistan (IMU), the Pakistan-based *Lashkar-e-Taiba*, and others. Both traditionally conceived right-wing and left-wing terrorist organizations are also present on the Web. Left-wing terror group sites include those maintained by the Popular Front for the Liberation of Palestine (PFLP), the Turkish-based Popular Democratic Liberation Front (DHKP/C), Peru's *Tupac Amaru*, and the Japanese Red Army (JRA). Right-wing terrorist groups who maintain an online presence—though much less numerous than their leftist counterparts—include the Colombian National Liberation Army (ELN) and the United Self-Defence Forces of Colombia (AUC), among others.[6] A relatively comprehensive list of all such sites, both official and unofficial, is maintained by an individual in the United States and is available online.[7]

3. Conceptualizing Terrorist Activity on the Web

The traditional mass media has long been a tool used by terrorists to pursue their goals. This is because terrorism has always been about communication. In fact, "Without communication there can be no terrorism."[8] Each new advancement in communication technology has resulted in new opportunities for terrorists to publicize their positions: from Marxist revolutionaries such as Brazil's Carlos Marighela's advice to his comrades to use photocopying machines to produce large numbers of pamphlets and manifestos to Hizbollah's establishment of its Al-Manar television station in the early 1990s. While seeking to convey a message through their "propaganda of the deed," terrorists must also employ written and spoken language in an effort to legitimize, rationalize and, ultimately, advertise their actions. Now, thanks to the new communications technologies, and the Internet in particular, terrorists are, for the first time, equal communication partners in the electronic agora.

Rachel Gibson and Stephen Ward identify five key properties of the Internet that render it different from traditional media:

(1) Volume: far larger volumes of information can be transferred easily compared with previous modes of communication.

(2) Speed: the ability to compress data and more space for transmitting data decrease the amount of time it takes to exchange information.

(3) Format: the ability to combine text, graphics, audio, and video means that in-depth, dynamic, and visually stimulating communication is possible simultaneously.

(4) Direction: the possibilities for two-way interactive communication are greatly expanded on the WWW as a result of the greater space and speed, but also due to the enhanced horizontal or lateral links arising out of hypertext linkage between sites.

(5) Individual Control: the opening up of control over the direction in the sending and receiving of information means that power is decentralized to the individual user who has the choice of not only what to view, but also what to publish.

"In summary, therefore, Web-based communication has the potential to be a more immediate, dynamic, in-depth, interactive, and unedited process than is possible in conventional media."[9]

What are terrorist groups attempting to do by gaining a foothold in cyberspace? In a recent report for the United States Institute of Peace titled *WWW.terror.net: How Modern Terrorism Uses the Internet* (2004),

Gabriel Weimann highlights the advantages offered by the Internet to terrorists: (1) ease of access; (2) the ability to evade regulation, censorship, and other forms of government control; (3) potentially huge audiences with a global spread; (4) anonymous intra-group communication; (5) rapid transfer of information; (6) inexpensive development and maintenance of Web sites; (7) a multimedia environment; and (8) the ability to shape coverage in the traditional mass media, which increasingly use the Web as a source for reporting.[10] Weimann goes on to identify eight different ways in which terrorists currently use the Internet, which are premised upon the distinctive properties of the Internet as identified by Gibson and Ward earlier. These are: psychological warfare, publicity and propaganda, data mining, fundraising, recruitment and mobilization, networking, information sharing, and planning and coordination.[11] Many of these uses rely on a functioning Web site, whether operated by terrorists and/or their supporters to engage in propaganda and raise funds or sites operated by others, but used by terrorists for data mining or planning and coordination purposes. If we aggregate Weimann's categories, we are left with four major—albeit sometimes overlapping—functions that terrorist groups might seek to pursue via their Web sites: information provision, resource generation, networking, and promoting participation.

Information Provision

This refers to efforts by terrorists to engage in publicity, propaganda and, ultimately, psychological warfare. The unmediated nature of the Internet, in conjunction with high levels of connectivity, renders it a communications medium unlike any other. There is a tendency in newspapers and on television for the primary sources of political information to be those who represent authority or who are members of the existing power structure. The British scholar Stuart Hall distinguishes between these "primary definers" (e.g., politicians, police spokesmen, government officials), and what he calls "secondary definers" (e.g., political or social activists, "reformers," terrorists) who reside outside the existing power structure. The latter are used much less frequently by the media than are primary definers, according to Hall.[12] So whereas modern terrorists can manipulate the media into devoting newsprint and airtime to their activities, political claims, and demands, the media in turn manipulates the terrorists: "The insurgent terrorist messages are transported to the public mainly by the media and the message is thereby almost invariably abbreviated, distorted or even transformed."[13] Journalists and TV presenters achieve this by playing up the violent spectacle at the expense of analysis, in order to attract consumers, thus undermining the terrorists' claim to legitimacy by depicting them as merely violent—oftentimes irrational and perhaps even psychotic—and not political.[14] With the advent of the Internet, however, the same groups can disseminate their information undiluted by the media and untouched by government sensors. This can take the form of historical information, profiles of leaders, manifestos, and so forth. But terrorists can also use the Internet as a tool of psychological warfare through spreading disinformation, delivering threats, and disseminating horrific images, such as the beheading of American entrepreneur Nick Berg in Iraq and U.S. journalist Daniel Pearl in Pakistan via their Web sites.[15] These functions are clearly improved by the Web's enhanced volume, increased speed of data transmission, low cost, relatively uncontrolled nature, and global reach.

Resource Generation

This refers to efforts by terrorist groups to raise funds for their activities. The immediacy and interactive nature of Internet communication, combined with its high-reach properties, opens up a huge potential for increased financial donations as has been demonstrated by a host of nonviolent political organizations and civil society actors.[16]

Networking

This refers to groups' efforts to flatten their organizational structures and act in a more decentralized manner through the use of the Internet, which allows dispersed actors to communicate quickly and coordinate effectively at low cost. The Internet allows not only for intragroup communication, but also intergroup connections. The Web enhances terrorists' capacities to transform their structures and build these links because of the alternative space it provides for discussion and the hypertext nature of the Web, which allows groups to link to their internal subgroups and external organizations around the globe from their central Web site.

Promoting Participation

This refers to groups' efforts to recruit and mobilize sympathizers to more actively support terrorist causes or activities. The Web offers a number of ways for achieving this: it makes information gathering easier by offering more information, more quickly, and in multimedia format; the global reach of the Web allows groups to publicize events to more people; and by increasing the possibilities for interactive communication, new opportunities for assisting groups are offered, along with more chances for contacting the group directly. Finally, through the use of discussion forums, it is also possible for members of the public—whether supporters or detractors of a group—to engage in debate with one another.[17]

The coding scheme described below is designed to address two questions: Are terrorist Web sites performing the functions identified above? How well or effectively are they performing these functions?[18]

4. Comparing Terrorist Web Sites: Methodology

Of the 36 organizations that currently appear on the U.S. State Department's list of Designated Foreign Terrorist Organizations, 15 maintain official sites.[19] Ten of these are available in English, and it is these sites that will be the subject of this analysis.[20] All ten groups, their countries of origin, and the URLs of their Web sites are listed in table 9.1.

The content analysis of the sites closely follows the coding scheme developed by Rachel Gibson and Stephen Ward in their article "A Proposed Methodology for Studying the Function and Effectiveness of Party and Candidate Web Sites," which appeared in the *Social Science Computer*

Table 9.1 Terrorist group Web sites

Terrorist group	Country/region of origin	URL of Web site
Aleph/Aum Shinrikyo	Japan	http://english.aleph.to
Basque Homeland and Liberty (ETA)	Spain	http://www.contrast.org/mirrors/ehj/ aehj/aehj.html
Revolutionary Armed Forces of Colombia (FARC)	Colombia	http://www.farc-ep.ch/pagina_ingles/
Hamas	Israeli-occupied territories	http://www.hamasonline.com
Hizbollah	Lebanon	http://www.moqawama.tv/page2/main.htm
Kach/KahaneChai	Israel, USA	http://www.kahane.org/home.html
Liberation Tigers of Tamil Eelam (LTTE)	Sri Lanka	http://www.eelamweb.com
New People's Army (NPA)	Philippines	http://www.philippinerevolution.org
Kurdish Workers Party (PKK)/Kongra-Gel	Turkey	http://www.kongra-gel.org/
Sendero Luminoso	Peru	http://www.csrp.org

Review in 2000. Although Gibson and Ward focus on political party and election candidate Web sites, they foresee their scheme as having broader applicability to the sites of other political actors such as, they say, "Internet groups, municipal governments, and civic or community-based pro-democracy advocates."[21] Gibson and Ward do not specifically refer to terrorist organizations; nonetheless, their general schema was judged to be applicable to these sites also.

Gibson and Ward's coding scheme seeks to gather evidence pertaining to basic questions applicable to all political Web sites: (1) what the purpose(s) of the sites are and (2) how effectively they deliver their contents. The scheme facilitates the comparison of sites based on indicators for information and communication flows and those for site delivery.

Function

To assess functionality, the coding scheme was organized around Web sites' broad direction of information and communication flow (ICF). Four categories of ICF are identified: downward, upward, lateral (inward or outward), and interactive. The first three categories of ICF are unidirectional (i.e., communication is predominantly one-way); downward from the organization to the individual user, upward from the user to the organization, outward from the organization to other bodies, or inward to internal groupings. The latter two flows may be described as lateral. Interactive ICFs are two-way or multidirectional contacts between groups and individuals whereby there is input from one side (usually the user) with the expectation of producing a response from the other side. Transactional communications such as donating, where the exchange is non-substantive and one-way, are considered to constitute an upward rather than an interactive ICF. Gibson and Ward draw a distinction between asynchronous or sequential interaction and synchronous or real-time exchanges within the category of interactive ICF. As a result of that distinction, which is maintained here, a search engine was considered an asynchronous interactive mode of communication because a response follows user input after a certain time delay and cannot then be subject to ʾdification, while chat rooms are considered synchronous interactive ˡes of communication because they allow for free-flowing exchanges in both inputs and responses are subject to continuous modification.[22] ʾe 9.2, "Information and Communication Flows on Ten Terrorist ˑes," is divided into five categories. The first category, ˑd information flows," is based largely on word counts of the ˑizational histories; available documents, such as manifestos, and so on; values or ideologies; organizational structures; details of operations; leader profiles; negative campaigning; and credit claiming. The figures for "Newsletters" and "Media releases" refer to the number of each available on the Web site, including archived copies. The availability of a FAQ (i.e., list of Frequently Asked Questions) was coded on a simple "present/absent" (1/0) basis. The number accompanying the category "Targeted pages" refers to the number of groups targeted. The second category is "Upward information flows" and refers to the presence or absence of donation mechanisms, merchandise for sale, and cookies coded on a (1/0) basis. Category three, "Lateral/horizontal information flows," is focused on sites' link structures, specifically the number of links to groups supportive of the organization's goals (i.e., "Partisan links"), the number of general information sites linked to from the terrorist site (i.e., "Reference links"), and the number of suborganizational groups linked to (i.e., "Internal links"). The final two categories deal with "Interactive Information Flows." Category four deals with the measure of asynchronous flows (i.e., sequential interaction): (1) the number of opportunities available to download logos, posters, and/or screensavers; (2) the presence or absence of online art galleries, photo archives or galleries, site searches, online games or gimmicks, e-mail lists, and bulletin boards; and (3) the number of addresses offered through which to initiate e-mail contact. "E-mail feedback" is classified using a four-point scale: presence of e-mail address (1), e-mail requesting comments (2), online form/poll (3), no reference (0). The final category, "Interactive information flows: synchronous" (i.e., real-time exchanges), identifies the presence or absence of chat rooms on the various sites measured on a simple (1/0) basis.

Delivery

The second issue of interest is the success of the terrorist Web sites in delivering the postulated functions. This was divided into six basic components: presentation and appearance, accessibility, navigability, freshness, and visibility.[23] Presentation and appearance refers to the "glitz factor." Gibson and Ward break this component down into two subcategories: flashiness (graphics emphasis) and dynamism (multimedia properties). The visual appeal and entertainment value that such properties add to a site are considered to make it more effective in delivering its message than, say, purely static, plain-text pages. The second component is accessibility. High levels of "glitz" will be undermined if a site is off-line, takes a long time to load, and various features or pages

Table 9.2 Information and communication flows on ten terrorist Web sites

	Aleph	*ETA*	*NPA*	*Hamas*
Downward information flows				
Organizational history	1,169	18,791	30,042	18,162
Documents	2,552	3,991	29,823	9,181
Values/ideology	5,238	3,226	19,375	5,184
Structure	1,596	0	247	0
Operations	0	0	0	0
Newsletters	0	0	79	0
Media releases	13	0	137	615
Leader profile	0	0	14,236	13,035
FAQ	0	0	1	0
Negative campaigning	0	16,951	0	16,515
Credit claiming	0	0	0	0
Targeted pages	0	1	0	0
Upward information flows				
Donation	0	0	0	0
Merchandise	0	0	0	0
Cookies	0	0	0	0
Lateral/horizontal information flows				
Partisan links	0	7	6	5
Reference links	0	15	0	0
Internal links	12	0	1	2
Interactive information flows: asynchronous				
Download logos/screensavers/ posters/pamphlets	0	0	0	642
Online art gallery	0	1	0	0
Online photo archive/gallery	0	1	1	0
Site search	0	0	0	1
Online games/gimmicks	0	1	1	1
E-mail contact	17	3	2	1
E-mail feedback	4	1	4	1
Join e-mail list	0	1	1	1
Bulletin board	0	0	0	0
Interactive information flows: synchronous				
Chat room	0	0	0	0

Hizbollah	Kach	PKK	LTTE	FARC	SL
0	0	0	12,844	4,222	8,368
0	0	3,842	10,289	8,170	36,803
0	1,550	12,382	2,653	9,376	14,126
0	0	0	133	4,617	0
108,896	0	0	5,512	0	8,944
0	0	0	0	4	9
0	0	1	15	12	0
0	1,237	427	28,261	0	23,255
0	0	0	1,526	0	0
705,836	0	0	1,156	8,699	24,367
108,896	0	0	5,682	0	0
0	0	0	1	0	1
0	1	0	0	0	0
0	1	0	1	0	1
0	0	1	0	0	0
2	19	21	0	0	10
0	6	0	3	0	0
23	1	1	0	0	0
0	3	0	10	0	11
0	0	0	0	0	1
1	1	0	1	0	0
1	1	1	0	0	1
1	1	0	1	0	1
1	1	0	4	1	0
1	4	3	1	3	3
0	1	0	1	0	0
0	1	0	0	0	0
0	0	0	0	0	0

are inaccessible. Third, navigability is an important component of any site. A site that is easy to move around and makes it simple to locate particular information communicates its message more effectively. Site maps and search engines are factors that assist efficient site navigation. Fourth, freshness is considered key to effective content delivery. Sites that are regularly updated will create more interest than those that are not. Stale sites deter repeat visits. Finally, measures of visibility of the site on the WWW were also included. To deliver its contents, a site must be relatively straightforward to locate. A site that is not visible on the Web is failing to deliver its contents.[24]

Table 9.3, "Terrorist Web Site Delivery," explores the effectiveness of terrorist Web sites in terms of their delivery of the functions stated earlier and utilizing the categories identified above. "Flashiness" was measured in terms of the total number of images appearing on the site, including those contained in photo archives and online art galleries. Images appearing on menu bars were counted only once if they were fixed as a frame to reappear on each page. The dynamism of sites was measured in terms of multimedia content using a four-point scale: moving icons (+1), audio (+2), video (+3), live streaming (+4). "Freshness" was classified on a six-point scale according to whether the site was updated daily (6), every one to two days (5), every three to seven days (4), every two weeks (3), monthly (2), every one to six months (1), or hadn't been updated for more than six months (0). Accessibility was broken down into three categories. A count was made of the number of languages, including English, in which each site was available. The second category explored the sites' accessibility in principle by measuring whether each site had a no-frame option (+1), text-only option (whole site) (+1), text-only documents to download or print (+1), and foreign language

Table 9.3 Site delivery indicators for ten terrorist Web sites

	Aleph	ETA	NPA	Hamas	Hizbollah	Kach	PKK	LTTE	FARC	SL
Graphics/flashiness	117	141	77	679	367		23	588	8	286
Multimedia/dynamism	0	6	6	6	6	6	0	6	0	5
Freshness	0	0	5	5	5	1	1	1	1	1
Languages	3	3	2	1	2	3	4	1	6	2
Accessibility (in principle)	1	1	1	0	1	1	2	0	1	2
Accessibility (in practice) (a)	1	1	1	1	1	1	1	1	1	1
(b) Kb	7	45.5	21	26	6	55	50.5	23	1	8
Navigability	3	1	4	3	3	1	3	2	2	5
Visibility (links in) (a)	19	128	38	26	21	5	8	247	0	180
(b)	27				60	152	43		72	29

translation (+1). On a more practical level, a simple (1/0) count was used to record whether a site was working or inaccessible on a given date (a) and a measure of the English home page in Kb was also recorded at that time (b). The number attached to "Navigability" is based on the following calculation: navigation tips (+1), number of search engines (+n), home page icon on each page (+1), major site area links/menu bar on each page (+1), site map/index (+1). Finally, "Visibility" was measured in terms of an advanced Google search measuring "links in" both to the top-level English-language page (a) and the home page of the group's main Web site (b), if such existed.

5. Analysis of Content

Downward Information Flows

So what is the content of terrorist Web sites? A majority of the sites analyzed provided historical background on the group and the conflict. This ranged from extensive background on Palestine, the land and its people, on the Hamas site, along with a brief profile of the group (approx. 500 words) to the Aleph site, which contained a brief "apology for the Aum Shinrikyo-related incidents" and concise details of "drastic reform" of the organization. The FARC site contained just a small amount of historical information and had not been updated to reflect the prominently displayed reference to the groups' fortieth anniversary "celebrations" on their overall homepage. This is in contrast to the large amount of background information to be found on the NPA site, including text and pictures relating to the thirty-fifth anniversary of the group's founding. Just three sites were devoid of substantive historical content; these were the sites maintained by Hizbollah, Kach, and the PKK. Hizbollah maintain a suite of Web sites and extensive background information on the group is provided on their Central Press Office site.[25] The Kach and PKK sites, on the other hand, appear to be more concerned with current news and events than explanation of their positions based on historical events. The lack of background information may also point to a presumption on the part of these sites' creators that visitors to their sites are already familiar with the groups' origins and the history of the respective conflicts.

Large amounts of "official" documentation were to be found on the Web sites of the leftist organizations. The Web site of Sendero Luminoso contained a section titled "Documents of the Communist Party of Peru," which included numerous reports and declarations of the group's

Central Committee, including the *Programme of the Communist Party of Peru* (1988). The NPA site also contained extensive documentation including a section entitled "Peace Talks Documents" (approx. 5,000 words) and another "Recent Statements," measuring more than 25,000 words. The LTTE site had available copies of two e-books entitled *Broken Promises* (1995) and *A Struggle for Justice*, the latter of which was advertised as available in hardcopy from the Tiger's International Secretariat in London.

A majority of the sites analyzed contained sections or documents dealing with the groups' values or ideology. Once again the leftist group—the NPA, Sendero Luminoso, PKK, and FAR—devoted large amounts of text to explaining their ideological stance. Hizbollah were the only group to make no overt mention of their values or ideology on the site analyzed, but a number of clear statements on these issues were included on their Central Press Office site. Implicitly, however, the contents of the site analyzed left one in no doubt as to the group's political and religious stance. Six of the ten sites in the study contained no information on the group's organizational structure. Two sites, those maintained by the NPA and the LTTE, contained very brief references to their groups' organizational configuration. As mentioned previously, the Aleph site contained information about the group's restructuring in the wake of the 1995 sarin gas attack on the Tokyo subway. In a somewhat similar vein, the FARC site contained quite a detailed rundown of their structure in a document that sought to prove the FARC's right to recognition as belligerents pursuant to the Geneva Conventions. In other words, both Aleph and FARC provided information on their organizational structure in order to make claims for legitimacy.

Details of terrorist operations were also absent from a majority of the sites analyzed. Just three groups provided information about their operations. The LTTE site provided analysis and photographs of the operation code-named "Unceasing Waves" that took place from 1996 to 2000 while the Sendero Luminoso site contained a section with text and pictures entitled "Reports from the Battlefield." The Hizbollah site stands out, however, as it contains more than 100,000 words devoted to "Military Operations." This section of the Hizbollah site provides a day-by-day accounting of Hizbollah operations from 1997 to the present. The following is a description of events on April 6, 2000:

> 12:00—The IR team of martyrs Mohammad Hassan Ghaddar and Hassan Abbas El-Haj attacked Aramta position with the rocket-propelled grenades striking its northern fortification and inflicting those who were inside it.
> 6:35—The fighters of Lebanese Resistance Brigades (LRB) targeted Rshaf

position with the machine guns and rocket-propelled grenades scoring accurate hits. Meanwhile, another group of LRB was falling upon the positions of Hemayed and Jamoussa with the suitable arms. Direct goals were chalked up, the fighters told.

The Hizbollah site also contains a gallery of photographs of dead "martyrs" numbering 153. While the Hamas site does not provide text relating to their operations, the site does contain 14 "martyrdom videos," that is, video footage of persons taken previous to their engaging in suicide bomb attacks.

Just three of the Web sites had newsletters available on their sites. Three copies of the newsletter *Resistencia* were available on the FARC site (Vol. 26, 29, 30). Issues of politics, economics, and culture were addressed in each issue. These included articles entitled "Variations on Plan Colombia," "Women and Their Struggle," "The Left and the Elections in the Dominican Republic," "Remembering History," and "Venezuela and Colombia: Two Brother Peoples that are Resisting the Imperialist Offensive Together." Nine issues of *Peru Action and News* were available in HTML format on the Sendero Luminoso (SL) Web site. The earliest available issue dated from Summer 1997 and the most recent available issue appeared in Winter 2002. Each newsletter was six to ten pages in length and contained political commentary, statements of the Committee to Support the Revolution in Peru (CSRP), news, and other information. The NPA site had the most extensive collection of newsletters with 79 copies available; all were downloadable in both html and pdf formats. These dated from 1998 to 2004. The site described the newsletter as follows:

Ang Bayan is the official news organ of the Communist Party of the Philippines issued by the CPP Central Committee. It provides news about the work of the Party as well as its analysis of and standpoint on current issues. *AB* comes out fortnightly. It is published originally in Pilipino [*sic*] and translated into Bisaya, Ilokano, Waray, Hiligaynon and English.

Subscriptions to *Ang Bayan* were also available via e-mail. A number of other sites also provided e-mail newsletters; these included ETA, Hamas, Kach, and the LTTE. None of these newsletters were posted online.

Six of the ten sites analyzed contained a profile of the group's leader. Some of these, such as those that appeared on the Sendero Luminoso and LTTE sites, were quite extensive. The Tamil Tiger leader, Veluppillai Prabhakaran, received extensive coverage on the LTTE site. The "National Leader" section of the site contained eight interviews with Prabhakaran,

"Speeches and Messages" dating from as far back as 1984, a selection of twenty quotes, a five-second video clip, and a selection of twenty-seven portrait photographs. The SL leader, Dr. Abimael Guzmán, has been imprisoned by the Peruvian government since 1992. The SL site had a large section devoted to the activities of the International Emergency Committee to Defend the Life of Dr. Abimael Guzmán (IEC) which contained reports, conference proceedings, published advertisements, leaflets, and emergency bulletins (1995–2001), while elsewhere on the site the text of Dr. Guzmán's 1992 "Speech from a Cage" was reproduced along with accompanying photographs. The Hamas site had a prominent link on its top page to a section of the site devoted to memorializing the group's recently deceased leader, Sheikh Achmed Yassin (1938–2004). This section contained a biography of Yassin, a selection of quotes, the text of five of Yassin's speeches, and a selection of reactions to his killing from around the globe. The leaders of both Aleph and Hizbollah have their own personal Web sites.[26] Neither the ETA nor the FARC Web sites identified or discussed the leadership of their organizations.

Only two of the ten sites displayed a list of Frequently Asked Questions (FAQ). The LTTE FAQ related to the group and its origins as opposed to the Web site. The list of questions addressed in the FAQ were as follows:

(1) What is Tamil Eelam?
(2) Why did Tamils in Sri Lanka want Tamil Eelam?
(3) Who is the leader of Tamil Eelam?
(4) Is Tamil Eelam a communist idea?
(5) What is the present state of Tamil Eelam?
(6) Is there religious freedom in Tamil Eelam?
(7) Can any one travel to Tamil Eelam?
(8) Who is LTTE?
(9) Where can I find more information?

The NPA FAQ (entitled "Q&A" and located on the menu bar in the top right of each page), on the other hand, dealt with technical issues such as downloading and unzipping files.

Those sites that show a "0" in the "Negative Campaigning" section of table 9.2 were not sites that were free of negative comments regarding their foes. Instead negative comments were spread haphazardly throughout these sites and were therefore not conducive to measurement in the same way as the negative campaigning on some of the other sites that was located in special sections or documents and therefore easily identified and measured. The ETA site, for example, contained numerous documents detailing instances of torture, unlawful killing, and other human rights abuses allegedly carried out by the Spanish authorities. In a similar vein, a large part of the SL site was taken up with criticism of the Peruvian government and its officials and their actions against SL members and supporters. The Hamas site had a section devoted to "Zionist Crimes," which contained 61 separate articles detailing alleged Israeli mistreatment of Palestinians. Some of the article titles are as follows:

"Occupation Forces Fire at Worshipers During Prayer"
"Zionist Terrorist Forces Wound Palestinian Baby"
"Palestinian Mother Arrested to Blackmail her Wanted Son"
"Zionist Terrorist Sniper Paralysis [*sic*] Palestinian Child"

The same section of the Hamas site also contained four videos entitled "Zionist Crimes on Video" (2 minutes 36 seconds), "Zionist Heli [*sic*] Bombing Ambulance" (25 seconds), "Zionist Terrorists Beating Child" (13 seconds), and "Zionists Terrorise Palestinians" (2 minutes 40 seconds).

By far the largest amount of negative campaigning was carried out on the Hizbollah site. A section entitled "Israeli Aggressions" contained hundreds of pages—over 700,000 words—detailing what appeared to be every act of Israeli aggression against the Lebanese since 1998. One of the two reports filed on January 15, 2002 is given below:

Eight "Israeli" warplanes violated Lebanese airspace on Monday, a statement issued by the Army Command said. The warplanes roared over the country, breaking the sound barrier over Beirut and Tripoli in separate sorties. The statement said the planes also swooped over south Lebanon and the Bekaa Valley. In a separate statement, the United Nations condemned similar violations, which occurred on Sunday after a lull that lasted 10 days. According to the statement, Staffan de Mistura, the UN secretary-general's personal representative for southern Lebanon, called upon "Israel" to cease such air violations across the UN-delineated Blue Line.

The list of alleged "aggressions" was enormous incorporating not just violations of airspace, but torture, unlawful detentions and killings, shootings, bombings, deportations, destruction of crops and livestock, beatings of women and children, and so forth.

The figure occupying Hizbollah's entry for "Credit Claiming" in table 9.2 is the same as the figure for "Operations." This is because detailing operations was judged to be a method of credit claiming. The LTTE entry for "Credit Claiming" is a composite figure made up of the figure for "Operations" with the addition of a small amount of text (approx. 170 words) that was deemed "credit claiming" and was found linked from the "LTTE" icon on the navigation bar at the top of the page. None of the other sites analyzed were judged to contain significant amounts of overt credit claiming.

Upward Information Flows

A number of sites solicited financial contributions, but none provided online donation facilities, such as a credit card payment option. A number of the sites that requested donations also had merchandise for sale. The Kach Web site had numerous requests for donations, including a pop-up box on the top page that read as follows:

> Make Donations. Israel needs you now more than ever. Support Kahane.org the only organisation that has a program that could save Israel. Help us legalise the Kahane views in Israel. Only one answer, and it is not fences or Oslo. All hostile Arabs who wish to destroy Israel must be removed from Israel.

Clicking on the pop-up brought one to a page requesting donations by mail to an address in Brooklyn, New York. A telephone number was also provided. The Kach site also had a "Shopping Centre." For sale were books, videotapes, audiotapes, t-shirts, jewelry, Israeli and Kahane Chai flags, and stickers. To purchase, one was requested to print out the order form provided and send it, along with a check or money order in US$, to the organization's Brooklyn, New York address.

There was a "Contributions" button located on the top page of the Hizbollah site, but this was not operational at the time the site was downloaded for analysis. A request for financial contributions was at one time included on Hizbollah's Al-Manar TV site and was accompanied by an account number for a bank in Beirut, Lebanon. However, all such requests for contributions now appear to have been scrubbed from Hizbollah's English-language Web sites. None of the Hizbollah sites provide items for sale.

The following request for support appeared on the top page of Sendero Luminoso's site:

> We're all-volunteer, from our national office staff to our student agitators—we rely on yearly membership dues, material purchases and contributions to pay our office rent, phone, postage and printing expenses. If you want to hook up with, support and/or join us, please contact us today by phone, fax or postal mail.

The "Materials" section of the site offered numerous items for sale including copies of the group's newsletter *Peru Action and News*, books and pamphlets, VHS videotapes, stickers, magnets, t-shirts, pins and buttons, and music CDs. To purchase, one was requested to print out the order form provided and send it, along with a check or money order in US$ made out to CSRP, to the organization's Berkeley, California address. "Volume discounts (up to 40% off) are available to bookstores, teachers, and to supporters for use in community outreach." A calculator was provided at the bottom of the page to help with the math.

The LTTE's "Online Store" had similar sorts of items for sale and operated in much the same manner as its Kach and SL equivalents, one's check or money order to be posted to an address in Toronto, Canada. The Aleph site had no items for sale, but requested that those who wished to donate do so to the charities established to aid victims of the 9/11 terrorist attacks in the United States. None of the other Web sites analyzed contained either requests for donations or merchandise for sale.

Just two of the ten sites analyzed installed cookies.[27] They were the Hamas and PKK sites.

Hyperlink Analysis: Lateral–Horizontal Information Flows

Hyperlink analysis has two measures: the number of links from a site and the number of citations linking to a site. The sites analyzed addressed special interests and many of them were therefore relatively self-contained or "close-ended" meaning that the sites generally did not offer extensive external links of either a partisan or nonpartisan nature. The FARC site, for example, was entirely self-contained. It offered no external links whatsoever, to the extent that once one had entered the English-language section of the site there was no clear way of navigating back to the site's top page as the "Home" link only returned one to the top English-language page. Not all of the ten sites analyzed were so close-ended, however. The Kach site had the greatest number of external links. A majority of these were of a partisan nature and appeared in the "Friendly Sites" section of the sidebar. The Kach site also contained six reference links, which appeared in the "News Network" section of the sidebar and allowed one to link to the newspapers *Ha'aretz* and the *Jerusalem Post*, among other news sources. The ETA site also had a relatively large number of reference links. However, these differed from those appearing on the Kach site in that they were links not to current affairs sources, but to sites such as the University of Minnesota Human Rights Library, the homepage of the UN High Commissioner for Human Rights, and Amnesty International

Spain. None of the other sites analyzed adopted a similar linkage practice. Linking to sites maintained by organizational subgroups is another practice that is not particularly popular among terrorist Web sites. This may be because a majority of the groups studied are centralized and their Web presence follows the same pattern, but may also stem from the fact that the present research focuses upon the groups' English-language sites and that subgroup sites are only available in indigenous languages. The Aleph site provided links to 12 "branch" sites throughout Japan, but these were only available in Japanese. The Hizbollah site, on the other hand, provided a links page containing links to the Web sites of some 23 constituent organizations and various representatives of the organization. These included links to Hizbollah's Al-Manar satellite television station,[28] Al-Nour radio,[29] and Al-Ahed magazine,[30] the homepage of the group's secretary general, Sayed Hassan Nasrollah, and the homepage of the group's deputy secretary general, Sheikh Naim Kasem,[31] among others. All these sites were available in English.

The number of citations to a site is a measure of the extent to which a site is recognized among other sites that deal with the same or similar issues. There are two major ways of determining the "popularity" of a site. The first is to measure the number of "hits" on or visits to a site. Many pages offer a "hit counter" that records the number of times a page has been visited in a given span of time, which number can serve as an indicator of the popularity of the page. This was not a viable method in this research, however, as none of the ten sites analyzed provided such a "hit counter."

This approach is severely disadvantaged in any event as it is relatively simple to manipulate hit counters. Further, the number shown does not indicate the number of visits by different surfers, but is the raw number of hits on the page. The upshot of this is that the page may legitimately have been hit a large number of times, but only by a small number of regular visitors. The second measure of popularity is to measure the number of links to a page from other pages. This was the method employed here. The top English-language page of each of the sites along with the sites' overall home page, if such existed, were subjected to a Google "Advanced Search" that allows one to find pages that link to specific URLs.[32]

In terms of visibility, some sites were considerably more prominent than others (see table 9.3). The LTTE site was the most prominent of the 10 sites analyzed with 240 "links in" in January 2004. The Sendero Luminoso, Kach, and ETA sites were also fairly prominent during the same period. The top English-language FARC page had no direct "links in," but the group's Spanish-language homepage acted as a cover page for all the FARC sites and this page had 72 "links in" in January 2004. The PKK site showed a very small number of "links in," at just eight, but this was due to the structure of the PKK sites, which did not have a cover page similar to the FARC site. However, it was possible to navigate from the top Kurdish-language page, which acted as the site's overall top page, to the top English-language page of the PKK site, and the former had just over 40 "links in" in January 2004.

Interactive Information Flows

Some sites were highly interactive while others were much less so. Just half of the sites analyzed provided site search facilities. The Kach site had the most interactive features, including a site search. There were posters and flyers for download, thousands of photographs (of the Kahane family, protests, parades, funerals, etc.), cartoons, jokes, "pre-state underground music," and so forth. Contact information was provided in the form of an e-mail address and a telephone number. The site also contained an online poll. In addition, the Kach site was the only site with an online gaming section, which contained five games in which players were supposed to kill Ehud Baraq, Shim'on Peres, and Yasir Arafat, among others. The aim of one of the games, entitled "Escape of the Oslo Criminals," was described as follows:

> The year is 2010. Red Alert ! Red Alert ! The insane and dangerous Oslo Architects have escaped from their High Security Mental Asylum and are heading towards PA! You must stop them from reaching the safety of their friends of the PLO and prevent the Israeli citizens from lynching them.

When challenged by a reporter about the games, David Ha'ivri, a Kach member, replied: "Each week, Jews are murdered. There are more dangerous things than this game. The people who appear in the games gave weapons to the terrorists who murder Jews. It's just a game for children on the Internet."[33]

Whereas none of the sites investigated had chat room facilities, the Kach site was the only site with a bulletin board forum. This forum was quite active with 610 members, 578 separate topics, and over 5,800 posts.

The Hamas sites had the most items available for download with an archive of over 600 screensavers available. Artistic renderings have long been important propagandistic devices.[34] This is reflected not just in the Hamas screensavers, but the online art galleries contained on two of the sites. There are 29 separate artworks displayed on the SL site, mainly paintings, line drawings, and a small number of wall murals. A majority of these were colorful, but crude posters with slogans such as "Break the chains! Unleash the fury of women as a mighty force for revolution!" and "Long live the invincible People's War!" They were contained in the sections "Art in Support of the Revolution" and "Revolutionary Art of Peru." Many of the images were also available as fridge magnets. According to the site's creators:

> The art displayed here was mainly created by imprisoned fighters and supporters of the PCP. The materials to produce these artworks had to be smuggled into the prisons by friends and family. The art has since made its way around the world. Many of the artists were killed in the prison massacres of June 1986 and September 1992.

The ETA site also had an online art gallery. However, this "virtual gallery" was a great deal more sophisticated than its SL equivalent. It contained ten video installations and photomontages with audio, accompanied by information about the various artists. One of the montages, "The Liberation of Navarre," featured a naked woman in grainy black and white curled in the fetal position, slowly unfolding the length of her body, only to find herself in an enclosed space, unable to escape. The gallery also contained a montage of photographs of wall murals, from scrawled words to complex paintings, accompanied by a short explanation of this practice.

Five of the sites analyzed had online photo galleries or archives. As mentioned earlier, the Kach site contained thousands of images of the Kahane family, the funerals of murdered Israelis (including the Kahanes), and the like. The Hizbollah site contained over 150 photos of dead "martyrs" along with an archive of some 200 still-images from Al-Manar television. The LTTE site also had an extensive photo archive containing over 400 images. This archive was searchable by both category and key word. Some of the categories included "Warrior Statues" (19 photos), "Elephant Pass Victory" (287 photos), "Tamil National Leader" (27 photos), "Liberation Tigers" (49 photos), and "Tiger Operations" (26 photos). These categories were then divided into subcategories. So, for example, "Liberation Tigers" was divided into "Black Tigers" (7 photos), "General Photos" (12 photos), "Men Fighters" (11 photos), "Sea Tigers" (7 photos), and "Women Fighters" (12 photos). There was also the facility to send these images as e-cards.

As mentioned, the Kahane site was the only site with an online gaming section, but a number of the other sites included less sophisticated games and gimmicks. The ETA site contained a clickable map of the Basque country and an interactive map of the city of Pamplona, along with real-time information on the weather in the area. This site also contained a Basque language primer. The Hamas site contained 13 poems linked from the site's top page; the NPA site also included poetry and two albums of "revolutionary" music. Like the NPA site, both the LTTE and SL sites also contained music recordings. The Hizbollah site contained four cartoons, while the Kach site contained eighty-four. A majority of the latter was pro-Israel and anti-Arab, while some 24 were anti-Semitic cartoons that had appeared in the Arab press. In addition to the musical offerings and e-cards mentioned above, the LTTE site also had clickable maps, an online quiz, and a "Memory of the Day" section, while the SL site offered free stickers and/or a free newsletter to anybody who wished to post the CSRP a stamped, addressed envelope.

The Aleph site had the most e-mail contacts, with 17 addresses listed. The LTTE provided four separate e-mail addresses, ETA supplied three, and the NPA two. The Hamas, Hizbollah, Kach, and FARC sites each provided one e-mail address. The PKK and SL sites were the only sites not to provide e-mail contact details. Instead, the SL site invited visitors to contact them via postal mail, phone, or fax. In addition to e-mail contact details, a number of the sites also provided online forms or polls. Sites soliciting such feedback included both SL and the PKK, along with Aleph, the NPA, Kach, and FARC. Half the sites analyzed offered visitors the opportunity to sign-up for e-mail newsletters. However, these newsletters were not archived on any of the five sites—ETA, NPA, Hamas, Kach, LTTE—that offered this facility and so their content remains unknown.

The least interactive sites were those maintained by the FARC and the PKK. These sites had no items for download, neither online art nor photo galleries, no games or gimmicks, and no e-mail lists. While the PKK site had a search facility, the FARC site did not even include this basic feature.

Terrorist Web Site Delivery

Half of the sites investigated could be described as "glitzy." The Kach site, due to its very large number of images, was the flashiest of the sites analyzed. Other sites containing large numbers of images were the Hamas, LTTE, Hizbollah, and Sendero Luminoso sites. With just eight images, the FARC site was the least glitzy of all.[35] Regarding the second component of the glitz factor, audio and video were available on six of the sites: ETA, NPA, Hamas, Hizbollah, Kach, LTTE, and SL. All these sites, excepting the SL site, also contained moving icons. The Aleph,

PKK, and FARC sites contained neither audio nor video, nor moving icons.

The NPA, Hamas, and Hizbollah sites were the most up-to-date. All three had new material added every one to two days. The Aleph and ETA sites, on the other hand, had not been updated for more than six months. In fact, most of the material on these sites appeared to date from 2001. The remaining sites had been updated at various points in the preceding six months.

Eight of the sites analyzed were available in more than one language. The Hamas and LTTE sites were only available in English. However, there are other Web sites associated with these groups available in an assortment of other languages, including Arabic and Tamil respectively. The FARC site had the most translations. It was available in English, Spanish, Italian, Portuguese, Russian, and German. However, the Portuguese and German sites were inaccessible at the time this research was undertaken. The PKK site was available in four languages: English, German, Kurdish, and Turkish. The Aleph, ETA, and Kach sites were all available in three languages. All three sites were available in English, while the Aleph and Kach sites were also available in Russian and the groups' native languages, Japanese and Hebrew respectively. The ETA site, while predominantly in English, also had Spanish and Basque language components. Three further sites were available in both English and the groups' native language. These were the NPA (Filipino), Hizbollah (Arabic), and Sendero Luminoso (Spanish) sites.

The top mark a site could have scored in terms of accessibility was four. However, none of the Web sites performed well in this category, and the top mark actually scored was two, by the PKK site, which had both foreign language translations and text-only documents for printing. The Hamas and LTTE sites, because they did not have foreign language translations, performed very poorly, receiving zero points, while the remainder of the sites scored just one point (for foreign language facilities). None of the sites were off-line during January 2004, the period during which the sites were downloaded for study. Gibson and Ward adopt a sensible rule of thumb when it comes to the time it takes for a home page to load. They say that a home page size greater than 30 Kb will mean the page contains multiple graphics and will therefore take a long time to load for the average home user.[36] Just three of the sites investigated had homepages greater than 30 Kb. The largest of these was the Kach site at 55 Kb, followed by the PKK site at 50.5 Kb, and lastly the ETA site at 45.5 Kb. The FARC homepage at just 1 Kb loads instantly,[37] as do the Hizbollah (6 Kb) and Aleph (7 Kb) pages.

If accessibility was not a top priority on any of the sites, navigability was an issue that received more attention. The top-scoring site was that maintained by the CSRP for Sendero Luminoso. The SL site included a search capacity, navigation tips, a home page icon on each page, a menu bar on each page, and a sitemap linked from the top page. The NPA site was also easily navigable due to the provision of navigation tips, a home page icon on each page, major site area links, and a site map linked from the top page. The most difficult sites to navigate were the ETA and Kach sites. The ETA site had a menu bar on each page, but no search facility or navigation tips, while the Kach site provided a search facility, but no site map or navigational tips, which would have increased the user-friendliness of this very large site.[38]

6. Conclusion

As far back as 1982, Alex Schmid and Janny De Graaf acceded:

> If terrorists want to send a message, they should be offered the opportunity to do so without them having to bomb and kill. Words are cheaper than lives. The public will not be instilled with terror if they see a terrorist speak; they are afraid if they see his victims and not himself . . . If the terrorists believe that they have a case, they will be eager to present it to the public. Democratic societies should not be afraid of this.[39]

Certainly those who maintained the Web sites analyzed here were eager to get their views across. But how well did these Web sites deliver the functions postulated at the beginning of the chapter? In terms of information provision, the sites were an unmitigated success. A majority of the sites contained large volumes of information about the groups' history, heroes, founders, mindsets, and motivations that would be difficult for most people to access without the aid of the Internet. If information provision was clearly the primary function of the sites, then promotion of participation was a close second. This refers not to the recruitment of persons to take part in terrorist activities, but the mobilization of supporters and sympathizers to more actively support the terrorists' causes whether through linking from their own sites to the terrorist sites, printing out and pasting up the posters supplied for download on a number of the sites in their local areas, or contacting the groups via the various avenues highlighted on the Web sites and getting more directly involved. Of course, funneling money to terrorist groups is also a form of participation. A number of the sites analyzed sought to raise funds for their activities via their Web sites either through directly soliciting donations or offering merchandise for sale. Perhaps the least satisfactory aspect of the Web sites analyzed, in terms of their postulated functions, was the use of the sites for networking purposes. Most of the sites analyzed were quite centralized and provided little or no links to either subgroups within the organization or to other, perhaps similar or sympathetic, groups around the globe. Having said that, some of the sites were linked to by quite a large number of other sites.

In terms of delivery, the sites differed quite markedly. A number of the sites were quite glitzy and had significant multimedia content, whereas others were static and dull. Whereas a small number of the Web sites were updated regularly, many were updated only intermittently, and two had not been updated for more than a year. Many of the sites were available in more than one language, thus giving them a global reach. However, the sites scored low on other measures of accessibility, such as the availability of text-only documents for printing. Easy navigation was a hallmark of a significant number of the sites, which provided search capacities, site maps, home page icons on each page, and major site area links.

Two sites stand out in terms of their functioning and effectiveness. These are the Kach and NPA sites. The Kach sites, although its design was somewhat amateur, delivered very effectively on the functions postulated. It was crammed with information and commentary; contained thousands of photographs of the aftermath of attacks on Israelis, the funerals of those killed in attacks, and the like, all meant to serve as evidence of the rightness of the group's ideological position; had an online gaming section and numerous other gimmicks, including an online store; and was the only site to have a functioning discussion forum. The NPA site, on the other hand, was considerably smaller than the Kach site, contained considerably less images, and had neither an online store nor a discussion forum. Nonetheless, the NPA site was remarkably well designed, both in terms of appearance and navigability, and was updated regularly. The site contained large amounts of information about the NPA and its activities; had a "Culture" section including musical recordings and poetry; contained copies of the group's newsletter stretching back a number of years; and provided numerous ways of contacting the organization, including the mobile phone number of the NPA Press Officer.

The FARC site was in marked contrast to the Kach and NPA Web sites. This site was amateurish both in its appearance and overall structure. It had not been updated for some time, was difficult to navigate, and contained only a small amount of information about the FARC and its activities. (In contrast to the English-language pages analyzed here, however, the FARC's Spanish-language site had a professional appearance, was regularly updated, was chock-full with information, and could be easily navigated.) The remainder of the sites analyzed met with varying, but generally high, levels of success in terms of their functioning and effectiveness.

What is clear from this analysis is that terrorists are not limiting themselves to the traditional means of communication; they increasingly employ the new media to pursue their goals. The terrorists of today, like those of yesteryear, are keen to exploit the traditional mass media while also recognizing the value of more direct communication channels. And, as has been pointed out, "if what matters is openness in the marketplace of ideas . . . then the Web delivers an equal opportunity soapbox."[40]

Notes

1. See Ariana Eunjung Cha, "Cyberspace Security Czar Worries About 'Digital Pearl Harbour'," *Washington Post*, November 5, 2001; Barton Gellman, "Qaeda Cyberterror Called Real Peril," *Washington Post*, June 28, 2002; Tania Hershman, "Cyberterrorism is Real Threat, Say Experts at Conference," *Israel Internet*, December 11, 2000; Jerrold M. Post, Erich Shaw, and Keven Ruby, "From Car Bombs to Logic Bombs: The Growing Threat from Information Terrorism," *Terrorism and Political Violence*, Vol. 12, No. 2 (Summer 2000); Dan Verton, *Black Ice: The Invisible Threat of Cyberterrorism* (California: McGraw Hill, 2003).

2. For an overview of terrorist use of the Net, see Maura Conway, "Reality Bytes: Cyberterrorism and Terrorist 'Use' of the Internet," *First Monday*, Vol. 7, No. 11 (November 2002), http://www.firstmonday.org/issues/issue7_11/conway/index.html; Technical Analysis Group, *Examining the Cyber Capabilities of Islamic Terrorist Groups* (Dartmouth College, NH: Institute for Security Technology, 2003), https://www.ists.dartmouth.edu/TAG/ITB/ITB_032004.pdf; Gabriel Weimann, *www.terror.net: How Modern Terrorism Uses the Internet* (Washington, D.C.: United States Institute of Peace, 2004), http://www.usip.org/pubs/specialreports/sr116.html.

3. A sampling of research on terrorist Web sites: Maura Conway, "Cybercortical Warfare: The Case of Hizbollah.org," *European Consortium for Political Research (ECPR) Joint Sessions of Workshops*, Edinburgh, March 28–April 2, 2003, http://www.essex.ac.uk/ecpr/events/jointsessions/paperarchive/edinburgh/ ws20/Conway.pdf; Brigitte Nacos, *Mass-Mediated Terrorism: The Central Role of the Media in Terrorism and Counterterrorism* (Oxford: Rowman & Littlefield, 2002); Yariv Tsfati and Gabriel Weimann, "www.terrorism.com: Terror on the Internet," *Studies in Conflict and Terrorism*, Vol. 25, No. 5

(September–October 2002); Michael Whine, "Cyberspace: A New Medium for Communication, Command, and Control by Extremists," *Studies in Conflict and Terrorism*, Vol. 22, No. 3 (August 1999), pp. 231–245; Michael Whine, "Islamist Organisations on the Internet," *Terrorism and Political Violence*, Vol. 11, No. 1 (1999), pp. 123–132.

4. See, e.g., W. Lance Bennett, "Communicating Global Activism: Strengths and Vulnerabilities of Networked Politics," *Information, Communication, and Society*, Vol. 6, No. 2 (2003), pp. 143–168; Harry M. Cleaver, "The Zapatista Effect: The Internet and the Rise of an Alternative Political Fabric," *Journal of International Affairs*, Vol. 51, No. 2 (Spring 1998), pp. 621–631; Nick Couldry and James Curran, eds., *Contesting Media Power* (New York: Rowman, 2003); Wim Van De Donk, Brian Loader, Paul Dixon, and Dieter Rucht, eds., *Cyberprotest: New Media, Citizens, and Social Movements* (London: Routledge, 2003); Peter I. Hajnal, ed., *Civil Society in the Information Age* (Aldershot: Ashgate, 2002); Leander Kahney, "Internet Stokes Anti-War Movement," *Wired News*, January 21, 2003, http://www.wired.com/news/ culture/ 0,1284,57310,00. html?tw=wn_ story_related; Sagi Leizerov, "Privacy Advocacy Groups Versus Intel: A Case Study of How Social Movements are Tactically Using the Internet to Fight Corporations," *Social Science Computer Review*, Vol. 18, No. 4 (Winter 2000), pp. 461–483; Wan-Ying Lin and William H. Dutton, "The 'Net' Effect in Politics: The 'Stop the Overlay' Campaign in Los Angeles," *Party Politics*, Vol. 9, No. 1 (2003), pp. 124–136.

5. Walter Laqueur, *The New Terrorism* (Oxford: Oxford University Press, 1999), p. 262.

6. There is a tendency to equate far-right or "hate" groups with terrorist groups, especially among Internet researchers. Such an equation does not hold up under scrutiny; Web sites maintained by terrorist and hate groups differ markedly in terms of appearance, content, functioning, and effectiveness. Analyses that uncritically lump terrorists and hate groups—and their Web sites—together include Kelly R. Damphousse and Brent L. Smith, "The Internet: A Terrorist Medium for the 21st Century," in Harvey W. Kushner, ed., *The Future of Terrorism: Violence in the New Millennium* (London: Sage, 1998), pp. 208–224; Brian Levin, "Cyberhate: A Legal and Historical Analysis of Extremists' Use of Computer Networks in America," *American Behavioral Scientist*, Vol. 45, No. 6 (2002), pp. 958–988; Nacos, *Mass-Mediated Terrorism*, pp. 103–130.

7. Bob Cromwell's "Separatist, Para-Military, Military, Intelligence, and Political Organisations," is available online at http://www.cromwellintl. com/security/netusers.html.

8. Alex P. Schmid and Janny De Graaf, *Violence as Communication: Insurgent Terrorism and the Western News Media* (London: Sage, 1982), p. 9.

9. Rachel Gibson and Stephen Ward, "A Proposed Methodology for Studying the Function and Effectiveness of Party and Candidate Web Sites," *Social Science Computer Review*, Vol. 18, No. 3 (Fall 2000), p. 304.

10. Weimann, *www.terror.net*, p. 3.

11. Ibid., pp. 5–11.

12. Ronald D. Crelinsten, "Power and Meaning: Terrorism as a Struggle Over Access to the Communication Structure," in Paul Wilkinson and A.M. Stewart, eds., *Contemporary Research on Terrorism* (Aberdeen: Aberdeen University Press, 1987), p. 420.

13. Schmid and De Graaf, *Violence as Communication*, p. 110.

14. Crelinsten, "Power and Meaning," p. 421.

15. Reuters, *Malaysia PM Says Web Terror Sites Unacceptable*, May 14, 2004, Weimann, *www.terror.net*, p. 5.

16. For example, the Internet provided a channel, not just for the American public, but publics worldwide, to reach out financially to those affected by the events of 9/11. The day before the attacks, the American Red Cross's Web site had 20,959 visitors and gathered $1,024. On the day of the attacks, the number of visitors skyrocketed to 243,974 with people making contributions at the rate of one per second. More than $1 million was contributed in the space of 12 hours, and the American Red Cross went on to raise $39.5 million in the following seven days. The most the organization had managed to raise online previously was $2.5 million, in response to the earthquakes in India and Central America earlier in 2001. A number of Internet companies also banded together to raise money for charities aiding victims of the attacks; more than $57 million was raised in the first week alone on the Web sites of six companies: Amazon.com, AOL Time Warner, Cisco Systems, eBay, Microsoft, and Yahoo.

17. Gibson and Ward, *A Proposed Methodology*, pp. 305–306; Weimann, *www.terror.net*, p. 8.

18. Gibson and Ward, *A Proposed Methodology*, p. 306.

19. Some sites are clearly more official than others. There is no doubt, e.g., that the Hizbollah Web sites were established and are maintained by the Hizbollah organization. The same is true of the LTTE site. Other sites were established and are maintained by organizations with close ties to the concomitant terrorist organization. This is true of the Committee to Support the Revolution in Peru (CSRP) who founded and maintain Sendero Luminoso's Web site. Sites such as the latter are of a quasi-official nature; sites not represented here are those founded and maintained by supporters who appear to have no direct ties to the groups for whom they cheerlead.

20. All Web sites were downloaded in January 2004 with the exception of the Hamas site, which was downloaded in May 2004. Since the contents are changing all the time, the present analysis can only provide a snapshot of Web sites at one point in time.

21. Gibson and Ward, *A Proposed Methodology*, p. 302.

22. Ibid., p. 306.

23. Gibson and Ward included a seventh category, responsiveness, which tested the speed and quality of the response to an e-mailed request for information.

This category was not included in this research as a number of researchers in this area advised me that, based on their experience, responses to such a general request were unlikely to be forthcoming. I will explore the issue of responsiveness in future research nonetheless.

24. Gibson and Ward, *A Proposed Methodology*, p. 308.
25. The CPO site is online at http://www.hizbollah.org.
26. Joyu Fumihiro's official site is online at http://www.joyu.to. Nasrollah's personal homepage may be accessed at http://www.nasrollah.org.
27. Cookies are pieces of information generated by a Web server and stored in the user's computer, ready for future access. They are embedded in the html information flowing back and forth between the user's computer and the servers and were devised to allow user-side customization of Web information. Cookies make use of user-specific information transmitted by the Web server onto the user's computer so that the information might be available for later access by itself or other servers. Web servers automatically gain access to relevant cookies whenever the user establishes a connection to them, usually in the form of Web requests. For more information on cookies, check out http://www.cookiecentral.com.
28. http://www.manartv.com
29. http://www.alnour.net/
30. http://www.alahed.org
31. http://www.naimkassem.org
32. Google was chosen because it is the world's leading Internet search engine. It ranks Web pages using software called PageRank. PageRank relies on the uniquely democratic nature of the Web by using its vast link structure as an indicator of an individual page's value. In essence, Google interprets a link from page A to page B as a vote, by page A, for page B. But, Google looks at more than the sheer volume of votes, or links a page receives; it also analyzes the page that casts the vote. Votes cast by pages that are themselves "important" weigh more heavily and help to make other pages "important." For more, see http://www.google.com/technology/index.html.
33. Foreign Broadcast Information Service, "Right-Wing Internet Site Urges Players to Kill Oslo 'Criminals,' Arafat," *FBIS-NES-2002–0214*, February 14, 2002.
34. See Karen S. Johnson-Cartee and Gary A. Copeland, *Strategic Political Communication: Rethinking Social Influence, Persuasion, and Propaganda* (Maryland: Rowman and Littlefield, 2004), pp. 141–142.
35. There are a number of limitations to using the raw number of graphics to judge flashiness; see Gibson and Ward, *A Proposed Methodology*, p. 313.
36. Ibid., p. 313.
37. The top FARC page (i.e., the Spanish-language home page from which all the other sites are linked) is slightly more graphical at 14 Kb.

38. "Visibility," the final site delivery variable, was addressed in the *Hyperlink Analyses* section above.
39. Schmid and De Graaf, *Violence as Communication*, p. 170.
40. Pippa Norris, *Digital Divide: Civic Engagement, Information Poverty, and the Internet Worldwide* (Cambridge: Cambridge University Press, 2001), p. 172.

CHAPTER 10

The News Media and "the Clash of Civilizations"

Philip Seib

"The call to jihad is rising in the streets of Europe, and is being answered," reported the *New York Times* in April 2004. The *Times* story quoted a Muslim cleric in Britain touting the "culture of martyrdom," an imam in Switzerland urging his followers to "impose the will of Islam on the godless society of the West," and another radical Islamist leader in Britain predicting that "our Muslim brothers from abroad will come one day and conquer here, and then we will live under Islam in dignity."[1]

For those who believe that a clash of civilizations—particularly between Islam and the non-Islamic West—is underway or at least approaching, the provocative comments in the *Times* article were evidence that "the clash" is not merely a figment of an overheated political imagination. Ever since Samuel Huntington presented his theory about such a clash in a *Foreign Affairs* article in 1993, debate has continued about whether his ideas are substantive or simplistic. For the news media, this debate is important because it helps shape their approach to covering the world.

1. News Coverage and the Huntington Debate

In Huntington's original article, which he refined and expanded in his 1996 book, *The Clash of Civilizations and the Remaking of World Order*, he argued "the clash of civilizations will dominate global politics. The fault lines between civilizations will be the battle lines of the future."[2] In the book, Huntington said "culture and cultural identities, which at the broadest level are civilization identities, are shaping the patterns of cohesion, disintegration, and conflict in the post–cold War world." Huntington's corollaries to this proposition, in summary form, are:

(1) "For the first time in history, global politics is both multipolar and multicivilizational."
(2) As the balance of power among civilizations shifts, the relative influence of the West is declining.
(3) A world order is emerging that is civilization-based.
(4) "Universalist pretensions" are increasingly bringing the West into conflict with other civilizations, especially the Islamic world and China.
(5) If the West is to survive, America must reaffirm its Western identity and unite with other Westerners in the face of challenges from other civilizations.[3]

One reason that Huntington's clash theory initially had appeal was that policymakers, the news media, and others were moving uncertainly into the post–cold war era without much sense of how the newest world order was taking shape. They were receptive to a new geopolitical scheme, particularly one that featured identifiable adversarial relationships that would supersede those being left behind.

The us-versus-them alignment of the cold war's half-century had been convenient for the news media as well as policymakers. The American perspective was that the bad guys operated from Moscow and its various outposts, while the good guys were based in Washington and allied countries. Not all the world accepted such a facile division, but those who did found it tidy and easy to understand. Many American news organizations shaped their coverage to conform to this worldview; there was cold war journalism just as there was cold war politics.

With the fall of the Berlin Wall, the demise of the Soviet Union, and other events marking the end of the cold war, the news media found themselves searching for new ways to approach international coverage. *New York Times* foreign editor Bernard Gwertzman sent a memo to his staff in December 1992 calling for adjustments in coverage: "In the old days, when certain countries were pawns in the cold war, their political orientation alone was reason enough for covering them. Now with their political orientation not quite as important, we don't want to forget them, but we have an opportunity to examine different aspects of a society more fully."[4]

But with the absence of the principal threat of the cold war—possible nuclear conflict between the two superpowers—interest in international news was less acute. Those "different aspects of a society" that Gwertzman cited *were* important, but news about them lacked urgency. New villains could be found from time to time—Saddam Hussein filled the bill nicely—but they were not part of a grand scenario such as that of the cold war.

Even the 1991 Gulf War seemed to take place in a narrow context. In response to an act of aggression that the American government judged to be against its interests, the United States built a coalition and smashed the aggressor. It was a fine showcase for America in its unipolar moment, but it seemed little more than a response to a singular aberrant act. Saddam Hussein's Iraq was not seen as representing any larger cultural or political force.

Nevertheless, something was percolating. In 1993, a car bomb killed seven and injured hundreds at the World Trade Center in New York. In 1995, an alleged plot to blow up a dozen U.S. aircraft was foiled. In 1995 and 1996, truck bombs were used in attacks on American training and residential facilities in Saudi Arabia. In 1998, U.S. embassies in Kenya and Tanzania were attacked with car bombs. In 2000, the U.S.S. *Cole* was attacked by suicide bombers in Yemen.

These and other terrorist incidents received heavy news coverage, but primarily as isolated events. Neither the government nor the news media "connected the dots." Although the attacks on the United States on September 11, 2001 represented an escalation, they were part of this continuum of terrorism. The attacks on American targets throughout the 1990s, as well as incidents directed at non-American targets (such as a 1995 assassination attempt against Egyptian president Hosni Mubarak), were parts of a radical Islamist agenda designed by Osama bin Laden and others. Bin Laden himself was a shadowy presence, but not invisible. He had been indicted for the embassy bombings and he granted interviews to American news organizations. He told CNN in 1997, "We declared jihad against the United States," and ABC in 1998, "We anticipate a black future for America."

Bin Laden does not in himself constitute a "civilization" that is clashing with the West. He can be dismissed as a murderer who has merely proclaimed himself to be a defender of Islam. There is, however, more to a decade of terrorism than one man's persistence. Whether Huntington's theory is validated by these terrorist events and whether Huntington's view of conflict should guide the planning of news coverage remains debatable.

Critics of Huntington's theory abound, focusing on a variety of issues, such as the idea that "civilizations" are superseding states. Johns Hopkins University professor Fouad Ajami said that Huntington "underestimated the tenacity of modernity and secularism."[5] Terrorism expert Richard Clarke has said that rather than there being a straightforward Islam-versus-West conflict, "we are seriously threatened by an ideological war within Islam. It is a civil war in which a radical Islamist faction is striking out at the West and at moderate Muslims. Once we recognize that the struggle within Islam—not a 'clash of civilizations' between East and West—is the phenomenon with which we must grapple, we can begin to develop a strategy and tactics for doing so."[6]

Scholars Ian Buruma and Avishai Margalit took a broader view. They wrote "radical Islamists no longer believe in the traditional Muslim division of the world between the peaceful domain of Islam and the war-filled domain of infidels. To them the whole world is now the domain of war. . . . The West is the main target. . . ."[7] Buruma and Margalit added that this radicalism is not going unchallenged and that "the fiercest battles will be fought inside the Muslim world."[8] International relations scholar Charles Kupchan said that "the ongoing struggle between the United States and Islamic radicals does not represent a clash of civilizations," but rather is the result of extremist groups preying upon discontent within Islamic states. "The underlying source of alienation," wrote Kupchan, "is homegrown—political and economic stagnation and the social cleavages it produces."[9]

Along similar lines Zbigniew Brzezinski has written

> the ferment within the Muslim world must be viewed primarily in a regional rather than a global perspective, and through a geopolitical rather than a theological prism. . . . Hostility toward the United States, while pervasive in some Muslim countries, originates more from specific political grievances—such as Iranian nationalist resentment over the U.S. backing of the Shah, Arab animus stimulated by U.S. support for Israel, or Pakistani feelings that the United States has been partial to India—than from a generalized religious bias.[10]

Journalist Thomas Friedman disagreed with Huntington's approach on different grounds, arguing that Huntington did not appreciate the effects of globalization on cultural interests and behavior. Huntington, Friedman wrote, "vastly underestimated how the power of states, the lure of global markets, the diffusion of technology, the rise of networks and the spread of global norms could trump [his] black-and-white (mostly black) projections."[11]

The debate about Huntington's clash theory continues, with Islam-related issues receiving the most attention, at least for now. Some observers see new fault lines that may contribute to cultural clashes. Niall Ferguson pointed to the declining population of current European Union members—it is projected to shrink by about 7.5 million by 2050, the most sustained drop since the Black Death in the fourteenth century—that will leave a vacuum that might be filled by Muslim immigrants. Concerning the consequences of this, Ferguson said, "A creeping Islamicization of a decadent Christendom is one conceivable result: while the old Europeans get even older and their religious faith weaker, the Muslim colonies within their cities get larger and more overt in their religious observance." Other possibilities, said Ferguson, include a backlash against immigration or perhaps "a happy fusion between rapidly secularized second-generation Muslims and their post-Christian neighbors." Each of the three could occur in various places, he added.[12]

In response to the initial wave of criticism that his *Foreign Affairs* article stimulated, Huntington stood his ground. "What ultimately counts for people," he wrote in late 1993, "is not political ideology or economic interest. Faith and family, blood and belief, are what people identify with and what they will fight and die for. And that is why the clash of civilizations is replacing the cold war as the central phenomenon of global politics, and why a civilizational paradigm provides, better than any alternative, a useful starting point for understanding and coping with the changes going on in the world."[13]

The supply of theories—and theories about theories—is inexhaustible. Fortunately for journalists, they need not—and should not—adopt just one as the foundation for building their approach to coverage. They should, however, become familiar with the diverse array of ideas about how the world is changing. The news media must go somewhere; they cannot simply remain at a standstill while yearning for the return of their neat cold war dichotomy.

In news coverage, as in politics, a vacuum exists if there is no "enemy." Professor Adeed Dawisha wrote "in the wake of the demise of international communism, the West saw radical Islam as perhaps its most dangerous adversary."[14] Thus, an enemy and so a vacuum no more. This was apparent immediately after the 2001 attacks, when mainstream American newspapers featured headlines such as these: "This Is a Religious War"; "Yes, This Is About Islam"; "Muslim Rage"; "The Deep Intellectual Roots of Islamic Terror"; "Kipling Knew What the U.S. May Now Learn"; "Jihad 101"; "The Revolt of Islam"; and so on. Several discussed the Crusades and were illustrated with pictures of Richard the Lion Heart.[15]

Events have pushed many in the news media toward a de facto adoption of the Huntington theory, regardless of its many critics. The 9/11 attacks, the resulting Afghanistan war, and the Iraq war begun in 2003 all lend themselves to political and journalistic shorthand: we have a new array of villains and they have Islam in common. That must mean that a clash of civilizations is underway.

2. How America Watches the World

It is difficult for Americans to make knowledgeable judgments about the existence of civilization-related clashes if the public knows little about the civilizations in question. Although the news media should not bear the entire burden of teaching the public about the world—the education system also has major responsibilities, which it consistently fails to fulfill—news coverage is a significant element in shaping the public's understanding of international events and issues. Aside from their occasional spurts of solid performance, American news organizations do a lousy job of breaking down the public's intellectual isolation.

The breadth of news coverage depends on news organizations' own view of the world, a view that is often too narrow. Expanding it will require a surge of ambition and a reversal of the reductions in international coverage. Media analyst Andrew Tyndall reported that in 1989 the ABC, CBS, and NBC evening newscasts presented 4,032 minutes of datelined coverage from other countries. That had dropped to as low as 1,382 minutes in 2000. With the attacks on the United States and the war in Afghanistan, the figure rose to 2,103 minutes in 2002, which was still only slightly more than half the total of 1989.[16]

Because of the U.S. invasion of Iraq, international coverage by American news organizations rose substantially in 2003, at least for Iraq-related stories. According to Tyndall's ADT Research, the big three U.S. television networks—ABC, CBS, and NBC—devoted 4,047 minutes of their principal weeknight newscasts to Iraq. But beyond Iraq, the networks' international reporting was negligible. For all of 2003, the Israeli–Palestinian conflict received 284 minutes, Afghanistan 80 minutes, the global AIDS epidemic 39 minutes, and global warming 15 minutes.[17]

From among these topics, consider what the public is likely to make of the Israeli–Palestinian story when coverage averages less than two minutes per week per network. The issues are complex and their impact is incendiary in parts of the world. A news organization that provides such scant coverage cannot hope to truly inform its audience and members of that audience cannot hope to truly understand what is going on.

Also in 2003, the news media virtually ignored humanitarian crises from Chad to Chechnya to Colombia and beyond that were identified by Doctors Without Borders in the organization's annual list of the ten most underreported stories.[18] When asked if the American public was suffering from compassion fatigue concerning such crises, Doctors Without Borders executive director Nicholas De Torrente said:

> If you have very quick, superficial coverage of very difficult, complex issues, then of course people will turn off and blank out and not be interested, and you'll see an ongoing litany of anarchy, chaos, crisis without rhyme or reason. However, if you do look at issues and devote resources and attention to them and try to understand them, then people will catch on . . . and there is a connection that is established.[19]

One aspect of the shrinkage of international coverage is the reduction in the number of foreign bureaus maintained by American news organizations, notably the big three television networks. As of mid-2003, ABC, CBS, and NBC each maintained six overseas bureaus with full-time correspondents, but since the peak of international coverage during the 1980s, each has closed bureaus or removed correspondents when there was not a full bureau in place. ABC did this in seven cities, including Moscow, Cairo, and Tokyo. CBS did it in four cities, including Beijing and Bonn. NBC followed suit in seven cities, including Paris and Rome.[20]

The weakness of international coverage is no secret within the news business. A 2002 study conducted for the Pew International Journalism Program found that among American newspaper editors, "nearly two-thirds of those responsible for assembling their newspaper's foreign news coverage rate the media's performance in this area as fair or poor."[21] When asked about their own news organization's performance in satisfying readers' interest in international news, 56 percent gave their own paper a rating of fair or poor (and only 2 percent rated their paper as excellent).[22]

Editors at newspapers with a circulation of at least 100,000 were particularly critical of television news. Sixty-seven percent of the editors said network television news did a fair or poor job of covering international events, while 40 percent said cable news coverage deserved only a fair or poor rating.[23] Overall, the study found, "the ratings given to international news coverage were significantly lower than those awarded to the media's coverage of sports, national, local, and business news."[24]

Such lackluster performance stands in contrast with what the editors perceived as an increase in the public's interest in international news, which contradicted the conventional wisdom that the American news audience resists learning about the rest of the world. In general, said the editors, only 7 percent of their readers were not too interested in international news.[25] Ninety-five percent of the editors said reader interest in international news had increased since the September 11, 2001 attacks, but 64 percent said that they believed that this interest would soon decline to pre–September 11 levels.[26] This reflects condescension on the part of journalists toward the public that in itself merits study, particularly in terms of the values governing the relationship between news media and the people they purportedly serve.

Another survey, conducted for the Project for Excellence in Journalism, found that by spring 2002, network television news had largely reverted to its pre–September 11 lineup of topics. The amount of hard news shrank, from 80 percent of stories in October 2001 to 52 percent in early 2002. Meanwhile, the number of "lifestyle" stories made a comeback. Such stories made up 18 percent of total network news stories in June 2001, 1 percent in October 2001, and back to 19 percent during the first 13 weeks of 2002.[27] This continued a trend that has been noticeable for more than a decade.

These findings indicate that in this age of globalization, when the news media's view of the world could and should become ever broader, intellectual isolationism has taken hold, at least in journalism and presumably other fields as well. When asked what obstacles kept them from increasing international coverage, 53 percent of the editors in the Pew survey cited cost. This was followed by lack of interest by senior editors and lack of experienced reporters, each cited by 9 percent of the editors.[28]

Regardless of the rationale that news executives offer for their limited coverage, news consumers are being denied tools they need to evaluate the state of the world. Shortly after the 2001 attacks on the United States, *Boston Globe* editor Martin Baron said that "most Americans are clueless when it comes to the politics and ideology in [the Muslim] world and, in that sense, I think we do bear some responsibility."[29]

Being clueless is not a good starting point when searching for answers to such persistent questions as "Why do they hate us?" and, for that matter, defining who "they" might be.

3. The Clash of Media Voices

When Egyptian president Hosni Mubarak toured Al-Jazeera's cramped headquarters in Qatar, he observed, "All this trouble from a matchbox like this."[30]

For Mubarak and other Arab leaders who prefer their news media com-
pliant, Al-Jazeera has caused plenty of trouble by fostering debate about
topics that many in the region—including many news organizations—
treat as being outside the news media's purview. On Al-Jazeera, everything from the role of women to the competence of governments is
addressed, often loudly. The station's motto is, "The opinion, and the
other opinion," which might seem commonplace in the West, but is
exceptional in the Arab media world.

The emir of Qatar, Sheikh Hamad bin Khalifa al-Thani, provided
$140 million to create Al-Jazeera, which began broadcasting in 1996.
When the emir touts Qatar as a progressive Islamic state that welcomes
Western investment, he can showcase Al-Jazeera as evidence of his
commitment to reform. He tolerates the station's independence, but Al-
Jazeera's bureaus have periodically been shut down by Middle Eastern gov-
ernments angered by its coverage. The station was seen mainly as a curiosity
until 2001, when its content began capturing international attention.
Shortly after the attacks on the United States, Libyan leader Muammar
Qaddafi went on Al-Jazeera to say that he thought the attacks were "horri-
fying, destructive," and that the United States had the right to retaliate.[31]

Al-Jazeera also played a leading role in coverage of the U.S. war
against Afghanistan. It was allowed to remain in Taliban-controlled
territory after Western journalists were ordered to leave. It presented live
coverage of the aftermath of American air strikes and emphasized civilian
casualties and reactions to the war.[32] It gained further notoriety by
broadcasting videotapes of Osama bin Laden. News organizations that
were unable to get closer than the fringes of the war turned to Al-Jazeera
for help, and the station's logo began appearing on newscast footage
around the world.

Its constituency was growing. While it covered Afghanistan, Al-Jazeera
also kept up its intensive reporting about the Israeli–Palestinian conflict,
with a pro-Palestinian slant (suicide bombings were referred to as
"commando operations") and emphasis on the mood on "the Arab street."
Arabs in the Middle East and scattered around the world increasingly
turned to Al-Jazeera.

This audience, eager for news featuring an outlook that they can identify with, is hard to define. Mohammed el-Nawawy and Adel Iskandar,
authors of a book about Al-Jazeera, wrote "the connections that bind the
300 million Arabs in twenty-two countries are often abstract. It's not a
military alliance, a political truce, an economic cooperative, or a simple
linguistic tie. It may not even be reduced to a common religion. Instead,
what brings Arabs together is a notion of joint destiny."[33]

The idea of joint destiny might seem to some skeptics as overrating Arab commonality. Debate about Arab unity—even just unity of aspirations—is similar to that concerning Muslim unity, which is a contentious issue related to the clash theory. Huntington talks about Islam in terms of "consciousness without cohesion," which he says is "a source of weakness to Islam and a source of threat to other civilizations."[34] News media and other communications tools might foster increased cohesion. Regardless of how the Arab population is characterized, there clearly is an audience for news presented from an Arab perspective, and with that audience, Al-Jazeera has credibility that eludes Western media.

Credibility and objectivity are not the same thing, and Al-Jazeera's coverage has a pronounced tilt. Speaking about the Iraq war, Faisal Bodi, senior editor for Al-Jazeera's Web site, said:

> Of all the major global networks, Al-Jazeera has been alone in proceeding from the premise that this war should be viewed as an illegal enterprise. It has broadcast the horror of the bombing campaign, the blown-out brains, the blood-spattered pavements, the screaming infants, and the corpses. . . . By reporting propaganda as fact, the mainstream media had simply mirrored the Blair/Bush fantasy that the people who have been starved by U.N. sanctions and deformed by depleted uranium since 1991 will greet them as saviors.

Bodi cited Al-Jazeera as "a corrective" to the official line that Western media embraced.[35]

Choices of words and images can shape the news and the audience's perception of events. Al-Jazeera did occasionally show some restraint. While other Arab media referred to the American-led coalition in Iraq as the "forces of aggression," Al-Jazeera used "invading forces."[36] This is not to say that Al-Jazeera pulled its punches; its coverage of the fighting—particularly its graphic depictions of casualties—fueled its critics' charges that it was sympathetic to Saddam Hussein's regime.

U.S. officials may have been unhappy with what they saw as Al-Jazeera's anti-American bias, but they recognized the station's clout with its more than 35 million viewers, and so set out to influence its coverage. This was part of the overall information strategy adopted by the American government, which was similar to the one that Saddam Hussein had hoped to employ—to appeal directly to the other side's public opinion and reduce the willingness to fight.[37] Using news coverage to show the other side that it could not win the war might accomplish that.

During the unsettled summer of 2003, tension persisted between the U.S. government and Al-Jazeera. In July, Deputy Defense Secretary

Paul Wolfowitz accused Al-Jazeera of "slanting the news" in favor of Saddam Hussein, and claimed that the channel's "very biased reporting" was "inciting violence against our troops" in Iraq.[38] In response, Al-Jazeera complained to the U.S. State Department that the channel's offices and staff in Iraq had been subjected to intimidation by American forces, including "strafing by gunfire, death threats, confiscation of news material, and multiple detentions and arrests."[39]

In September 2003, the interim Iraqi government banned Al-Jazeera (and another Arab news channel, Al-Arabiya) from government facilities and news conferences. The Iraqi Governing Council said that the stations had incited violence against the council and had fanned animosities between Shiite and Sunni Muslims.[40]

Despite such controversies, Al-Jazeera has established itself as a major media player. In addition to its large viewership, visits to its Web site increased from one million each day before 9/11 to seven million daily soon after.[41] When the Iraq war began, Internet search engines reported a surge in queries about Al-Jazeera. Lycos announced that "Al-Jazeera" had been the subject of three times more searches than "sex."[42] Hackers also targeted the Al-Jazeera site, diverting visitors to a page featuring an American flag.

Al-Jazeera emerged from the war with vastly increased name recognition and a growing audience. It remained controversial, however, within the Middle East as well as elsewhere, and that damaged its economic health. In Saudi Arabia, which constitutes 60 percent of the Persian Gulf region's advertising market, advertising on Al-Jazeera is unofficially banned because of the station's tendency to jab at Saudi officialdom. Kuwait and Bahrain have imposed similar bans. When worldwide interest in the region is high, Al-Jazeera can make money by selling footage to other news organizations, and its forthcoming English-language service may attract new ad revenues.[43] The emir of Qatar continues to value Al-Jazeera as a highly visible advertisement for his country's liberalization, so he makes sure that the station can cover its $30 million annual operating costs.

Al-Jazeera's most important contributions so far may be its establishment of Arab media as a viable alternative to Western news organizations and its role in attracting global recognition of Arab media voices. As recently as the 1991 Gulf War, much of the Middle Eastern news audience had few alternatives to CNN, the BBC, and other Western media that dominated the supply of information. Al-Jazeera is now seen as their legitimate competitor.

The Al-Jazeera story is important because clashes between civilizations can occur in ways other than armed conflict. There can be clashes of perspective, the beginnings and outcomes of which are affected by information flows; how people see the world shapes their attitudes toward other cultures. When Al-Jazeera covered the Iraq war in 2003 and beyond, it did so with a spin that its audience had not seen during the Gulf War a decade earlier. Although there was no effort to paint Saddam Hussein as a hero, the coverage certainly did not feature the boosterism that colored much of American war journalism. Instead, Al-Jazeera presented a distinctively Arab view of the war, with graphic reports about civilian casualties and later about mistreatment of Iraqi prisoners by American and British forces.

And always on Al-Jazeera there was the undercurrent of news about events in Israel, with reporting that was pointedly sympathetic to the Palestinians. Discussion of the Israeli–Palestinian conflict in terms of its effect on the overall U.S.–Arab relationship was notably missing from much of the American news coverage and political debate. City University of New York professor Ervand Abrahamian observed that post-9/11 coverage by the *New York Times*, among others, "scrupulously avoided anything connecting the rise of radical political Islam with Israel and Palestine."[44]

4. The Internet Factor

Policies and events themselves, not simply the reporting of them, influence political attitudes. News coverage in itself will not create or prevent intercultural tensions, but the flow of information has effect, and that flow and its effect have been enhanced considerably by the Internet. As an interactive medium as well as conventional information provider, the Internet can bring unprecedented cohesion to the most far-flung community. Scholar Gary R. Bunt has noted that "it is through a digital interface that an increasing number of people will view their religion and their place in the Muslim worlds, affiliated to wider communities in which 'the West' becomes, at least in cyberspace, increasingly redundant."[45] As the Internet continues to reduce the significance of national borders and other boundaries, the entire array of global media and information technology may help create virtual communities that are as worthy of coverage as traditional states have been.

During the past few years, Internet usage has increased dramatically in some Islamic countries, but as of early 2004 it still lagged far behind the levels of access in much of the rest of the world. No predominantly Islamic country ranks in the top 25 nations in terms of percentage of population with access to the Internet. In the entire Middle East, minus

Israel, only 5 percent of the population has Internet access. In large, predominantly Muslim countries elsewhere, the rate was even lower: for example, 3.6 percent in Indonesia and 1 percent in Pakistan. Statistics about the growth of Internet use are more substantial: from 2000–04, use in Iran increased almost 1,200 percent and in Saudi Arabia 610 percent. But the figures from Pakistan illustrate how far Internet use still needs to grow. Although usage in that country increased more than 1,000 percent during the four years, in real numbers the expansion was from 133,900 to 1.5 million users (out of a total population of more than 157 million).[46]

Assuming that Internet use in Islamic countries will grow significantly during the coming years, the ummah—the worldwide Islamic population—might become a virtual community with technology-based cohesion. Whether this population will be insular or participate in the larger global community will be a crucial factor in determining the future character of Islam. Those observers who believe that the clash of civilizations will occur might consider any new unification within Islam to be a threat, while those who are skeptical about the clash theory might argue that the Internet will enhance the potency of globalizing influences and lead Islamic states and people toward greater integration with the rest of the world.

Online news providers will be players in this process. Despite the efforts of some governments, such as that of Saudi Arabia, to block access to certain online news venues, the Internet is increasingly hard to obstruct. It may help democratize intellectual life in ways that no government official (or religious leader) can wholly control. News is becoming more of a global product, and, as with satellite television channels, the Web could help defuse civilizational clashes by providing information that undermines myths and stereotypes. IslamOnline and many other sources are available to those in the West and elsewhere, serving as educational tools that provide insights about Islamic life. Even without relying on mainstream news media, the individual news consumer can get information directly from sources such as this as well as from governments, NGOs, interest groups, bloggers, and others.

So much information is available that it is bound to have some effect. Whether it can offset deep-rooted hostility and misunderstanding remains to be seen.

5. Looking Ahead: How the News Media May Adjust

The continued debate about the clash theory gives news organizations, particularly in the United States, an opportunity to reassess post–cold war—and now post-9/11—alignments of political and cultural forces throughout the world. In doing so, the news media—like policymakers and the public—should guard against accepting convenient stereotypes and judging civilizational differences in simplistic ways. When Huntington's first clash article appeared in 1993, it seemed to support inchoate fears and reinforce Western predispositions about "the others." But just because the public may be prepared to accept an idea does not mean that the news media should treat it uncritically.

Many in the Muslim world, wrote Georgetown University professor John L. Esposito, saw Huntington as "articulating what they always thought was the West's attitude toward Islam."[47] What had been a cautious approach on the part of the public became, in some instances, overt hostility after 9/11. Particularly in light of the anti-Muslim hate crimes that occurred in the United States, the American news media had a responsibility not to fuel anger and instead present balanced perspectives on Islam.

News organizations' performance was mixed. Although some of the coverage seemed to be based on the desire to identify an enemy, some of it provided the news audience with useful information about Islam. Georgetown professor John Voll commented in late 2001 that coverage was improving somewhat. He noted that Islam "was treated in the past as very exotic, backward, and medieval." Western news coverage, he said, was grounded in the arrogant attitude that "an effective, modern form of Islam was inconceivable, and that in order to be modern, it had to be a carbon copy of the West."[48]

One problem with the news media's and public's view of Huntington's clash theory is that excerpts can be found to suit the political mood of the moment, regardless of how they fit into the broader context of his work. Huntington has contributed to this problem by sometimes using sweeping statements that are the academic equivalent of the politician's sound bite—rhetorically stirring, intellectually imprecise. For example: "The underlying problem for the West is not Islamic fundamentalism. It is Islam, a different civilization whose people are convinced of the superiority of their culture and are obsessed with the inferiority of their power."[49] Why is this a "problem for the West"? Who are these "people" who are so convinced?

The news media's treatment of Huntington's outlook may render it even hotter and more simplistic. Media versions of Huntington's ideas have come to be regarded by some as conventional wisdom and have elicited responses from Islamic leaders. Mustafa Ceric, the Grand Mufti of Bosnia, observed "the current perception in the West that not all

Muslims are terrorists but all terrorists are Muslims is not only morally and politically corrupt, but also factually unsustainable." Ceric also said that Islam should not be labeled a "terrorist religion" because "the violent small minority of any faith does not represent the peaceful great majority of that faith."[50]

Huntington's clash is not solely between the West and Islam. In *The Clash of Civilizations*, he provided maps and descriptions of his version of how the world is divided. He wrote "Western ideas of individualism, liberalism, constitutionalism, human rights, equality, liberty, the rule of law, democracy, free markets, the separation of church and state, often have little resonance in Islamic, Confucian, Japanese, Hindu, Buddhist, or Orthodox cultures."[51] Some scholars and policymakers are also looking beyond Islam as they try to anticipate where crises may arise. Zbigniew Brzezinski has written about "the volatile character of Japanese and Korean nationalisms" that "could turn anti-American, igniting a regional Asianist identity that defines itself in terms of independence from American hegemony." That analysis may be speculative, but such a problem for the United States certainly is possible. This is just the kind of issue that news organizations should examine and plan coverage for before the crisis explodes, rather than waiting and then having to respond frantically.

Even in the Islam–West relationship, facets of civilizational clashes exist beyond those of greatest concern to Huntington. Citing findings of the World Values Survey, scholars Ronald Inglehart and Pippa Norris wrote "when it comes to attitudes toward gender equality and sexual liberalization, the cultural gap between Islam and the West widens into a chasm."[52] This is yet another approach to cultural conflict that the news media must deal with if they are going to present a comprehensive picture of the state of the world to the public.

Emerging from these and other plausible examples of civilizational conflict—current or prospective—is a complex mandate for twenty-first-century journalism. For starters, the volume of international news coverage must become more consistent. Anyone thinking that the 2003 Iraq war might mark a lasting turnaround in international news coverage will probably be disappointed. News coverage of major crises evaporates quickly. Using coverage around the time of the 1991 Gulf War as an example, the Tyndall Report found that network news coverage of Iraq went from 1,177 minutes during January 1991 to 48 minutes in August of that year.[53] Coverage of Afghanistan also illustrates the short attention span of many news organizations. According to the Tyndall Report, in November 2001, Afghanistan received 306 minutes of coverage; in January 2002, 106 minutes; in February 2002, 28 minutes; in January 2003, 11 minutes; in March 2003, 1 minute. Comparable declines occurred in American newspapers, and the drop off is even more precipitous if the coverage appearing in the *New York Times* and *The Washington Post* is excluded.[54]

The news media today confront an international community that is more amorphous than in the past. Today's "bad guys" (as defined by Western governments and media) such as Al-Qaeda may have no home that can be identified on a map. That produces disorientation among policymakers and news executives. It is hard to plan policy or design news coverage without being able to rely on traditional tools such as maps and lists of foreign ministry officials around the world.

Further complicating the task of understanding the world are the evolving communities of interest, such as the European Union and Mercosur, which make coverage of transnational entities important. Other aspects of globalization take that a step farther, as supranational economic and political interests become more significant. Giant corporations transcend nationality and are governed through cyberspace. Humanitarian emergencies in remote places that would have escaped notice in the past now come into the world's living rooms as "virtual" crises. Non-state "armies" of terrorists compensate for their small numbers by being able to disregard borders and use media to enhance the impact of their actions.

These issues extend beyond the civilizational conflicts that Huntington describes. Policymakers and journalists have similar interests in grappling with these matters. While governments decide how to adapt to these new realities, the news business must realign its own priorities if journalists are to help the public develop a better sense of what is going on in the world.

Samuel Huntington's definitions may be questioned and his conclusions challenged, but he performed a considerable service by pushing policymakers and journalists toward undertaking more sophisticated analyses of how the world works. Perhaps the result will be more thoughtful policy and more comprehensive news coverage. Any improvement along these lines would be welcome.

Notes

1. Patrick E. Tyler and Don Van Natta Jr., "Militants in Europe Openly Call for Jihad and Rule of Islam," *New York Times*, April 26, 2004, A1.
2. Samuel P. Huntington, "The Clash of Civilizations?" *Foreign Affairs*, Vol. 72, No. 3 (Summer 1993), p. 22.

3. Samuel P. Huntington, *The Clash of Civilizations and the Remaking of World Order* (New York: Simon and Schuster, 1996), p. 20.

4. Bernard Gwertzman, "Memo to the *Times* Foreign Staff," *Media Studies Journal*, Vol. 7, No. 4 (Fall 1993), p. 34.

5. Fouad Ajami, "The Summoning," *Foreign Affairs*, Vol. 72, No. 4 (September–October 1993), p. 25.

6. Richard A. Clarke, "The Wrong Debate on Terrorism," *New York Times*, April 25, 2004, WK15.

7. Ian Buruma and Avishai Margalit, *Occidentalism* (New York: Penguin, 2004), p. 126.

8. Buruma and Margalit, *Occidentalism*, 147.

9. Charles A. Kupchan, *The End of the American Era* (New York: Knopf, 2002), p. 70.

10. Zbigniew Brzezinski, *The Choice: Global Domination or Global Leadership* (New York: Basic Books, 2004), p. 59.

11. Thomas L. Friedman, *The Lexus and the Olive Tree* (New York: Farrar Straus Giroux, 1999), p. xvii.

12. Niall Ferguson, "Eurabia?" *New York Times Magazine*, April 4, 2004, p. 14.

13. Samuel P. Huntington, "If Not Civilizations, What?" *Foreign Affairs*, Vol. 72, No. 5 (November–December 1993), p. 93.

14. Adeed Dawisha, "Arab Nationalism and Islamism: Competitive Past, Uncertain Future," *International Studies Review*, Vol. 2, No. 3 (Fall 2000), p. 89.

15. Ervand Abrahamian, "The U.S. Media, Samuel Huntington, and September 11," *Middle East Report*, No. 223 (Summer 2002), p. 62.

16. Howard Kurtz, "For Media After Iraq, A Case of Shell Shock," *Washington Post*, April 28, 2003, A1.

17. Jim Lobe, "Iraq Blotted Out Rest of the World in 2003 TV News," Inter Press Service News Agency, www.ipsnews.net/print.asp?idnews=21802

18. Doctors Without Borders, "Top 10 Most Underreported Humanitarian Stories of 2003," www.doctorswithoutborders.org

19. Terence Smith, "The Unreported Stories," *The News Hour*, March 4, 2002.

20. Lucinda Fleeson, "Bureau of Missing Bureaus," *American Journalism Review*, Vol. 25, No. 7 (October/November 2003), p. 34.

21. Dwight L. Morris and Associates, "America and the World: The Impact of September 11 on U.S. Coverage of International News," survey conducted for the Pew International Journalism Program, June 2002, p. 3.

22. Ibid., p. 9.

23. Ibid., p. 2.

24. Ibid., p. 3.

25. Ibid., p. 17.

26. Ibid., pp. 13–14.

27. Project for Excellence in Journalism, "The War on Terrorism: The Not So New Television News Landscape," May 23, 2002, www.journalism.org/resources/reports/landscape/month.asp

28. Morris and Associates, "America and the World," p. 22.
29. David Shaw, "Foreign News Shrinks in Era of Globalization," *Los Angeles Times*, September 27, 2001, A20.
30. Brian Whitaker, "Battle Station," *Guardian*, February 7, 2003.
31. Mohammed el-Nawawy and Adel Iskandar, *Al-Jazeera* (Boulder, CO: Westview, 2002), p. 100.
32. Neil Hickey, "Perspectives on War," *Columbia Journalism Review*, (March/April 2002), p. 40.
33. el-Nawawy and Iskandar, *Al-Jazeera*, p. 20.
34. Huntington, *The Clash of Civilizations*, p. 177.
35. Faisal Bodi, "Al-Jazeera Tells the Truth About War," *Guardian*, March 28, 2003.
36. Ian Black, "Television Agendas Shape Images of War," *Guardian*, March 27, 2003.
37. Michael Dobbs, "In Fight for World Opinion, Results Are Mixed for U.S.," *Washington Post*, March 24, 2003, A27.
38. Dominic Timms, "Wolfowitz Sparks Fury from Al-Jazeera," *Guardian*, Tuesday, July 29, 2003.
39. E.A. Torriero, "U.S., Media at Odds Over Iraq Coverage," *Chicago Tribune*, August 1, 2003.
40. Alissa J. Rubin, "Iraqis Defend Media Ban, Allege Incitement," *Los Angeles Times*, September 25, 2003, A1.
41. el-Nawawy and Iskandar, *Al-Jazeera*, p. 163.
42. Peter Svensson, "Al-Jazeera Site Most Sought After," *Editor and Publisher*, April 2, 2003.
43. "All That Jazeera," *Economist*, June 21, 2003, p. 60.
44. Abrahamian, "The U.S. Media, Samuel Huntington, and September 11," p. 63.
45. Gary R. Bunt, *Islam in the Digital Age* (London: Pluto Press, 2003), p. 211.
46. www.internetworldstats.com
47. John L. Esposito, *Unholy War: Terror in the Name of Islam* (New York: Oxford University Press, 2002), p. 126.
48. Alina Tugend, "Explaining the Rage," *American Journalism Review* (December 2001), p. 26.
49. Huntington, *The Clash of Civilizations*, p. 217.
50. Mustafa Ceric, "Islam Against Terrorism," speech delivered to the Euro-Atlantic Partnership Council, Vienna, Austria, June 14, 2002.
51. Huntington, "The Clash of Civilizations?" p. 40.
52. Ronald Inglehart and Pippa Norris, "The True Clash of Civilizations," *Foreign Policy* (March–April 2003), p. 67.
53. Howard Kurtz, "For Media After Iraq, A Case of Shell Shock," *Washington Post*, April 28, 2003, A1.
54. Kurtz, "For Media After Iraq," A1; Lori Robertson, "Whatever Happened to Afghanistan?" *American Journalism Review*, Vol. 25, No. 5 (June–July 2003), p. 25.

Contributors

Sean Aday is assistant professor of Media and Public Affairs at the George Washington University.

W. Lance Bennett is the Ruddick C. Lawrence Professor of Communication and professor of Political Science at the University of Washington. He is also the director of the Center for Communication and Civic Engagement.

Robin Brown is senior lecturer in International Communications in the Institute of Communications Studies, University of Leeds.

Maura Conway is a Ph.D. candidate in the Department of Political Science at Trinity College, Dublin, Ireland and a teaching fellow in the School of International Relations at the University of St. Andrews, Scotland.

Kathy Fitzpatrick is associate professor and director of the MA in Public Relations and Advertising at DePaul University in Chicago.

Eytan Gilboa is professor of communication and government at Bar-Ilan University.

Cinny Kennard is assistant professor at the Annenberg School for Communication at the University of Southern California and is manager of NPR West.

Tamara Kosic is a student of political science and journalism at DePaul University.

Steven Livingston is director of the School of Media and Public Affairs at George Washington University and associate professor of Media and International Affairs.

Sheila Murphy is a social psychologist and associate professor at the Annenberg School for Communication of the University of Southern California.

W. Lucas Robinson is a researcher and lecturer within the F.U.N.K. Centre at Agder University College.

Jayne Rodgers is lecturer in International Communications at the University of Leeds.

Jan de Ridder is associate professor in the Department of Communication at the University of Amsterdam.

Nel Ruigrok is a Ph.D. student at the Amsterdam School of Communication Research at the University of Amsterdam.

Otto Scholten is associate professor in the Department of Communication at the University of Amsterdam.

Philip Seib is the Lucius W. Nieman Professor of Journalism at Marquette University.

Index